CORE READY LESSON SETS

A Staircase to Standards Success for English Language Arts

The Road to Knowledge: Information and Research

Pam Allyn

Executive Director of LitLife and LitWorld

PEARSON

Boston • Columbus • Indianapolis • New York • San Francisco • Upper Saddle River
Amsterdam • Cape Town • Dubai • London • Madrid • Milan • Munich • Paris • Montreal • Toronto
Delhi • Mexico City • São Paulo • Sydney • Hong Kong • Seoul • Singapore • Taipei • Tokyo

Vice President, Editor in Chief: Aurora Martínez Ramos
Acquisitions Editor: Kathryn Boice
Associate Sponsoring Editor: Barbara Strickland
Editorial Assistant: Katherine Wiley
Senior Marketing Manager: Christine Gatchell
Production Editor: Karen Mason
Project Coordination, Editorial Services, and Text Design: Electronic Publishing Services Inc., NYC
Art Rendering and Electronic Page Makeup: Jouve
Cover Designer: Diane Lorenzo and Jenny Hart
Grade Band Opening and Lesson Set Illustrations: Steve Morrison

Text Credits: The Common Core State Standards for the English Language Arts are © Copyright 2010. National Governors Association Center for Best Practices and Council of Chief State School Officers. All rights reserved. Page xix, "5 Principles for Teaching Content to English Language Learners." by Jim Cummins, Retrieved from www.PearsonELL.com. Reprinted with permission.

Photo Credits: All photos not credited are courtesy of the author.

Library of Congress Cataloging-in-Publication Data
Allyn, Pam.
  The road to knowledge: Information and research / Pam Allyn.
    p. cm. — (Core ready lesson sets for grades 3 to 5)
  ISBN-13: 978-0-13-290755-2
  ISBN-10: 0-13-290755-0
  1. Language arts (Elementary)–Curricula–United States. 2. Language arts (Elementary)–Activity programs–United States. I. Title.

LB1576.A6145 2014
372.6—dc23
                                              2012024754

ISBN 10: 0-13-290755-0
ISBN 13: 978-0-13-290755-2

About the Author

Pam Allyn is an authority in the field of literacy education and a world-renowned expert in home and school literacy connections. As a motivational speaker, expert consultant, author, teacher, and humanitarian advocating for children, she is transforming the way we think about literacy as a tool for communication and knowledge building.

Pam currently serves as the executive director of LitLife, a national literacy development organization providing research-based professional development for K–12 educators. She founded and leads LitWorld, a groundbreaking global literacy initiative that reaches children across the United States and in more than 60 countries. Her methods for helping all students achieve success as readers and writers have brought her acclaim both in the United States and internationally. Pam is also recognized for founding the highly acclaimed initiative Books for Boys for the nation's most struggling readers.

Pam is the author of 11 books for educators and parents, including the award-winning *What to Read When: The Books and Stories to Read with Your Child—And All the Best Times to Read Them* (Penguin Avery), *Pam Allyn's Best Books for Boys* (Scholastic), and *Your Child's Writing Life: How to Inspire Confidence, Creativity, and Skill at Every Age* (Penguin Avery). Her work has been featured on "Good Morning America," "The Today Show," "Oprah Radio," *The Huffington Post*, *The New York Times*, and across the blogosphere.

About the Core Ready Series

Core Ready is a dynamic series of books providing educators with critical tools for navigating the Common Core State Standards. The foundational text, *Be Core Ready: Powerful, Effective Steps to Implementing and Achieving the Common Core State Standards*, provides practical strategies for how to implement core ideas to make all students college- and career-ready scholars. The *Core Ready Lesson Sets*, including three grade bands with four books per grade band, provide an easy-to-use way to access and organize all of the content within the standards. Readers see how to take complex concepts related to the standards and turn them into practical, specific, everyday instruction.

Acknowledgments

I thank the team at Pearson for believing in the Core Ready vision. Aurora Martinez is a passionate and radiant leader who makes all things possible. Thanks to Karen Mason for her superb dedication to this work, to Christine Gatchell, Kathryn Boice, and Krista Clark for their great energy, and to Karla Walsh, Carrie Fox, Melinda Durham, Amy Pavelich, and their amazing team at Electronic Publishing Services Inc. for their wonderful care for this project.

Thanks to my colleagues at LitLife, most especially to the dream team on this project: Carolyn Greenberg, Jen Scoggin, Katie Cunningham, and Debbie Lera. They are teachers, leaders, and big thinkers who never forget it is about children first. I am blessed to work with them. Many, many thanks to Flynn Berry, Megan Karges, David Wilcox, Shannon Bishop, Rebekah Coleman, Marie Miller, Erin Harding, Danny Miller, and Jim Allyn for glorious input at every step.

I would like to thank our reviewers who provided valuable feedback: Christine H. Davis, Hillcrest Elementary (Logan, Utah); Wendy Fiore, Chester Elementary School in Connecticut; Keli Garas-York, Buffalo State College in New York; Karen Gibson, Springfield Public Schools in Illinois; Timothy M. Haag, Greater Albany Public Schools, New York; Katie Klaus Salika Lawrence, William Paterson University of New Jersey; Edward Karl Schultz, Midwestern State University (Wichita Falls, TX) Elizabeth Smith, Saint Joseph's College in New York; and Rhonda M. Sutton, East Stroudsburg University in Pennsylvania. Finally, I thank Steve Morrison for his extraordinary illustrations which were, like everything else about everyone who has participated in the creation of this series, so perfect all together.

Contents

Grade 3   What Matters Most: Research and Analysis in Informational Text   1

Reading Lessons 15

Writing Lessons 112

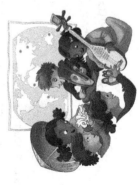

Grade 5 Knowledge Quest: Navigating and Integrating Multiple Sources as Researchers 139

Reading Lessons 152

Writing Lessons 180

Appendixes

Welcome

Welcome to *Core Ready Lesson Sets for Grades 3 to 5: A Staircase to Standards Success for English Language Arts—The Road to Knowledge: Information and Research.* Here you will find the rich and detailed lesson plans, and the specifics and daily activities within them, that you can use instantly to make the Core Ready instruction come to life.

The Four Doors to the Common Core State Standards

We have synthesized the expanse of the Common Core State Standards document into four essential doors to the English Language Arts. These Four Doors organize the CCSS into curriculum, identifying the most critical capacities our students need for the 21st century—skills, understandings, and strategies for reading, writing, speaking, and listening across subject areas. "The Four Doors to the Core" group the CCSS into lesson sets that match the outcomes every college and career-ready student must have. The magic of the Four Doors is that they bring together reading, writing, speaking, and listening skills together into integrated lesson sets. Rather than face an overwhelming array of individual standards, teachers, students, parents, and administrators together can use the Four Doors to create the kind of curriculum that simplifies the schedule and changes lives. The Four Doors to the Core are described below.

▶ **The Road to Knowledge: *Information and Research***

This Door to the Core—The Road to Knowledge—encompasses research and information and the skills and strategies students need to **build strong content knowledge and compose informational text** as suggested by the Common Core State Standards.

▶ **The Power to Persuade: *Opinion and Argument***

This Door to the Core—The Power to Persuade—encompasses instruction that explores the purposes, techniques, and strategies to **become effective readers and writers of various types of opinion text** as delineated in the Common Core State Standards.

▶ **The Shape of Story: *Yesterday and Today***

This Door to the Core—The Shape of Story—encompasses exploration of a variety of genres with the corresponding craft, structures, and strategies one needs to be a **successful consumer and producer of literary text** as required by the Common Core State Standards.

▶ **The Journey to Meaning: *Comprehension and Critique***

This Door to the Core—The Journey to Meaning—encompasses the strategies and skills our students need to **comprehend, critique, and compose literary text** as outlined in the Common Core State Standards.

Get Ready to Travel the Road to Knowledge:
Information and Research

We know our students are going to need to navigate informational texts and be able to cite evidence from elementary school through adulthood. But up until now, this has not been a major focus of students' instructional time in school. Much of their reading and writing instruction has focused on fiction and the whole-class novel. With the Common Core State Standards comes a huge turning point. I have been campaigning for years for schools to add more informational texts to classroom and school libraries and to encourage teachers to read aloud from informational texts. Such books will take learning to a new level. Teachers and students will now focus on informational texts and research in ways that will enliven, inform, and inspire.

We will guide students to read and listen carefully to glean key ideas and details and notice patterns of events, ideas, and concepts in a variety of informational text types. Students will learn to use text features and text structure

with purpose to access information efficiently and effectively. They will become thoughtful researchers who integrate information from multiple sources in preparation for writing, speaking, and visual presentation. They will learn to take notes, summarize, paraphrase, and cite resources.

Students will synthesize their ideas and research in clear, well-organized informative and explanatory writing pieces and presentations. They will share ideas logically and support them with details, graphics, and multimedia. They will study content vocabulary and employ domain-specific language and transitional phrases to effectively convey and link information. They will share their writing and thinking with others orally and by using appropriate tools and technologies. We live in an information age, and this lesson set will help students to successfully navigate and grow in this ever-changing world.

Walk Through a Lesson Set

This section is meant to take the reader through the major features of the lesson set with snapshots of design elements/icons, etc. to illustrate.

Why This Lesson Set?

This section establishes the rationale for the lesson set and provides helpful background information about the lesson set focus.

Common Core State Standards Alignment

All of the Common Core State Standards addressed in the lesson set are listed here, including the individual grade-level standards.

Essential Skill Lenses
(PARCC Framework)

This table provides specific examples of how in this lesson set, Core Ready students will build the essential skills required by the Partnership for Assessment of Readiness for College and Careers (PARCC), a multi-state coalition that is currently developing Core Standards–aligned assessments that are slated to replace many statewide assessments across the United States. This alignment helps to ensure that Core Ready students will be prepared when states begin to use these assessments.

Core Questions

Core Questions are thought-provoking, open-ended questions students will explore across the lesson set. We expect students' responses to the Core Questions to evolve as their experience and understanding become richer with each

lesson. For best results, post these questions somewhere in your classroom and use them to focus your instruction.

Ready to Get Started?

This is a brief and inspiring pep talk intended to set the stage for teachers and provide insight about learners at this grade level.

Lesson Set Goals

Here you will find a list of goals for student learning summarized in clear language in three to five observable behaviors for each reading and writing lesson set, listed with corresponding Common Core State Standards that the goals address.

Choosing Core Texts

For best practice to occur and for all our students to achieve success, all teaching of reading and writing should be grounded in the study of quality literature. Here you will find lists of books, poems, articles, and other texts for you and your students to use for modeling and close reading to achieve the instructional goals of the lesson set. We also explain the types of texts that will focus and enrich your students' reading and writing during this lesson set. Any text that is used specifically as an exemplar in a lesson appears here in the first list. We also recommend additional texts with similar features and qualities to supplement your work in this lesson set.

Teacher's Notes

This section relays a personal message from us to you, the teacher, meant to give the big picture of what the lesson set is all about, the impact we hope it will have on students, and tips or reminders to facilitate your teaching.

Core Message to Students

This segment speaks directly to students, providing background knowledge and rationale about the lesson set to come. We encourage you to share this message with your students to set the stage for their learning.

Building Academic Language

This section provides a list of key terms and phrases chosen to help your students read, write, listen, and speak during the course of the lesson set. Introduce these terms to your students in context gradually; scaffold their use by making them visible to everyone, with bulletin boards and manipulatives; and encourage students to use the new words as they communicate during your study together. See the glossary at the end of each grade's lesson set for more information about important lesson vocabulary.

Recognition

The successful conclusion of each grade's lesson set is a time for recognition. Find specific suggestions for how to plan meaningful recognition opportunities for your students here.

Assessment

In this section you will find information about where to find assessment tools in every lesson set, along with suggestions specific to that grade.

Also see the Reading Lessons and Writing Lessons sections to find Milestone Performance Assessments for monitoring progress and for standards-aligned reading and writing rubrics.

Core Support for Diverse Learners

Here we provide guidance for how to pace and plan instruction and provide materials that will help all students in your class be successful during the lessons.

Complementary Core Methods

This segment offers specific ideas for how to use key instructional structures (read-aloud, shared reading, shared writing, etc.) to reach the goals of the lessons.

Core Connections at Home

This section suggests ways to keep caregivers at home informed and involved.

The Reading and Writing Lessons

Each set of reading and writing lessons is separated into two sections with the following contents for either reading or writing:

- The Core I.D.E.A. / Daily Instruction at a Glance table

- Reading and writing rubrics aligned to unit goals and Common Core State Standards

- Detailed lesson plans (10 for reading, 10 for writing, and 1 Language Companion Lesson)

What to Look for in the Core I.D.E.A. / Daily Instruction at a Glance Table

Specifies the I.D.E.A. framework stage for each lesson

Lists any extra teacher support found in the lesson:
- Milestone Assessment
- Speaking and listening opportunities
- Suggestions for English Language Learner (ELL) support
- Technology suggestions
- Close reading opportunity

Lists the standards that align with the lesson

States the teaching objective of each lesson

Indicates the lesson number

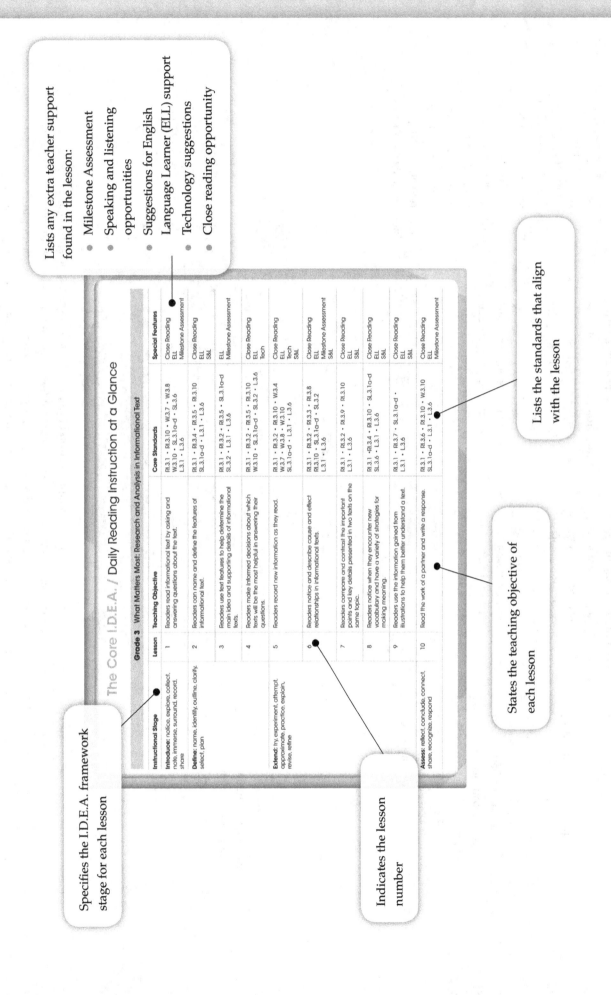

The Core I.D.E.A. / Daily Reading Instruction at a Glance

Grade 3 What Matters Most: Research and Analysis in Informational Text

Instructional Stage	Lesson	Teaching Objective	Core Standards	Special Features
Introduce: notice, explore, collect, note, immerse, surround, record, share	1	Readers read informational text by asking and answering questions about the text.	RI.3.1 · RI.3.10 · W.3.7 · W.3.8 W.3.10 · SL.3.1a-d · SL.3.6 L.3.1 · L.3.6	Close Reading ELL Milestone Assessment
Define: name, identify, outline, clarify, select, plan	2	Readers can name and define the features of informational text.	RI.3.1 · RI.3.4 · RI.3.5 · RI.3.10 SL.3.1a-d · L.3.1 · L.3.6	Close Reading ELL S&L
	3	Readers use text features to help determine the main idea and supporting details of informational texts.	RI.3.1 · RI.3.2 · RI.3.5 · SL.3.1a-d SL.3.2 · L.3.1 · L.3.6	ELL Milestone Assessment
	4	Readers make informed decisions about which texts will be the most helpful in answering their questions.	RI.3.1 · RI.3.2 · RI.3.5 · RI.3.10 W.3.10 · SL.3.1a-d · SL.3.2 · L.3.6	Close Reading ELL Tech
Extend: try, experiment, attempt, approximate, practice, explain, revise, refine	5	Readers record new information as they read.	RI.3.1 · RI.3.2 · RI.3.8 · W.3.4 W.3.7 · W.3.8 · W.3.10 SL.3.1a-d · L.3.1 · L.3.6	Close Reading ELL Tech S&L
	6	Readers notice and describe cause and effect relationships in informational texts.	RI.3.1 · RI.3.2 · RI.3.3 · RI.3.8 RI.3.10 · SL.3.1a-d · SL.3.2 L.3.1 · L.3.6	Close Reading ELL Milestone Assessment S&L
	7	Readers compare and contrast the important points and key details presented in two texts on the same topic.	RI.3.1 · RI.3.2 · RI.3.9 · RI.3.10 L.3.1 · L.3.6	Close Reading ELL S&L
	8	Readers notice when they encounter new vocabulary and have a variety of strategies for making meaning.	RI.3.1 · RI.3.4 · RI.3.10 · SL.3.1a-d SL.3.6 · L.3.1 · L.3.6	Close Reading ELL S&L
	9	Readers use the information gained from illustrations to help them better understand a text.	RI.3.1 · RI.3.7 · SL.3.1a-d · L.3.1 · L.3.6	Close Reading ELL S&L
Assess: reflect, conclude, connect, share, recognize, respond	10	Read the work of a partner and write a response.	RI.3.1 · RI.3.6 · RI.3.10 · W.3.10 SL.3.1a-d · L.3.1 · L.3.6	Close Reading ELL Milestone Assessment

What to Look for in the Reading and Writing Rubrics

In both the reading and writing lesson sets, we provide a discipline-specific performance rubric, including performance descriptors for four levels of proficiency. A score of 3 ("Achieving") indicates that by the end of the lesson set, a student has demonstrated solid evidence of success with the elements of the task or concept and can perform independently when required by the standards.

Lesson set goals

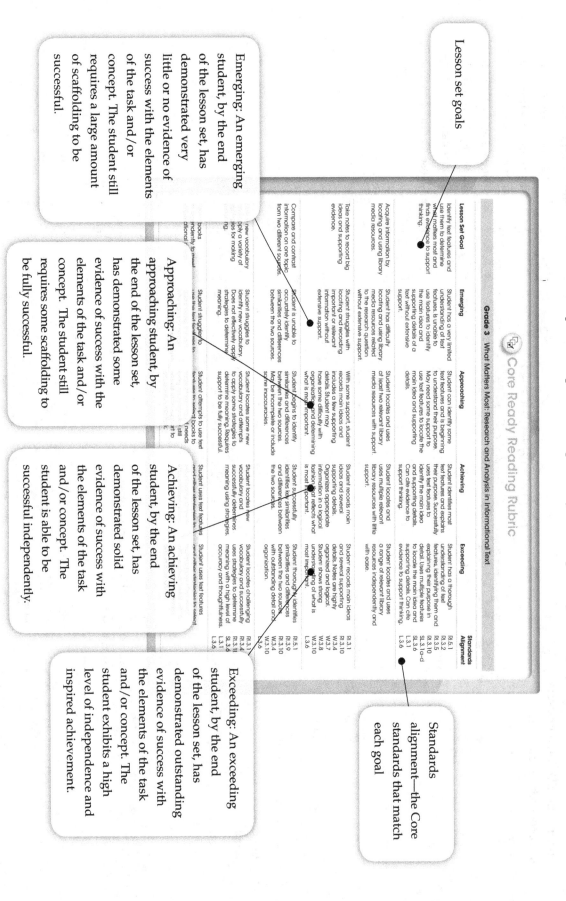

Emerging: An emerging student, by the end of the lesson set, has demonstrated very little or no evidence of success with the elements of the task and/or concept. The student still requires a large amount of scaffolding to be successful.

Approaching: An approaching student, by the end of the lesson set, has demonstrated some evidence of success with the elements of the task and/or concept. The student still requires some scaffolding to be fully successful.

Achieving: An achieving student, by the end of the lesson set, has demonstrated solid evidence of success with the elements of the task and/or concept. The student is able to be successful independently.

Exceeding: An exceeding student, by the end of the lesson set, has demonstrated outstanding evidence of success with the elements of the task and/or concept. The student exhibits a high level of independence and inspired achievement.

Standards alignment—the Core standards that match each goal

What to Look for in the Detailed Lesson Plans

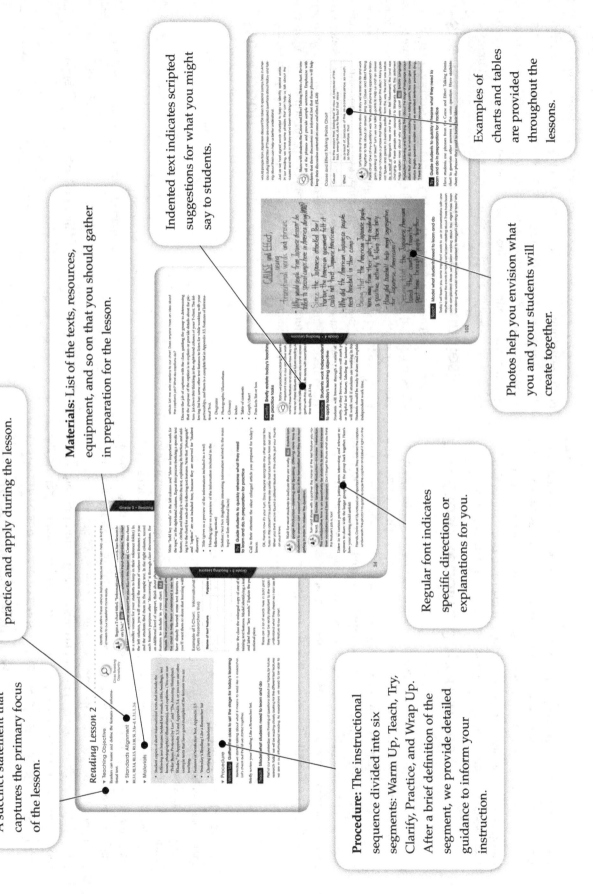

Teaching Objective: A succinct statement that captures the primary focus of the lesson.

Standards Alignment: A list of the standards that the students will practice and apply during the lesson.

Materials: List of the texts, resources, equipment, and so on that you should gather in preparation for the lesson.

Procedure: The instructional sequence divided into six segments: Warm Up, Teach, Try, Clarify, Practice, and Wrap Up. After a brief definition of the segment, we provide detailed guidance to inform your instruction.

Indented text indicates scripted suggestions for what you might say to students.

Regular font indicates specific directions or explanations for you.

Examples of charts and tables are provided throughout the lessons.

Photos help you envision what you and your students will create together.

Special Features Marked with an Icon

Look for these icons to help you find the following important elements within each lesson set.

Suggestions for English language learners	
Speaking and listening opportunity	
Suggestions for technology integration	
Assessment opportunity	
Close reading opportunity	

ELL Support

Across the lesson set, we highlight specific strategies embedded in the lesson to shelter instruction for ELL students. Based on Jim Cummins's *Five Principles for Teaching Content to English Language Learners* (www.pearsonschool.com), these strategies will help ELL students participate successfully in the whole-group lesson and will support the development of their language skills. Wherever you see this icon, you can expect to find which of the 5 Principles is being employed alongside helpful advice and information to support your English Language Learners in any lesson you teach. (See Figure 1 for a complete list with descriptions of the Five Principles for Teaching Content to English Language Learners).

Speaking and Listening Opportunities

Speaking and listening skills are essential for career- and college-ready students, yet these two capacities are frequently underrepresented in classrooms. We have embedded frequent opportunities for students to grow in these areas. Look for the Speaking and Listening icon to see where. Also, see the appendix of any Core Ready lesson set book for a standards-aligned checklist to help you assess student performance in these areas.

Technology Options

The Common Core State Standards require that students use technology strategically and capably, and for today's student, this is essential work across the disciplines. Each lesson set provides several suggestions, marked with the Technology icon, for how to build student technology skills and enhance the lessons with various technological tools. Beside each English Language Arts Goal we list for students, we present both high- and low-tech options for your classroom. Although we strongly advocate using a high-tech approach, we recognize that circumstances of funding, training, or even those annoying times when equipment just refuses to function may make it difficult to rely completely on technology. Therefore, we also suggest a low-tech method to achieve the goal—tools that are easily available and inexpensive or free.

Milestone Assessments

Every lesson set includes several suggested Milestone Performance Assessments to assess students' progress toward the lesson set goals. Each of these performance-based assessments aligns directly with one or more Common Core State Standards for reading or writing. With each milestone assessment, we include a checklist of indicators for you to observe with specific guidelines for where to gather the evidence. See each grade's appendix for "copy and clip" masters of these checklists.

Close Reading Opportunities

Every lesson set includes several lessons that require focused, text-based reading where teachers model and students practice reading closely to determine what the text says explicitly, making logical inferences from it, and citing specific textual evidence when writing or speaking to support conclusions drawn from the text. This icon marks a Close Reading opportunity.

Figure 1 Five Principles for Teaching Content to English Language Learners

1. Identify and Communicate Content and Language Objectives

When presenting content objectives.

- Simplify language (active voice, use same terms consistently)
- Paraphrase
- Repeat
- Avoid idioms and slang
- Be aware of homophones and multiple-meaning words
- Clarify (with simplified language, gestures, visuals)
- Check for understanding

When working with language objectives focus on

- Key content vocabulary
- Academic vocabulary found across the curriculum
- Language form and function essential for the lesson

2. Frontload the Lesson

Provide opportunities to frontload or preteach lesson elements.

- Activate prior knowledge by connecting to students' academic, cultural, or personal experiences
- Build background by explaining new vocabulary or unfamiliar facts and concepts
- Preview text by reviewing visuals, headings, and/or highlighted text
- Set a purpose for reading by clarifying comprehension questions at the end of the lesson
- Make connections by helping students see relationships between the lesson and other aspects of their lives

3. Provide Comprehensible Input

Make oral and written content accessible by providing support.

- Visuals: photos, illustrations, cartoons, multimedia
- Graphics: graphs, charts, tables
- Organizers: graphic organizers, outlines
- Summaries: text, audio, native language
- Audio: recordings, read-alouds
- Audiovisual aids: videos, dramatizations, props, gestures
- Models: demonstrations and modeling
- Experiences: hands-on learning opportunities, field trips

4. Enable Language Production

Structure opportunities for oral practice with language and content.

Listening and speaking

- Make listening input understandable with a variety of support
- Model language
- Allow wait time for students to plan what they say

Reading and writing

- Tailor the task to each student's proficiency level
- Provide support and scaffolding
- Expect different products from students with different levels of proficiency

Increasing interaction

- Provide collaborative tasks so students can work together
- Encourage the development of relationships with peers
- Lower anxiety levels to enable learning, as indicated by brain research

5. Assess for Content and Language Understanding

Monitor progress and provide reteaching and intervention when necessary.

Diagnostic Assessment

- Determine appropriate placement
- Identify strengths and challenges

Formative Assessment

- Check comprehension in ongoing manner
- Use appropriate instruction and pacing

Summative Assessments

- Provide alternative types of assessment when possible, such as projects and portfolios
- Provide practice before administering formal tests

Accommodations

- Provide extra time
- Use bilingual dictionaries
- Offer oral presentation of written material

Source: Jim Cummins, "Five Principles for Teaching Content to English Language Learners." Retrieved from www.pearsonELL.com. Reprinted with permission.

Language Companion Lesson

Each lesson set includes a Language Companion Lesson as a resource and model for explicit teaching of language standards within the context of each lesson set topic.

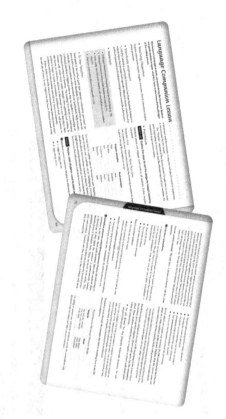

Glossary

A glossary of key terms is provided with each grade's lesson set.

Appendixes

We have provided a variety of resources in the appendixes, including masters for graphic organizers and charts, sample texts for close reading, a Speaking and Listening Performance Checklist, bibliographical information for the research and texts we mention within the lesson sets, Clip-Apart Milestone Performance Assessments that can be copied, and other resources specific to the lesson sets. The Appendixes pages, along with other teaching tools, will be available as downloadable PDFs in the PDToolkit. For information, visit the PDToolkit for Pam Allyn's *Be Core Ready Series* at **http://pdtoolkit.pearson.com.**

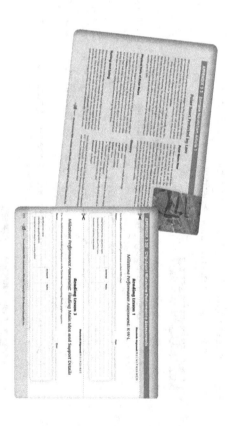

FAQs about the Core Ready Lesson Sets

Q How does Core Ready ensure alignment with the Common Core State Standards?

A We have carefully examined, analyzed, and synthesized the standards to create for all students rich, engaging learning experiences—many of which touch on multiple standards—with the goal that within a single grade level, Core Ready students will experience the full breadth of Core Standards in reading, writing, speaking, and listening. Every grade-level standard in these three areas is listed in one or more of the lessons for that grade level, and most appear in multiple lessons.

As the Common Core document on "Focus and coherence in instruction and assessment" states, not every standard appears as a stand-alone instruction and assessment objective:

> While the Standards delineate specific expectations in reading, writing, speaking, listening, and language, each standard need not be a separate focus for instruction and assessment. Often, several standards can be addressed by a single rich task. (CCSS, p. 5)

We consider every standard we list in the Common Core State Standards Alignment section to be an integral part of what students must do in order to achieve one or more instructional objective of the multifaceted tasks that make up each lesson set.

Q How do you address Foundational Standards for Reading and Language Standards?

A When applicable, Foundational Skills for Reading Standards and Language Standards may be listed with a lesson; however, the full range of Reading Foundations and Language Standards is outside the scope of these lesson sets.

We recommend that teachers plan opportunities for students to build Reading Foundational Skills by exploring grade-level appropriate skills in the context of the core texts from each lesson set and applying this knowledge to their independent reading and writing. Schools may also wish to acquire

developmentally appropriate curricular materials specific to this area. *Words Their Way* by Donald Bear et al. is an excellent example of a program that addresses this need.

Regarding the teaching and application of language standards, we stand with the position of the National Council of Teachers of English:

> the use of isolated grammar and usage exercises not supported by theory and research is a deterrent to the improvement of students' speaking and writing and that, in order to improve both of these, class time at all levels must be devoted to opportunities for meaningful listening, speaking, reading, and writing. (NCTE Position Statement on the Teaching of Grammar, 1998–2009)

The primary goal of grammar study is to improve writing and speaking skills. Students acquire such skills best not from isolated drill and practice of grammar rules, but from engagement in authentic language experiences requiring active participation in reading, writing, listening, and speaking.

> The inclusion of Language standards in their own strand should not be taken as an indication that skills related to conventions, effective language use, and vocabulary are unimportant to reading, writing, speaking, and listening; indeed, they are inseparable from such contexts. (CCSS, p. 25)

Q What are the Language Companion Lessons?

A The Core Ready Lesson Sets provide the type of authentic integrated experiences that will help all students expand their language skills.

Explicit instruction in selected language concepts benefits students as they try to navigate the complex rules and requirements of conventional English. To this end, we have provided Language Companion Lessons, one per grade, as resources and models for the explicit teaching of language standards within the context of each lesson set topic.

When choosing teaching objectives for the Language Companion Lessons, we considered a few factors. First, we made sure to include a lesson for each of the standards listed in the Language Progressive Skills, which are specially marked in the standards as being particularly likely to require extended attention over time. The inclusion of these growth-targeted standards will help Core Ready teachers start addressing these important topics.

Second, we made sure that the lesson set and Language Companion Lessons were compatible in focus so that students could immediately connect and apply the language learning to their reading and writing experiences. For example, a lesson on punctuating dialogue would not be a very good match for a lesson set on writing editorials—while dialogue might be included in editorials, it is not very common. A lesson on using domain-specific words would be a better language match for that lesson. Teaching this lesson will enhance your students' language use during the lesson set. The Language Companion Lessons can also be used as models for teaching other language standards that couple well with the content of the lesson set.

Q How do you address the Common Core State Standard requirements for text complexity (Standard 10)?

A We have reflected the Core requirements by suggesting texts that meet the standards' call for appropriate text complexity for the lesson set grade level. In addition to our own suggestions for grade-level appropriate text, we have used many exemplars from Appendix B of the Common Core State Standards across each lesson set book.

We support the Common Core State Standards' assertion that the ability to read complex text independently and proficiently is essential for high achievement in college and the workplace and important in numerous life tasks. To this end, we also agree with the Core Standards tenet that all students deserve opportunities to read and engage with high-quality literature. We stand firmly, however, by years of research that suggests that students who are learning to read need extended practice (Allington, 2009; Kuhn et al., 2006) with texts that they can read with accuracy and comprehension (Allington, 2012; Ehri, Dreyer, Flugman, & Gross, 2007) in order to improve their abilities. This means time spent reading appropriately leveled text, which may be above, within, or below grade level depending on an individual's needs and skills. This type of differentiation typically takes place in small-group and independent settings.

Q Do I have to use the core texts recommended in the lesson set? What if I can't get a text or I have a different one in mind?

A Although we always provide specific suggestions for texts that we feel will serve you and your students well for each lesson, there is always room to make thoughtful substitutions. Can't find the text cited in the lesson? No problem. Use the Already Have a great piece in your classroom collection? description of what to look for in the introduction to guide you to substitute texts you already own or already love.

Q Are teachers required to use the text exemplars listed by the Common Core State Standards in Appendix B?

A The writers of the Core Standards intended the text exemplars as models of appropriate texts for each grade band, not a required list, as stated below:

> The choices should serve as useful guideposts in helping educators select texts of similar complexity, quality, and range for their own classrooms. They expressly do not represent a partial or complete reading list. (Common Core, 2011, p. 2)

We have included some of the Appendix B texts in the lesson sets alongside our own choices of texts that meet the parameters suggested by the exemplars.

Q You include an icon for speaking and listening opportunities and strategies to support ELLs in only some lessons, yet there seem to be lots of speaking and listening and similar ELL strategies in practically every lesson. Why don't you mark every instance with an icon?

A Icons are added where we felt teachers should purposefully focus their instruction and attention on a particular element. Core Ready Lessons are rich with practices that strengthen speaking, listening, and language skills, such as conversing with a classmate, but we do not include an icon in every instance. We hope that by highlighting effective practices in selected lessons, we will increase teachers' awareness of how to build speaking, listening, and language skills in any lesson they teach.

Q Must the lesson sets be taught in any particular order?

A Each set of 10 reading and writing lessons has been designed to be modular; that is, the sequence in which you teach the lesson sets may vary in response to local curricular needs, testing schedules, or other factors that influence a school calendar. However, that being said, we offer a suggested set of calendar options for you in our online PDToolkit. We make specific, strongly encouraged suggestions in regard to the K–2 lessons in particular.

Q Should the individual lessons be taught in the order they appear in the book?

A Yes. The lessons within the Core Ready lesson sets are arranged in a purposeful sequence that reflects respected models of how students learn, such as the "gradual release of responsibility" model (Pearson and Gallagher, 1993) and "cognitive apprenticeship theory" (Collins, Brown, & Newman, 1989). Across the lessons, the teacher guides the students toward increasing levels of independence with the lesson set goals. The teaching objectives of each lesson generally build on the knowledge gained in the previous lesson and many student products are developed in a series of steps across multiple lessons. Therefore, the lessons are designed to be taught as a set and are best delivered in the sequence we provide.

There are four stages in a Core Ready lesson set: Introduce, Define, Extend, and Assess. We use the acronym I.D.E.A. to refer to this structure. Each stage is described below. For a much more detailed description of these stages, please see the foundational book of this series, *Be Core Ready: Powerful, Effective Steps to Implementing and Achieving the Common Core State Standards.*

▶ **Introduce** The Introduce stage activates students' background knowledge and builds a big-picture understanding of the topic of study.

▶ **Define** The Define stage provides students with essential knowledge, terms, and structures that will guide their learning about the topic across the unit.

▶ **Extend** If you compare the types of lessons found in the Define stage of the unit to a road map to learning, the Extend stage might be likened to a series of guided day trips designed to help students become increasingly independent travelers. This is the phase in which students apply and refine the skills and strategies they need to achieve the goals of the unit.

▶ **Assess** The Assess stage serves to wrap up each lesson set in a meaningful way intended to encourage students to recognize and commit to how they have grown as readers, writers, listeners, and speakers.

Q Is it important to teach both the reading and the writing lessons?

A The reading and writing lesson sets are strategically connected, and we have long advocated teaching reading and writing in an integrated manner. That is, what we study with our classes in reading is directly related to what we study in writing. For example, a reading lesson set on successful reading of folktales is taught alongside writing lessons on how to write folktales. Or a set of reading lessons on determining theme in traditional text is accompanied by lessons on theme-related written response to literature.

We have found that the confluence of reading and writing benefits both students and teachers. Each area, reading or writing, helps students be more successful in the other via the natural connections that students make between the two disciplines. A reading experience helps students gain knowledge that helps them develop and enhance the content and structure of connected writing tasks. As students read folktales, for example, they gain a sense of the literary elements, author's purpose, and craft techniques that they will need to consider and include as they write folktales. Likewise, a close study of how to write folktales raises student awareness of what to expect in this genre, leading them be more confident and perceptive readers.

Teachers intuitively understand that such connections help students, but often, curricular materials do not align reading and writing together. Core Ready's dynamically integrated reading and writing lesson sets make it easy for teachers to help students see important connections clearly and immediately. "In reading yesterday, we talked about how folktales usually include magic and fantasy. Today in writing, you begin to imagine how magic and fantasy can be an important part of your original tale."

Because of the close relationship between our reading and writing lesson sets, we strongly recommend that they be taught side by side. Is it possible to teach *just* the reading lessons or *just* the writing lessons? In most cases, with some adjustments, this could be done, but again, we recommend that reading and writing be presented simultaneously to maximize the benefits for students and teachers.

Q You provide a lot of specific guidelines for what teachers should say aloud and do during the lessons. Should I follow those specifications exactly?

A It depends. There are all kinds of cooks out there. Some like to follow the recipe to the letter. Some like to refer to a recipe and immediately improvise with the ingredients and procedure. Others like to follow a recipe exactly the first time, and figure out places they want to modify next time to suit their tastes and needs. It is much the same with teachers and lesson plans. We expect that some teachers will adopt these plans as written and others will adapt them to suit their teaching style, needs, and resources. The quotes and directions are there to model how the teaching *might* go. The most non-negotiable elements by far are the teaching objectives and standards alignment. If you keep your eye on those as your ultimate destinations, there are many roads that will get you there. These lessons are designed to guide you along the way.

Q Are the lessons meant to be taught in one class period? If not, what are your suggestions for timing?

A Each lesson provides guidelines for six instructional segments: Warm Up, Teach, Try, Clarify, Practice, and Wrap Up. As your students become actively engaged in the rich content of the lessons, you are often likely to find that one class period will not be enough time to complete all of these segments thoroughly. It is perfectly OK to split the segments over two or more periods.

We encourage you to use your professional judgment to decide how to allocate your time teaching these lessons. There are, however, a few rules of thumb that will make your teaching more successful:

1. *Make every effort to include all six segments of the lesson.* There is a purposeful flow and gradual release of responsibility embedded in every lesson to guide students to build independence. Skipping sections interrupts this flow and reduces the likelihood that students will achieve the objectives of the lesson.

2. *Don't let the whole-group segments at the beginning of the lesson (Warm Up, Teach, Try, Clarify) eat up all of your time.* As a group, many teachers have a tendency to go on too long with the whole class lesson. Come on—you know we are talking to you! Nearly all of us are guilty of this from time to time. Just one more example, ask a couple more questions to check understanding, address a few more wayward student comments—we've all been there! Try to keep the whole-group instruction sharply focused with a succinct demonstration (Teach) and rehearsal (Try) of the teaching objective. Your students' attention span is limited, and you need to get "off the stage" so that they can get to what is arguably the most important part of the lessons. Which brings us to . . .

3. *Allow ample time for independent practice.* Although courtside instruction and pep talks from the coach are helpful to a budding basketball player, nothing builds a player's skills like playing the game. Likewise, while young readers and writers certainly need your teaching and guidance, what they really need most is to *read and write*—eyes on the text, pencils on paper, actively thinking and engaging in the reading and writing process *themselves*. This is where the students get to apply the teaching objective of the lesson on their own using their own texts or writing. This is where they work through the hard stuff of reading and writing that builds capacity, confidence, and stamina—focused practice, collaboration with other learners, making and revising mistakes, making choices, and revising their thinking and understanding of how language works. It is perfectly OK and necessary for you to coach from the sidelines, but if students are to become independent readers and writers, they must have extended time working independently. How much time is "ample" time? Depending on the grade level, we usually allocate about half of the total lesson time to independent practice. So, within 80 minutes spent on all six lesson segments, about 35 to 40 minutes should be in independent practice. Younger students and students who are unaccustomed to working independently will need to build up to longer periods of independent work. While your students are working independently, you may be holding teaching conferences with individual students, working with small groups to differentiate instruction, or making assessment notes to inform your planning.

A variety of options for allocating lesson plan time are in the table on the next page. All are based on a 50-minute class period. If you have more or less time, scale up or scale down the number of minutes accordingly, keeping proportions similar.

Timing Guidelines for a Lesson

	Days (Minutes)	Lesson Segment (Minutes)
A lesson that includes all six segments in one 50-minute session	Day 1 (50)	Warm Up (3), Teach (10), Try (5), Clarify (2), Practice (25), Wrap Up (5)
A lesson that spans 2 days	Day 1 (50)	Warm Up (10), Teach (20), Try (15), Clarify (5)
	Day 2 (50)	Practice (45), Wrap Up (5)
A lesson that spans 3 days with extended time for the independent practice	Day 1 (50)	Warm Up (10), Teach (20), Try (15), Clarify (5)
	Day 2 (50)	Practice (50)
	Day 3 (50)	Additional Practice (40), Wrap Up (10)
A lesson that spans 2 days, plus a reteach based on Milestone Performance Assessment data to allow students more time to achieve the teaching objective	Day 1 (50)	Warm Up (10), Teach (20), Try (15), Clarify (5)
	Day 2 (50)	Practice (45), Wrap Up (5)
	Day 3 (50)	Reteach Based on Milestone Data Warm Up (3), Teach (10), Try (5), Clarify (2), Practice (25), Wrap Up (5)

PD TOOLKIT™

Accompanying *Core Ready for Grades 3–5*, there is an online resource site with media tools that, together with the text, provides you with the tools you need to implement the lesson sets.

The PDToolkit for Pam Allyn's *Core Ready Series* is available free for 12 months after you use the password that comes with the box set for each grade band. After that, you can purchase access for an additional 12 months. If you did not purchase the box set, you can purchase a 12-month subscription at **http://pdtoolkit.pearson.com**. Be sure to explore and download the resources available at the website. Currently the following resources are available:

- Pearson Children's and Young Adult Literature Database
- Videos
- PowerPoint Presentations
- Student Artifacts
- Photos and Visual Media
- Handouts, Forms, and Posters to supplement your Core-aligned lesson plans
- Lessons and Homework Assignments
- Close Reading Guides and Samples
- Children's Core Literature Recommendations

In the future, we will continue to add additional resources. To learn more, please visit **http://pdtoolkit.pearson.com.**

Common Core State Standards Alignment

Available in the PDToolkit is a matrix that details the Common Core State Standards alignment for each Core Ready lesson set in all of the Core Ready books. See sample shown below.

Common Core Language Arts Standards Alignment

Standard Number	Standard	The Road to Knowledge (RK)	The Power to Persuade (PP)	The Shape of Story (SS)	The Journey to Meaning (JM)
Reading Literature					
RL.3.1	Ask and answer questions to demonstrate understanding of a text, referring explicitly to the text as the basis for the answers.	•	•		
RL.3.2	Recount stories, including fables, folktales, and myths from diverse cultures; determine the central message, lesson, or moral and explain how it is conveyed through key details in the text.		•	•	
RL.3.3	Describe characters in a story (e.g., their traits, motivations, or feelings) and explain how their actions contribute to the sequence of events.	•			•
RL.3.4	Determine the meaning of words and phrases as they are used in a text, distinguishing literal from nonliteral language.		•		•
RL.3.5	Refer to parts of stories, dramas, and poems when writing or speaking about a text, using terms such as chapter, scene, and stanza; describe how each successive part builds on earlier sections.	•		•	
RL.3.6	Distinguish their own point of view from that of the narrator or those of the characters.	•	•	•	•
RL.3.7	Explain how specific aspects of a text's illustrations contribute to what is conveyed by the words in a story (e.g., create mood, emphasize aspects of a character or setting).		•		•
RL.3.8	(Not applicable to literature)				
RL.3.9	Compare and contrast the themes, settings, and plots of stories written by the same author about the same or similar characters (e.g., in books from a series).	•	•		
RL.3.10	By the end of the year, read and comprehend literature, including stories, dramas, and poetry, at the high end of the grades 2–3 text complexity band independently and proficiently.	•	•	•	•

Grade 3

What Matters Most:
Research and Analysis in Informational Text

Introduction

This lesson set will build on the knowledge of nonfiction reading and writing students have gained in previous grades by focusing on a specific variety of informational text. Frequently, the terms *nonfiction* and *informational text* are used interchangeably. The Common Core State Standards characterize informational text at the K–5 level broadly as including "biographies and autobiographies; books about history, social studies, science, and the arts; technical texts, including directions, forms and information displayed in graphs, charts, or maps; and digital sources on a range of topics." In this lesson set, students will focus on the variety of informational text designed to convey knowledge about a given topic in an instructional way. The information in these texts is organized in clusters of like information and marked with features to guide and inform the reader such as headings, bold print, graphics, captions, and the like. This is in contrast to what the Common Core State Standards term "literary non-fiction," which includes "exposition, argument, and functional text in the form of personal essays, speeches, opinion pieces, essays about art or literature, biographies, memoirs, journalism, and historical, scientific, technical, or economic accounts (including digital sources) written for a broad audience."

Why This Lesson Set?

In this lesson set, students will:

- Use text features to read and navigate a wide variety of informational texts
- Read closely and think analytically to determine the big ideas in informational text
- Choose topics and generate research question
- Build note-taking and research skills as they gather information from multiple sources
- Use their research to create and present informational articles

Informational texts come in many formats—including books, magazine articles, and Internet websites. Learning to navigate informational texts is vital for success later in school. Students will be expected to remember and interpret information from textbooks as they move through the grades, and success with this genre is an essential part of being college-ready. Nonfiction text represents the vast majority of reading and writing done by adults and a large portion of the passages that students encounter on standardized tests (Hoyt, Mooney, & Parks, 2003). If we are going to prepare students to be successful in school and in their reading and writing lives beyond school, we need to devote time and creative energy to teaching them the skills they need in order to be successful readers and writers of informational texts.

Focusing on research skills is an important vehicle for teaching students about informational texts. You may be wondering, how do we teach children to do research in elementary school? In this lesson set, we examine the nature of research and explain ways to make research accessible and enjoyable for third graders. Research is a form of inquiry. That is, it is a process of ongoing questioning and a discipline for seeking answers. Our natural curiosity about the world is what

should drive our research in third grade and beyond. Once a question is sparked, research requires a disciplined look at a range of sources to gain an in-depth understanding of the topic being investigated. The research process involves a mastery of skills, including thinking skills and an array of literacy skills. In the end, research is meant to be shared, whether you are an academic scholar at the university level or a third grader engaged in research for the first time.

We teach research to make students independent problem solvers inside and outside the classroom. We teach research to inspire students to be lifelong inquirers who recognize that there is more than one answer to a question. We teach research as a form of purposeful, thoughtful learning that requires deep investigation over time. We teach research to guide students while they determine what they want to know and how to go about finding the answers. As teachers, we can set guidelines and model the process, but we believe the topics and questions must be driven by what students want to know. Our initial role as teachers is to work with students on what burning questions they have. As we engage students in the research process, we empower them to synthesize information, come to their own conclusions, develop their own opinions grounded in evidence, and gain respect for the beliefs and opinions of others.

Helping students understand what they read is a hallmark of grade 3. In this lesson set, the focus of big ideas and evidence to prove them in informational texts will help students in any genre moving forward. In grades K–2,

children begin to master the decoding skills described in the standards for reading foundational skills. Students in grade 3 apply these skills to negotiate multi-syllabic words, which in turn increases their fluency and confidence when reading new and unfamiliar material. By focusing on the big ideas in informational texts, students have an opportunity to practice these skills in a focused way.

In support of the reading standards, students are taught within this lesson set to ask questions of one another, to deepen their understanding of the big ideas and supporting details that prove them. Students will have many opportunities to read aloud fluently and offer appropriate elaboration on the ideas of classmates by building on what has been said before. By focusing on what matters most in a text, students will develop a deeper understanding of how informational texts are structured and what strategies they can employ to determine the main idea.

Through writing an informational article, students will become better readers of informational text. More specifically, this lesson set provides students the opportunity to write articles based on their research. Through the writing process, students will practice using text features to convey the big idea to their readers. In addition, the importance of paragraphing to cluster information will be emphasized, as well as the use of a variety of sentence types to help hook readers and then guide them to what matters most in the article.

Common Core State Standards Alignment

Reading Standards

RI.3.1 Ask and answer questions to demonstrate understanding of a text, referring explicitly to the text as the basis for the answers.

RI.3.2 Determine the main idea of a text; recount the key details and explain how they support the main idea.

RI.3.3 Describe the relationship between a series of historical events, scientific ideas or concepts, or steps in technical procedures in a text, using language that pertains to time, sequence, and cause/effect.

RI.3.4 Determine the meaning of general academic and domain-specific words and phrases in a text relevant to a grade 3 topic or subject area.

RI.3.5 Use text features and search tools (e.g., key words, sidebars, hyperlinks) to locate information relevant to a given topic efficiently.

RI.3.6 Distinguish their own point of view from that of the author of a text.

RI.3.7 Use information gained from illustrations (e.g., maps, photographs) and the words in a text to demonstrate

understanding of the text (e.g., where, when, why, and how key events occur).

RI.3.8 Describe the logical connection between particular sentences and paragraphs in a text (e.g., comparison, cause/effect, first/second/third in a sequence).

RI.3.9 Compare and contrast the most important points and key details presented in two texts on the same topic.

RI.3.10 By the end of the year, read and comprehend informational texts, including history/social studies, science, and technical texts, at the high end of the grades 2–3 text complexity band independently and proficiently.

Writing Standards

W.3.2 Write information/explanatory texts to examine a topic and convey ideas and information clearly.

a. Introduce a topic and group related information together; include illustrations when useful to aiding comprehension.

b. Develop the topic with facts, definitions, and details.

c. Use linking words and phrases (e.g., also, another, and, more, but) to connect ideas within categories of information.

d. Provide a concluding statement or section.

W.3.4 With guidance and support from adults, produce writing in which the development and organization are appropriate to the task and purpose.

W.3.5 With guidance and support from peers and adults, develop and strengthen writing as needed by planning, revising, and editing.

W.3.7 Conduct short research projects that build knowledge about a topic.

W.3.8 Recall information from experiences or gather information from print and digital sources; take brief notes on sources and sort evidence into provided categories.

W.3.10 Write routinely over extended time frames (time for research, reflection, and revision) and shorter time frames (a single sitting or a day or two) for a range of discipline-specific tasks, purposes, and audiences.

Speaking and Listening Standards

SL.3.1 Engage effectively in a range of collaborative discussions (one-on-one, in groups, and teacher-led) with diverse partners on grade 3 topics and texts, building on others' ideas and expressing their own clearly.

a. Come to discussions prepared, having read or studied required materials; explicitly draw on that preparation and other information known about the topic to explore ideas under discussion.

b. Follow agreed-upon rules for discussions (e.g., gaining the floor in respectful ways, listening to others with care, speaking one at a time about the topics and texts under discussion).

c. Ask questions to check understanding of information presented, stay on topic, and link their comments to the remarks of others.

d. Explain their own ideas and understanding in light of the discussion.

SL.3.2 Determine the main ideas and supporting details of a text read aloud or information presented in diverse media and formats including visual, quantitative, and oral presentations.

SL.3.6 Speak in complete sentences when appropriate to task and situation in order to provide requested detail or clarification.

Language Standards

L.3.1 Demonstrate command of the conventions of standard English grammar and usage when writing or speaking.

a. Explain the function of nouns, pronouns, verbs, adjectives, and adverbs in general and their functions in particular sentences.

b. Form and use regular and irregular plural nouns.

c. Use abstract nouns (e.g., childhood).

d. Form and use regular and irregular verbs.

e. Form and use the simple (e.g., I walked; I walk; I will walk) verb tenses.

f. Ensure subject-verb and pronoun-antecedent agreement.

g. Form and use comparative and superlative adjectives and adverbs, and choose between them depending on what is to be modified.

h. Use coordinating and subordinating conjunctions.

i. Produce simple, compound, and complex sentences.

L.3.2 Demonstrate command of the conventions of standard English capitalization, punctuation, and spelling when writing.

a. Capitalize appropriate words in titles.

b. Use commas in addresses.

c. Use commas and quotation marks in dialogue.

d. Form and use possessives.

e. Use conventional spelling for high-frequency and other studied words and for adding suffixes to base words (e.g., sitting, smiled, cries, happiness).

f. Use spelling patterns and generalizations (e.g., word families, position-based spellings, syllable patterns, ending rules, meaningful word parts) in writing words.

g. Consult reference materials, including beginning dictionaries, as needed to check and correct spellings.

L.3.3 Use knowledge of language and its conventions when writing, speaking, reading, or listening.

a. Choose words and phrases for effect.

b. Recognize and observe differences between the conventions of spoken and written standard English.

L.3.6 Acquire and use accurately grade-appropriate conversational, general academic, and domain-specific words and phrases, including those that signal spatial and temporal relationships (e.g., After dinner that night we went looking for them).

Essential Skill Lenses (PARCC Framework)

As part of its proposal to the U.S. Department of Education, the multi-state Partnership for Assessment of Readiness for College and Careers (PARCC) has developed model content frameworks for English Language Arts to serve as a bridge between the Common Core State Standards and the PARCC assessments, in development at the time of this publication. In the grade 3 to 5 lesson sets, we expect students to engage in reading and writing through eight PARCC specified skill lenses that are rooted in the standards. The following table details how each skill lens is addressed across the lesson set.

	Reading	Writing
Cite Evidence	Students cite the text as evidence throughout this lesson set. In particular, students use text as evidence to identify the main idea and details that support the main idea in nonfiction passages.	Students cite specific evidence from their reading when writing their informational articles.
Analyze Content	Students carefully analyze complex content area texts to identify the main idea.	Students analyze what they have read with careful attention to the most important information in nonfiction texts.
Study and Apply Grammar and Usage	Emphasis will be placed on conventional elements frequently found in informational texts, such as effective paragraphing to cluster information, and the production of simple, compound, and complex sentences.	When writing their own informational news articles, students apply grammar lessons from reading, in particular how to create a solid paragraph and how to vary sentences for effect.
Study and Apply Vocabulary	Specific academic language is included with this lesson set. It is expected that students be exposed to and successfully incorporate these terms into their speaking and writing during this study.	Students are expected to choose precise language to strengthen their writing.
Conduct Discussions	Rules and behaviors that foster productive conversation are a crucial element of this study.	Students continuously engage in conversations about what they see as the main idea and details that support the main idea in informational texts.
Report Findings	Students share what matters most in informational texts on a daily basis with partners and in whole-class discussions.	By writing informational news articles, students will report on the findings from their nonfiction research.
Phonics and Word Recognition	Plan opportunities for students to build Reading Foundational Skills by exploring grade-level appropriate skills in the context of the Core Texts from each lesson set and applying this knowledge to their independent reading.	Encourage students to apply Reading Foundational Skills in the context of their daily writing.
Fluency and Stamina	Fluency and stamina are emphasized throughout the lesson set. Content area texts can easily be scaffolded. Provide students with short texts, building up to longer texts as the lesson set progresses. This will help students build greater fluency and stamina within this genre.	There are many opportunities for short, quick writes as well as longer, more extended writing with their independently written articles. When reading their articles aloud, students will be encouraged to read accurately, with an appropriate pace, and with expression.

© pressman / Fotolia

Core Questions

Third graders need an introduction to the essential skill set of reading informational texts and writing their own research-based articles. The following questions should remain at the core of your teaching. Refer back to them often, encouraging your class to share their thinking as it evolves.

- How do we determine what matters most in an informational text?
- What text features can guide my thinking around the big ideas?
- What evidence can I find to support my thinking about the big ideas?
- What does it mean to conduct research?
- What are the steps I should follow in the research process to determine the big ideas and form my own opinions?
- How do I translate my research into an informational article?
- What can I learn from reading informational articles to help me write my own?

Ready to Get Started?

Let's tap into our students' natural curiosity and desire to learn. . . .

Third graders love gaining new information. They love learning new facts and sharing them with one another. Third graders are also observing the world in new ways and are beginning to ask questions that have many possible answers. You will find that your students are eager to gain the skills needed to find answers to the questions they have on their own, that they are able to integrate their background knowledge with new content, and love learning about historical and scientific topics. Third grade is an ideal time to tap into your students' natural curiosity and their zest for learning new information.

Lesson Set Goals

Within this lesson set, there are many goals we as teachers want to help our students reach.

Reading Goals

- Identify text features and use them to determine what matters most and finds evidence to support thinking. (RI.3.2, RI.3.5, RI.3.10, RI.5.1, SL.3.1a–d, SL.3.6, L.3.1, L.3.6)
- Acquire information by locating and using library media resources.
- Take notes to record big ideas and supporting evidence. (RI.3.1, RI.3.10, W.3.4, W.3.7, W.3.8, W.3.10, L.3.6)
- Compare and contrast information on one topic from two different sources. (RI.3.9, RI.3.10, RI.5.1, W.3.4, W.3.10, L.3.6)
- Notice new vocabulary and apply a variety of strategies for making meaning. (RI.3.1, RI.3.4, RI.3.10, SL.3.6, L.3.1, L.3.6)
- Select books independently to meet informational needs.
- Use illustrations and pictures to gain a deeper understanding of the text. (RI.3.1, RI.3.7, RI.3.10, L.3.6)
- Identify and describe cause and effect relationships in informational text. (RI.3.1, RI.3.3, RI.3.8, RI.3.10, SL.3.1a–d, SL.3.2, SL.3.6, L.3.1, L.3.6)
- Ask and answer questions to demonstrate understanding of a text, referring explicitly to the text as the basis for the answers. (RI.3.1)

- By the end of the year, read and comprehend a variety of literature at the high end of the grades 2–3 text complexity band independently and proficiently. (RL.3.10)
- Write routinely over extended time frames (time for research, reflection, and revision) and shorter time frames (a single sitting or a day or two) for a range of discipline-specific tasks, purposes and audiences. (W.3.10)
- In collaborative discussions, demonstrate evidence of preparation for discussion and exhibit responsibility to the rules and roles of conversation. (SL.3.1a, SL.3.1b)
- In collaborative discussions, share and develop ideas in a manner that enhances understanding of topic. Contribute and respond to the content of the conversation in a productive and focused manner. (SL.3.1c, SL.3.1d)
- Speak in complete sentences when appropriate and demonstrate a command of standard English grammar and usage. (SL.3.6, L.3.1)
- Acquire and accurately use grade-appropriate conversational, general academic, and domain-specific vocabulary and phrases. (L.3.6)

Writing Goals

- Take notes to record big ideas and supporting evidence. (RI.3.1, RI.3.10, W.3.4, W.3.7, W.3.8, W.3.10, L.3.6)
- Write an informational article that includes a headline, lead, and clincher. (W.3.2a, W.3.2d, W.3.4, W.3.7, W.3.10)
- Produce clear, well-organized, and well-developed informational article. (W.3.2, W.3.7, W.3.10)
- Write labels and captions for graphics. (W.3.4, W.3.10)
- Develop the topic with facts, definitions, and details and use linking words and phrases. (W.3.2b, W.3.2c, W.3.10)
- With guidance and support from peers and adults, plan, revise, and edit—paying close attention to the conventions of standard English and clarity of the writing's development. (W.3.5)
- With guidance and support from adults and peers, create a visual presentation of the final story. (W.3.4, W.3.6, SL.3.1a–d, SL.3.6, L.3.1, L.3.6)

- Ask and answer questions to demonstrate understanding of a text, referring explicitly to the text as the basis for the answers. (RI.3.1)
- By the end of the year, read and comprehend a variety of informational texts at the high end of the grades 2–3 text complexity band independently and proficiently. (RI.3.10)
- Write routinely over extended time frames (time for research, reflection, and revision) and shorter time frames (a single sitting or a day or two) for a range of discipline-specific tasks, purposes, and audiences. (W.3.10)
- In collaborative discussions, demonstrate evidence of preparation for discussion and exhibit responsibility to the rules and roles of conversation. (SL.3.1a, SL.3.1b)
- In collaborative discussions, share and develop ideas in a manner that enhances understanding of topic. Contribute and respond to the content of the conversation in a productive and focused manner. (SL.3.1c, SL.3.1d)
- Speak in complete sentences when appropriate and demonstrate a command of standard English grammar and usage. (SL.3.6, L.3.1)
- Demonstrate knowledge of standard English and its conventions. (L.3.1, L.3.2, L.3.3)
- Acquire and accurately use grade-appropriate conversational, general academic, and domain-specific vocabulary and phrases. (L.3.6)

Choosing Core Texts

For this lesson set, you will need to gather informational books and informational articles for your class to explore during independent practice. Try to select texts that represent a range of topics that may interest your students—you know them best, after all! Also think about gathering texts of varying difficulty, so that everyone can find something appropriate and readable. Comb your classroom reading collection, reach out to your school librarian, and look to your local public library to assist you in collecting enough resources. In addition to informational books, there are a number of excellent magazines written for this age group that expose students to informational articles, including *National Geographic Kids*, *Time for Kids*, and *Scholastic News*. You can also search your local newspapers for feature articles that demonstrate the

> In the "Information Age" the importance of being able to "read and write informational texts critically and well cannot be overstated. Informational literacy is central to success, and even survival, in schooling, the workplace and the community.

—Nell Dube,
Michigan State University

skills you're going to focus on in this lesson set: a focused topic that is of interest to third graders, engaging hook, use of research, interesting language, an effective conclusion. Look for articles that make good use of text features such as titles, headings, subheadings, text boxes, charts, diagrams, graphs, font variety, and captions.

For the purposes of modeling each lesson with a common set of texts, we've chosen the general topic of the environment. You could change the topic of this lesson set and corresponding texts to match your local curriculum and resources. The teaching objectives in each reading and writing lesson can be applied to any informational texts or topics that interest your students. The following is a list of books and articles we use throughout the lesson sets. The articles and videos mentioned are available online from National Geographic Kids.

Books

Kids Care!: 75 Ways to Make a Difference for People, Animals & the Environment by Rebecca Olien

Not Your Typical Book About the Environment by Elin Kelsey

Articles

"The Case of the Missing Bees" (Time for Kids)

"A Chat with Jane Goodall" (Time for Kids)

"Drinking Water: Bottled or from the Tap" by Catherine Clarke Fox

"Green Tips" (Time for Kids)

"Polar Bears Listed as Threatened" (National Geographic News)

"Rainforest Rescue" (Scholastic News)

"This Bulb" (video available online at National Geographic Kids)

"Young Voices on Climate Change" (video available online at National Geographic Kids)

"Zipper's Green Tips" by Emily Busch, David George Gordon, and Catherine D. Hughes

Other books we recommend on the topic of the environment include:

365 Ways to Live Green for Kids: Saving the Environment at Home, School, or at Play—Every Day! by Sheri Amsel

The Adventures of a Plastic Bottle: A Story about Recycling by Alison Inches

Garbage and Recycling (Young Discoverers: Environmental Facts and Experiments) by Rosie Harlow

The Good Garden: How One Family Went from Hunger to Having Enough by Katie Smith Milway

The Mangrove Tree: Planting Trees to Feed Families by Susan L. Roth and Cindy Trumbore

Michael Recycle by Ellie Bethel

One Well: The Story of Water on Earth by Rochelle Strauss

The Scrap Kins Build-It Book by Brian Yanish

Where Do Recyclable Materials Go? by Sabbithry Persad

Why Should I Protect Nature by Jen Green

Why Should I Recycle by Jen Green

Why Should I Save Energy by Jen Green

Why Should I Save Water by Jen Green

A Note about Addressing Reading Standard 10: Range of Reading and Level of Text Complexity

This lesson set provides all students with opportunities to work with texts deemed appropriate for their grade level, as well as texts at their specific reading level. Through shared experiences and focused instruction, all students engage with and comprehend a wide range of texts within their grade-level complexity band. We suggest a variety of high-quality complex text to use within the whole-group lessons and recommend a variety of additional titles under Choosing Core Texts to extend and enrich instruction. During independent practice and in small-group collaborations, however, research strongly suggests that all students need to work with texts they can read with a high level of accuracy and comprehension (i.e., at their developmentally appropriate instructional level), in order to significantly improve their reading skill (Allington, 2012; Ehri, Dreyer, Flugman, & Gross, 2007). Depending on individual needs and skills, students' reading levels may be above, within, or below their grade-level band.

Goal	Low-Tech	High-Tech
Students engage with a variety of informational texts around a specific topic of interest.	Students work with the following sources: • Books • Printed copies of online informational articles • Articles from appropriate children's magazines and newspapers.	Students work with the following sources: • Books • Printed copies of online informational articles • Articles from appropriate children's magazines and newspapers In addition, students search the Internet for additional sources, using key words and following hyperlinks to find the most relevant material.

Teacher's Notes

Third grade is an important first step in the ability of our students to do research. In previous grades, research takes the form of questioning and group research but does not necessarily culminate in a final product developed over time that students create independently. Third grade provides that bridge year for students. The following steps are important for student research:

- Immersion in what informational text is all about
- Asking questions
- Narrowing the topic
- Creating key words
- Locating sources
- Locating information within sources
- Recording information—note taking
- Organizing information
- Coming to conclusions
- Presenting information

The following materials will help you organize the research process for students:

- Student research folders
- Ready to Review baskets for submission
- Reminder charts that review key concepts and guidelines to scaffold student independence

Core Message to Students

Before the first lesson, use this as a shared reading or read-aloud to set the stage and engage students in discussion about your upcoming study. See Appendix 3.1 for an enlarged version to reproduce and share with students.

Who has ever had a burning question and desperately needed an answer? What did you do? Did you talk to someone who you thought was an expert on the topic? Did you go the library or log on to the Internet to find what you were looking for? In this lesson set we're all going to be journalists—first by asking questions and then by seeking the answers. Journalists research, write, and report on the information they've learned on a topic. As journalists we're going to read and write about a topic of great importance in our world today. In this lesson set, your questions are going to be as important as the answers we find. So, let's think about, 'What do we want to know?'

Questions for Close Reading

The Core Ready lessons include many rich opportunities to engage students in close reading of text that requires them to ask and answer questions, draw conclusions, and use specific text evidence to support their thinking (Reading Anchor Standard 1). These opportunities are marked with a close reading icon. You may wish to extend these experiences using our recommended Core Texts or with texts of your choosing. Use the following questions as a resource to guide students through close reading experiences in any informational text.

- What is the purpose of this text?
- What is the most important information in the text?
- How is this text set up? Do you recognize a pattern or structure?
- What is the main idea of this text? What is the main idea of this section? How do you know?
- What details support the main idea?
- What information is interesting but not necessarily important to the main idea?
- What features are built in to help the reader understand the information?
- What vocabulary is unfamiliar to you? How can you find out what these words mean?
- Does the text appear to be complete? What could you add?
- How do you think the author prepared to write this? What resources were used?
- Do you detect bias? Why do you think so?
- How is this information important to you?

Building Academic Language

Academic language use will build your students' comprehension of the focus of this lesson set and facilitate their ability to talk and write about what they learn. Rather than introduce all the Core Words at once, slowly add them to a learning wall as your teaching unfolds. See the glossary at the end of this chapter for complete definitions of the words. Also listed here are sentence frames that may be included as a handout to scaffold student use of the content words or on a sentence wall (Carrier and Tatum, 2006), a research-proven

Core Words

article	layout
caption	lay out
diagram	main idea
evidence	nonfiction
fact	opinion
glossary	outline
hypothesis	paraphrase
index	quote
informational text	research
	supporting detail
	table of contents
	tables
	template

Core Phrases

- The main idea of this article is _____.
- My favorite part of the article is _____ because _____.
- This article reminds me of another article we've read called _____ because _____.
- I think this because _____ (textual evidence to support your thinking).

strategy for English language learners (Lewis, 1993; Nattinger, 1980). Some students, especially English language learners, may need explicit practice in using the sentence frames. Encourage all students to use these words and phrases regularly in their conversations and writing.

Recognition

At the end of the lesson set, it is important to recognize the hard work your students have put into their learning and the way they've thought about themselves and others. At the end of the reading lessons, students will be creating a class handbook, *Reading Like a Researcher*, that incorporates the class charts created during this lesson set. This will be a great tool as students embark on their independent research project. At the end of the writing lessons, students will be creating their own newsletters that combine text and images to explain what they've learned on an important topic of interest such as the environment. These will be wonderful publications to share with the other grades. Your students will be the toast of the school!

Assessment

Assessment in this lesson set is both ongoing and culminating, meaning that as teachers we are constantly kid-watching and observing how students make meaning and how they are interpreting new material. Throughout this lesson set, look for performance-based evaluation aids called Milestone Performance Assessments, each marked with an assessment icon. Milestone Performance Assessments are opportunities to notice and record data on standards-aligned indicators during the course of the lesson set. Use the results of these assessments to determine how well students are progressing toward the goals of the lesson set. Adjust the pace of your teaching and plan instructional support as needed.

In addition, we encourage you to use the Core Ready Reading Rubric and Core Ready Writing Rubric (also marked with an assessment icon) that are provided with each lesson set to evaluate overall student performance on the standards-aligned lesson set goals. In this lesson set, the finalized informational articles are an important piece for performance-based assessment that can be analyzed and then placed in a portfolio of student work.

In addition, we have provided a Speaking and Listening Performance Checklist in Appendix 3.20 that provides observable Core Standards–aligned indicators for you to use when assessing student performance as speakers and listeners. There are multiple opportunities in every Core Ready Lesson Set to make such observations. Use the checklist in its entirety to gather performance data over time or choose appropriate indicators to create a customized checklist to match a specific learning experience.

Core Support for Diverse Learners

This lesson set was created with the needs of a wide variety of learners in mind. Throughout the day-by-day lessons, you'll find examples of visual supports, graphic organizers, highlighted speaking and listening opportunities, and research-driven English language learner supports aimed at scaffolding instruction for all learners. Also, we urge you to consider the following areas of challenge with which your students may need guided support. The following sections are written to spotlight important considerations as you move through the lesson sets.

Reading

Choosing texts that are at students' reading levels is essential for their reading success and reading identity. When finding texts, make sure you have various levels, cultures, and native language text represented in your classroom library. Your students or some of your students may benefit from repeated exposure to a lesson's teaching objective over several days. This can be accomplished with the whole class or in small-group settings.

Closely monitor your students who are reading below grade level to determine whether they are reading with accuracy and fluency to support comprehension. Encourage students to use context to confirm or self-correct word recognition and understanding and to reread when necessary. Refer to the Common Core Foundational Skills Standards both at the grade 3 level as well as kindergarten, grade 1, and grade 2 standards for direct, explicit foundational skills support that your students who read below grade level may need.

Informational texts can often have unfamiliar words that will require teacher support to decode and understand. While our Core Words provide overarching informational text vocabulary, it is essential to preview the informational texts that readers who are below grade level will independently read during this lesson set. Consider providing your third graders with highlighters so that they can record words that they know and words that are unfamiliar. For many students, this may mean words that they do not know the meaning of; however, students working to decode multisyllabic words should be encouraged to highlight or record words that they are unsure of reading. In this way, you can provide ongoing support for them as developing readers while building independence. In addition, students reading below grade level or students who struggle with organization of ideas may need a great deal of help with their independent research. You may want to pair students with a research partner.

Establishing routines will be essential for all learners but will be especially important for emerging readers needing consistent opportunities to process the information required to conduct research. Frequently monitor students who need extra support. Condense the main ideas and key concepts from readings for students who need adaptations. In addition, emphasize and repeat the steps required for research for students who need repeated practice. For those students who need more scaffolding, consider forming small groups of students and conducting small-group research rather than independent projects. Work closely with the school librarian to find sources at all levels.

As you continue your work with students, use observational notes and reading assessment data to create two to three specific short-term goals for your students with diverse needs. For example, as stated previously, these goals may be related to increasing word accuracy, building vocabulary, improving fluency, or enhancing comprehension. Throughout this lesson set, tailor your individualized and small-group instruction set so that it addresses and evaluates student progress toward these goals. Diverse learners may need a great deal of help with their independent research. You may want to pair students with a research partner.

Writing

Inspired writers are motivated writers. Allowing students to choose the topic of their writing is critical for their ultimate success and their positive development of identity as a writer. When immersing your students in a new genre, form, or purpose for writing, be sure to emphasize the meaning and function this particular type of writing may have in their own lives. Many of your students will also benefit from exposure to strong mentor texts, examples of your own writing, and the experience of sharing their own work—both the final product and in process.

Many of your students will significantly benefit from the opportunity to sketch the main idea of their news article before adding text. For example, some students will require extra support in writing to move from drawing to writing or to move from a graphic organizer to sentences. This is especially helpful for visual learners and students who need to "sketch to stretch." Even your most proficient writers can benefit from this step, but many of your resistant writers will feel more comfortable with getting their ideas on paper through drawing first. Giving students some sentence starters (see the Core Words and Core Phrases) can vastly help them focus their ideas and have the stamina to get their thoughts on paper:

- The main idea is _____.
- One important detail is _____.
- Another important detail is _____.

As your students move from determining their ideas for their news articles and begin crafting their piece, provide your students with a variety of paper choices that are third grade appropriate. For students with fine motor control issues, providing students with a variety of paper choices that have handwriting lines with a dotted line in the middle can offer support as letter formation may require significant energy for some writers. Also consider having some students type and electronically publish their articles rather than handwrite them if that is a medium more conducive to their writing success.

We want our third graders to communicate their news articles to an audience and supporting them as developing writers is essential. In addition to providing students with topic choice and the opportunity to draw prior to writing, we can provide further scaffolding by having students orally rehearse their ideas to us or to a peer. For some students, the oral rehearsal will provide a springboard to writing. For others, they will have greater success dictating their news article to you.

As with the reading lessons, your students may benefit from several days on a single lesson's teaching objective. This can be done with the whole class or in small-group settings.

English Language Learners

Although it is always our goal as teachers to get to know all of our students deeply both in and out of the classroom setting, this work is perhaps more critical when considering our English language learners. Honoring families' cultural traditions and experiences is important to getting to know, understand, and work with your students in meaningful ways. This can be supported through a library that represents a wide range of levels, cultures, and native language text.

English language learners are learning about folktales alongside native English speakers in your classroom, but they are also simultaneously learning English. For our English language learners, it is essential to simultaneously develop their ability to easily hold conversations about their reading and writing and build their academic language base. Goldenberg (2010) defines "academic English" as the more abstract, complex, and challenging language that permits us to participate successfully in mainstream classroom instruction. English language learners will over time be responsible for understanding and producing academic English both orally and in writing. However, language acquisition is a process and our English language learners range in their development of English language proficiency. We urge you to consider your students along a spectrum of language acquisition from those new to this country to those who are proficient conversationally to those who have native-like proficiency. When planning instruction, consider the role of native language in the language acquisition process. You can support the tie to native language by pairing ELLs with other native speakers and supporting them in translating their thoughts.

Refer to the English language learner icons throughout this lesson set for ways to shelter instruction for English language learners. These elements will help English language learners participate successfully in the whole-group lesson and support the development of their language skills. Although these moments during instruction are designed to support English language learners, many schools are adding a separate ELD (English language development) block targeted at oral English language development to further support their students in language acquisition.

Students with growing English proficiency will benefit from an environment (or other central informational topic) word wall to build vocabulary (see the Core Words and Core Phrases). A sentence word wall to give them sentence starters to help with conversation will also offer students another layer of support. Some students may benefit from having their own personalized copies of these words to keep in their reading or writing notebooks for quick reference. Visual aids will further support students and give them a reference to what words are important to this study and what they mean.

Some students will benefit from several days on the same teaching objective. You may consider gathering small groups of readers or writers for repeated instruction or using one-on-one conferences as an opportunity to revisit teaching objectives. You can also consider pre teaching vocabulary and content to preview teaching objectives before the lesson. This offers time for ELLs to clarify their questions and understand the background knowledge they may bring to the lesson.

Complementary Core Methods

Read-Aloud

Take this opportunity to share a wide variety of informational texts during read-aloud. Make sure to include texts that vary in length, topic, and presentation style. Use your knowledge of students' interests to select texts that will inspire and excite your class. When appropriate, use your read-aloud as another chance for students to practice one or two of the following skills:

- Predict a text's potential content by skimming the text features
- Determine the main idea and key details of a text
- Ask and answer questions about a text using the portions of the text as evidence in your responses
- Identify and explore the meaning of new vocabulary
- Generate a list of key words to use in a search for additional information on the same topic

Shared Reading

Shared reading provides a wonderful opportunity to conduct a mini-study on a topic of general interest for the class. In particular, it can also provide the chance to link science or social studies content to the work you are doing in this lesson set. Think about selecting a range of short texts that match your current lesson set in either social studies or science. Use shared reading to reinforce the idea of "reading to learn" (versus "learning to read"). In the following list are some prompts you may want to use in your conversations about these texts:

- What is the main idea of this text? What are the supporting details?
- After reading this text, what questions do we still have about our topic?
- What new vocabulary did we take away from this text? How can we use this new vocabulary?
- Let's summarize what we just learned in our own words . . .

Shared reading can also be a great place to specifically highlight the linking words found within a shared text and to discuss how they connect ideas within a specific category of information.

Shared Writing

Shared Writing provides another opportunity to link to your work in social studies or science. Use this time to:

- Create shared lists of prior knowledge around a content area topic of study
- Generate key words to use in an Internet search

- Jot notes about a shared reading
- Organize notes into logical categories
- Compose questions about a topic for further investigation
- Craft answers to shared questions
- Revise shared writing to link ideas together, creating more complex sentences with words and phrases such as *also, another, and, more, but*

Core Connections at Home

Ask students to bring a piece of informational text from home. Who reads this text? Why do they read it? For homework, have students list what other sorts of informational text they see at home.

Invite families to spend time in their local library or online at home researching a topic of shared interest. Does the student have a family member with the same hobby or passion?

Have students share their final writing projects with their families during a special Recognition period. Ask families to write a letter to their child describing what they learned from their student's presentation. Display these letters alongside students' final work.

> *A mind is a fire to be kindled,*
> *not a vessel to be filled.*
>
> —Plutarch

Grade 3

Reading Lessons

The Core I.D.E.A. / Daily Reading Instruction at a Glance table on the next page highlights teaching objectives and standards alignment for all 10 lessons across the four stages (Introduce, Define, Extend, and Assess) of each lesson set. This table also indicates which lessons contain special features to support English language learners (ELLs), formative (Milestone) assessments, speaking and listening (S&L) skills, and technology use (Tech).

The Core Ready Reading Rubric that follows next is designed to help you record each student's overall understanding across four levels of achievement (emerging, approaching, achieving, exceeding) as it relates to the lesson set goals. We recommend that you use this rubric at the end of the lesson set as a performance-based assessment tool. Use the Milestone Performance Assessments as tools during the lesson set to help you gauge student progress toward these goals, and to reteach and differentiate as needed. See the foundational book, *Be Core Ready: Powerful, Effective Steps to Implementing and Achieving the Common Core State Standards*, for more information about the Core Ready Reading and Writing Rubrics.

The Core I.D.E.A. / Daily Reading Instruction at a Glance

Grade 3   What Matters Most: Research and Analysis in Informational Text

Instructional Stage	Lesson	Teaching Objective	Core Standards	Special Features
Introduce: notice, explore, collect, note, immerse, surround, record, share	1	Readers read informational text by asking and answering questions about the text.	RI.3.1 • RI.3.10 • W.3.7 • W.3.8 • L.3.1 • SL.3.1a–d • SL.3.6	Close Reading ELL Milestone Assessment
Define: name, identify, outline, clarify, select, plan	2	Readers can name and define the features of informational text.	RI.3.1 • RI.3.4 • RI.3.5 • RI.3.10 SL.3.1a–d • L.3.1 • L.3.6	Close Reading ELL S&L
	3	Readers use text features to help determine the main idea and supporting details of informational texts.	RI.3.1 • RI.3.2 • RI.3.5 • SL.3.1a–d SL.3.2 • L.3.1 • L.3.6	Close Reading ELL Tech
	4	Readers make informed decisions about which texts will be the most helpful in answering their questions.	RI.3.1 • RI.3.2 • RI.3.5 • RI.3.10 W.3.10 • SL.3.1a–d • SL.3.2 • L.3.6	Close Reading ELL Milestone Assessment
Extend: try, experiment, attempt, approximate, practice, explain, revise, refine	5	Readers record new information as they read.	RI.3.1 • RI.3.2 • RI.3.3 • RI.3.10 W.3.7 • W.3.8 • W.3.10 SL.3.1a–d • L.3.1 • L.3.6	Close Reading ELL Tech S&L
	6	Readers notice and describe cause and effect relationships in informational texts.	RI.3.1 • RI.3.2 • RI.3.3 • RI.3.8 RI.3.10 • SL.3.1a–d • SL.3.2 L.3.1 • L.3.6	Close Reading ELL Milestone Assessment S&L
	7	Readers compare and contrast the important points and key details presented in two texts on the same topic.	RI.3.1 • RI.3.2 • RI.3.9 • RI.3.10 L.3.1 • L.3.6	Close Reading ELL S&L
	8	Readers notice when they encounter new vocabulary and have a variety of strategies for making meaning.	RI.3.1 • RI.3.4 • RI.3.10 • SL.3.1a–d SL.3.6 • L.3.1 • L.3.6	Close Reading ELL S&L
	9	Readers use the information gained from illustrations to help them better understand a text.	RI.3.1 • RI.3.7 • SL.3.1a–d • L.3.1 • L.3.6	Close Reading ELL S&L
Assess: reflect, conclude, connect, share, recognize, respond	10	Read the work of a partner and write a response.	RI.3.1 • RI.3.6 • RI.3.10 • W.3.10 SL.3.1a–d • L.3.1 • L.3.6	Close Reading ELL Milestone Assessment

Core Ready Reading Rubric

Grade 3 What Matters Most: Research and Analysis in Informational Text

Lesson Set Goal	Emerging	Approaching	Achieving	Exceeding	Standards Alignment
Identify text features and use them to determine what matters most and find evidence to support thinking.	Student has a very limited understanding of text features. Is unable to use features to identify the main idea and supporting details of a text without extensive support.	Student can identify some text features and is beginning to understand their purpose. May need some support to use text features to locate the main idea and supporting details.	Student identifies most text features and explains their purpose. Successfully uses text features to identify the main idea and supporting details. Can cite evidence to support thinking.	Student has a thorough understanding of text features, identifying them and explaining their purpose in detail. Uses multiple features to locate the main idea and supporting details. Can cite evidence to support thinking.	RI.5.1 RI.3.2 RI.3.5 RI.3.10 SL.3.1a–d SL.3.6 L.3.1 L.3.6
Acquire information by locating and using library media resources.	Student has difficulty locating and using library media resources related to the research question without extensive support.	Student locates and uses at least two relevant library media resources with support.	Student locates and uses multiple relevant library resources with little support.	Student locates and uses a range of relevant library resources independently and with ease.	
Take notes to record big ideas and supporting evidence.	Student struggles with locating and recording important or relevant information without extensive support.	With some support, student records main ideas and includes a few supporting details. Student may have some difficulty with organization and determining what is most important.	Student records main ideas and several supporting details. Organizes appropriate information in a logical fashion that reflects what is most important.	Student records main ideas and several supporting details. Notes are highly organized and logical. Student shows strong understanding of what is most important.	RI.3.1 RI.3.10 W.3.4 W.3.7 W.3.8 W.3.10 L.3.6
Compare and contrast information on one topic from two different sources.	Student is unable to accurately identify similarities and differences between the two sources.	Student begins to identify similarities and differences between the two sources. May be incomplete or include some inaccuracies.	Student successfully identifies key similarities and differences between the two sources.	Student thoroughly identifies similarities and differences between the two sources with outstanding detail and organization.	RI.5.1 RI.3.9 RI.3.10 W.3.4 W.3.10 L.3.6
Notice new vocabulary and apply a variety of strategies for making meaning.	Student struggles to identify new vocabulary. Does not effectively apply strategies to determine meaning.	Student locates some new vocabulary and attempts to apply some strategies to determine meaning. Requires support to be fully successful.	Student locates new vocabulary and successfully determines meaning using strategies.	Student locates challenging vocabulary and successfully uses strategies to determine meaning with a high level of accuracy and thoughtfulness.	RI.3.1 RI.3.4 RI.3.10 SL.3.6 L.3.1 L.3.6
Select books independently to meet informational needs.	Student struggles to use the text features to select books to meet informational needs without extensive support.	Student attempts to use text features to select books to meet informational needs independently. May still require some support to accomplish this task.	Student uses text features and other strategies to select books to meet informational needs.	Student uses text features and other strategies to select multiple books that meet informational needs with a high level of effectiveness and independence.	

Core Ready Reading Rubric, Grade 3, *continued*

Lesson Set Goal	Emerging	Approaching	Achieving	Exceeding	Standards Alignment
Use illustrations and pictures to gain a deeper understanding of the text.	Student is beginning to develop an understanding of how pictures, but struggles to use the images to deepen his or her understanding of the text.	With support, student is able to answer specific questions about how pictures help readers to better understand the words on the page.	Student has a clear understanding of how illustrations or pictures can help readers gain a deeper understanding of the text and consistently and independently uses images to gain a deeper understanding of texts.	Student shows an exceptional understanding of how illustrations and pictures help readers gain a deeper understanding of the text and independently applies this strategy to understanding of texts.	RI.3.1 RI.3.7 RI.3.10 L.3.6
Identify and describe cause and effect relationships in informational text.	Student struggles to identify important events or differentiate cause and effect in informational texts.	Student has a limited ability to identify important events and determine cause and effect relationships. May confuse the two terms or miss key events at times.	Student is able to identify important events and describe cause and effect relationships with accuracy most of the time.	Student consistently identifies important events and describes cause and effect relationships with accuracy and specific text evidence from multiple texts. May notice subtle patterns and relationships.	RI.3.1 RI.3.3 RI.3.8 RI.3.10 SL.3.1a–d SL.3.2 SL.3.6 L.3.1 L.3.6
Ask and answer questions to demonstrate understanding of a text, referring explicitly to the text as the basis for the answers.	Student shows little or no evidence of active, purposeful reading or searching the text for specific information and evidence. Student makes little or no attempt to ask or answer questions about the text. Text evidence is minimal or nonexistent.	Student shows some evidence of active purposeful reading and searching the text for specific information and evidence. Student may be able to ask or answer some questions about the text accurately, but may not provide sufficient textual evidence to support thinking.	Student shows solid evidence of active, purposeful reading and searching the text for specific information and evidence. Student usually asks and answers questions accurately and provides appropriate textual evidence to support thinking.	Student demonstrates exceptional evidence of active, purposeful reading and searching the text for specific information and evidence. Student asks and answers questions with accuracy and provides appropriate, detailed, and thoughtful textual evidence to support thinking.	RI.3.1
By the end of the year, independently and proficiently read and comprehend a variety of informational texts at the high end of the grades 2–3 text complexity band.	Student shows little or no evidence of reading and comprehending texts appropriate for the grade 3 text complexity band.	Student shows inconsistent evidence of independently and proficiently reading and comprehending texts appropriate for the grade 3 text complexity band.	Student shows solid evidence of independently and proficiently reading and comprehending texts appropriate for the grade 3 text complexity band.	Student shows solid evidence of independent and proficiently reading and comprehending texts above the grade 3 text complexity band.	RI.3.10
Write routinely over extended time frames (time for research, reflection, and revision) and shorter time frames (a single sitting or a day or two) for a range of discipline-specific tasks, purposes, and audiences.	Student shows little or no evidence of writing routinely for short and long time frames for a range of discipline-specific tasks, purposes, and audiences.	Student shows some evidence of writing routinely for short and long time frames for a range of discipline-specific tasks, purposes, and audiences.	Student shows solid evidence of writing routinely for short and long time frames for a range of discipline-specific tasks, purposes, and audiences.	Student shows exceptional evidence of consistently and accurately writing for short and long time frames for a range of discipline-specific tasks, purposes, and audiences.	W.3.10

Lesson Set Goal	Emerging	Approaching	Achieving	Exceeding	Standards Alignment
In collaborative discussions, demonstrate evidence of preparation for discussion and exhibit responsibility to the rules and roles of conversation.	In collaborative discussions, student comes unprepared and often disregards the rules and roles of conversation.	In collaborative discussions, student's preparation may be evident but ineffective or inconsistent. May occasionally disregard the rules and roles of conversation.	In collaborative discussions, student prepares adequately and draws on the preparation and other information about the topic to explore ideas under discussion. Usually observes the rules and roles of conversation.	In collaborative discussions, student arrives extremely well prepared for discussions and draws on the preparation and other information about the topic to explore ideas under discussion. Always observes the rules and roles of conversation.	SL.3.1a SL.3.1b
In collaborative discussions, share and develop ideas in a manner that enhances understanding of topic. Contribute and respond to the content of the conversation in a productive and focused manner.	Student shows little or no evidence of engaging in collaborative discussions and makes little or no attempt to ask and answer questions, stay on topic, link comments to the remarks of others, or to explain his or her own ideas and understanding in light of the discussion.	Student shows some evidence of engaging in collaborative discussions and, with marginal success, attempts to ask questions to check understanding of information presented, to stay on topic, link comments to the remarks of others, and explain his or her own ideas and understanding in light of the discussion.	Student engages in a range of collaborative discussions and asks questions to check understanding of information presented, stays on topic most of the time, frequently links his or her comments to the remarks of others, and explains his or her own ideas and understanding in light of the discussion.	Student effectively and consistently engages in a range of collaborative discussions and asks thoughtful and high-level questions to check understanding of information presented. Always stays on topic and, with great insight and attention to the comments of others, links his or her comments to them, and explains his or her own ideas and understanding in light of the discussion.	SL.3.1c SL.3.1d
Speak in complete sentences when appropriate and demonstrate a command of standard English grammar and usage.	Student shows little or no evidence of attempting to speak in complete sentences. Student demonstrates little or no command of standard English grammar and usage.	Student attempts to speak in complete sentences when appropriate and demonstrates some command of standard English grammar and usage.	Student speaks in complete sentences when appropriate and demonstrates a command of standard English grammar and usage.	Student always speaks in complete sentences when appropriate and demonstrates an extraordinary command of the conventions of standard English grammar and usage.	SL.3.6 L.3.1
Demonstrate knowledge of standard English and its conventions.	Student demonstrates little or no knowledge of standard English and its conventions.	Student demonstrates some evidence of knowledge of standard English and its conventions.	Student consistently demonstrates knowledge of standard English and its conventions.	Student demonstrates an exceptional understanding of standard English and its conventions.	L.3.1 L.3.2 L.3.3
Acquire and accurately use grade-appropriate conversational, general academic, and domain-specific vocabulary and phrases.	Student shows little or no evidence of the acquisition or use of grade-appropriate conversational and academic language.	Student shows some evidence of the acquisition and use of grade-appropriate conversational and academic language.	Student shows solid evidence of the acquisition and use of grade-appropriate conversational and academic language.	Student shows a high level of sophistication and precision with the acquisition and use of grade-appropriate conversational and academic language.	L.3.6

Note: See the Core Ready Rubrics chart in the Walk Through for descriptions of category headers.

Reading Lesson 1

▼ Teaching Objective

Readers read an informational text by asking and answering questions about the text.

▼ Standards Alignment

RI.3.1, RI.3.10, W.3.4, W.3.7, W.3.8, W.3.10, SL.3.1a–d, SL.3.6, L.3.1, L.3.6

Close Reading Opportunity

▼ Materials

- Student copies of a blank K-W-L sheet (Appendix 3.2)
- Enlarged copy of blank K-W-L sheet (using chart paper or on an interactive whiteboard)
- Blank chart material for creating a Reading Like a Researcher list
- Charting supplies or interactive whiteboard
- *Not Your Typical Book about the Environment* by Elin Kelsey
- A variety of nonfiction texts for independent reading
- Copy of the Milestone Performance Assessment chart entitled "K-W-L," which you will use to assess student understanding of how to use a K-W-L sheet

▼ To the Teacher

Third graders *love* reading nonfiction! From finding fun facts about things that are creepy crawly to reading about places far away, children love to delve more deeply into the topics that interest them most. Today you will be launching your reading lesson set focused around the strategies good readers use to delve deeply into informational texts. More specifically, over the next few weeks you will guide your class to practice a variety of skills that include asking and answering questions about a topic using the text as evidence, identifying the main idea and supporting details of a text, and making meaning with new vocabulary words. Throughout the lessons, you will also see an emphasis on the close reading of texts to determine the big ideas and supporting details.

▼ Procedure

Warm Up Gather the class to set the stage for today's learning

Gather your students and announce that for the next few weeks you are going to be reading like researchers. "We're going to be investigating and learning about all sorts of topics! Take a look at some of the fantastic books I've found for us to explore!" Briefly preview for the class the baskets of books that represent the range of topics that they may choose to pursue further.

Teach Model what students need to learn and do

Explain that research can sometimes be hard work, so researchers always make sure to choose a topic that interests them. On the whiteboard, begin to create a list with the title "Reading Like a Researcher."

© Jacek Chabraszewski / Fotolia

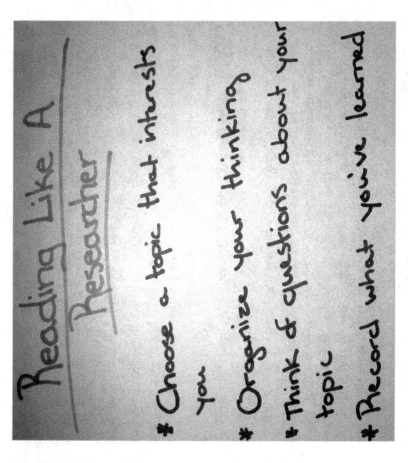

Reading Like A Researcher

* Choose a topic that interests you

* Organize your thinking

* Think of questions about your topic

* Record what you've learned

ELL Provide Comprehensible Input—Graphics. This chart helps ELLs to brainstorm as a group, sharing background knowledge and vocabulary that will help them form their thoughts around different topics. Keeping this chart visible will offer support throughout the lesson set. Write "Choose a topic that interests you" on the list. Take a minute or two to model choosing a topic of interest for the class to study collectively over the course of this lesson set. (Note: We use the topic of the environment as an example throughout the reading and writing lesson sets in this book; however, you can choose to substitute any other topic of high interest for your class.)

OK, now that we've chosen a topic to study, it's time to organize our thinking.

Add "Organize your thinking" to your list about Reading Like a Researcher. Model the use of the K-W-L sheet using an enlarged version (see next page). **ELL** Provide Comprehensible Input—Organizers. K-W-L charts offer a time to elicit background knowledge from your ELLs. This can also be a time to tie this knowledge to their native language if possible.

A K-W-L sheet is a simple three-column chart. The first column, K, is for listing prior knowledge of a topic—what you already *know*. The second column, W, is for listing what you *want* to know about the topic. The third column, L, is for what you have *learned* about the topic.

Focus on the first column of the chart, the K. With the students, generate a list of things that they already know about the topic. You should begin to model what to list, but after a few items, invite students to contribute. Sometimes students (and adults!) have misconceptions about a topic that they believe to be fact. If you or your students detect any inaccuracies in the information shared, you might kindly explain that you are not so sure if this information is true, and encourage students to explore it further in their upcoming research. After all, this is what research is all about!

Save the W and L columns for your students to do with you during the "Try" segment of this lesson.

Try Guide students to quickly rehearse what they need to learn and do in preparation for practice

Now it's time for our next step in reading like a researcher. We need to think of some questions that we want to find the answers to—we can list them in the second column of our K-W-L. And let me add this step to our list of Reading Like a Researcher.

Add "Think of questions about your topic" to your Reading Like a Researcher list. Ask students to turn and talk—they should come up with a question they have about the topic you've chosen to study. **ELL** Enable Language Production—Increasing Interaction. This is a good opportunity to listen in and see how to best scaffold and support language structures in partnerships. It is also an opportunity to understand the amount of language your ELLs bring to the topic they are discussing. Once you've given students adequate time to share with each other, solicit a few ideas from the class, adding them to the W column of your K-W-L chart as you go.

K-W-L Chart

Knowledge of the Topic	What I Would Like to Know	Learned

Explain to the class that you've left the L column, the section for listing what you've learned, blank on purpose. Let them know that you will come back to this column at the end of your reading time today, once you've had the chance to do some thinking, reading, and learning.

Clarify Briefly restate today's teaching objective and explain the practice tasks

Draw the students' attention back to the Reading Like a Researcher list.

Today we've been digging into what it means to read like a researcher. We started by choosing a topic to read about that interests us. Then, using a K-W-L chart, we listed what we already know about the topic and added questions for future research about it. When you're exploring informational text today, I'd like you to read like a researcher—choose to linger in a book that interests you. Use a K-W-L chart to organize your thinking and then get reading!

Practice Students work independently and/or in small groups to apply today's teaching objective

Students will independently explore a variety of informational texts. They will fill out the K and W columns of their K-W-L sheet and use their remaining time to read.

Wrap Up Check understanding as you guide students to briefly share what they have learned and produced today

Ask students to have handy the book they chose to linger in today, their K-W-L chart, and a writing tool. Gather your class and focus their attention back on your Reading Like a Researcher list. Tell them that the next step in reading like a researcher is to record what you've learned as you read. Add "Record what you've learned" to the Reading Like a Researcher list.

Wasn't it nice to spend some time lingering in a book you're really interested in? I spent some time reading *Not Your Typical Book about the Environment*. I want to wrap up our time today by thinking about what we've learned in our books. Before I forget, I'm going to jot my new learning in the L column of my chart. The L stands for what I learned.

Model jotting a brief note about your learning in the L column. Give the class a few moments to do some thinking and jotting on their own K-W-L sheets. Then collect their work. Set aside time to look through your students' work using the Milestone Performance Assessment to decide if they were successful in activating prior knowledge and generating simple questions about a topic to decide whether you need to spend more time supporting these skills. **ELL** Assess for Content and Language Understanding—Formative Assessment. This is the time you will understand the language supports and scaffolds needed for upcoming work.

Milestone Performance Assessment

K-W-L

Use this checklist to assess student performance on K-W-L sheets.

Standards Alignment: RI.3.1, W.3.7, W.3.8, W.3.10

	Achieved	Notes
List facts they know about the topic.		
Generate questions about their topic.		
Record what they learned.		

Reading Lesson 2

▶ Teaching Objective

Readers can name and define the features of informational text.

▶ Standards Alignment

RI.3.1, RI.3.4, RI.3.5, RI.3.10, SL.3.1a–d, L.3.1, L.3.6

▶ Materials

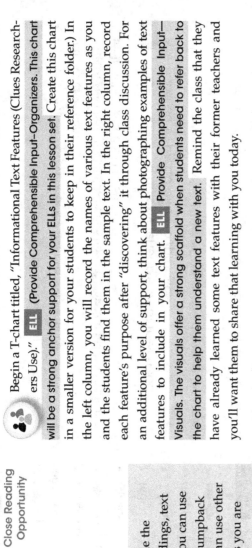

- Student copies of short informational texts that include the following text features: bolded key words, a title, headings, text boxes, photograph(s)/illustration(s), and captions. (You can use "Polar Bears Protected by Law" and "The Amazing Humpback Whales," in Appendix 3.3 and Appendix 3.4, or you can use other example texts that have good examples of the features you are teaching.

- Features of Nonfiction Text, Appendix 3.5
- Yesterday's Reading Like a Researcher list
- Charting paper or whiteboard

▶ Procedure

Warm Up Gather the class to set the stage for today's learning

Yesterday, we started talking about what it means to read like a researcher. Let's check out the list we started together.

Briefly review your Reading Like a Researcher list.

Teach Model what students need to learn and do

Part of our work yesterday was thinking of questions about our topics, for future research. Today we will be reading closely looking for the different text features we see in our informational reading. As researchers we need to be able to

identify and define these various features because they can help us find the answers to our questions more easily.

Close Reading Opportunity

Begin a T-chart titled, "Informational Text Features (Clues Researchers Use)." **ELL** (Provide Comprehensible Input-Organizers. This chart will be a strong anchor support for your ELLs in this lesson set. Create this chart in a smaller version for your students to keep in their reference folder.) In the left column, you will record the names of various text features as you and the students find them in the sample text. In the right column, record each feature's purpose after "discovering" it through class discussion. For an additional level of support, think about photographing examples of text features to include in your chart. **ELL** Provide Comprehensible Input—Visuals. The visuals offer a strong scaffold when students need to refer back to the chart to help them understand a new text. Remind the class that they have already learned some text features with their former teachers and you'll want them to share that learning with you today.

Example of T-Chart: Informational Text Features (Clues Researchers Use)

Name of text feature	Purpose of that feature

Show the class the enlarged copy of one of the short informational texts containing text features. Model identifying a feature. Circle bold words in the text and label them "key words." Explain the purpose of bold words in an informational piece.

There are a lot of words here in bold print. When words are bold, that means they must be really important to the topic I'm studying. I want to make sure I understand what they mean so I can use them the right way. Let me add this text feature to our chart.

Write "bold key words" in the left column and "show us important words for the topic" in the right-hand column. Repeat this process (noticing a specific text feature, circling and labeling it within the text, explaining its function, and adding it to the chart) for each of the following text features. Note that "photograph" and "caption" are not included here, because they are reserved for "student discovery."

- Title (gives us a preview of the information included in a text)
- Heading (give us a preview of the information included in the following section)
- Sidebar/text box (highlights interesting information related to the main topic or lists additional facts)

Call to their attention the other enlarged article you prepared for today's lesson.

Try Guide students to quickly rehearse what they need to learn and do, in preparation for practice

OK, friends, now it's your turn. Does anyone recognize any other special features in *this* article? I'm sure there are some that look familiar from last year.... When you think you've found a different feature in this article, put your thumb on your knee.

Wait for most students to indicate they are ready. **ELL** Enable Language Production—Listening and Speaking. Offering more time for students to answer can support your ELLs in the translation that they are navigating in order to answer the question.

Turn and share with a partner the name of the text feature you noticed. **ELL** Enable Language Production—Increase Interaction. This collaborative time is an opportunity for students to learn and increase their vocabulary around their discussion. Don't forget to share what you think the feature's job is, too!

Listen in to various partnerships, jotting down interesting and relevant responses to share with the larger group. Call the group back together. Here's how your sharing could unfold:

Friends, Carla and Lily noticed an important feature. They noticed the caption underneath the photo! I'm going to circle the caption and label it right on the article. Let me add *captions* to our chart. Does anyone have an idea about the caption's job? What do captions do?

Discuss the job of captions with the class, guiding the group to determining that the purpose of the caption is to explain or provide details about the picture. Jot down this thinking in the right-hand column of your T-chart. The following list has some other text features to listen for while working with your partnerships, and there is a complete list in Appendix 3.5, Features of Informational Text.

- Diagrams
- Photographs/illustrations
- Glossary
- Index
- Table of contents
- Graph/chart
- Fun facts list or box

Clarify Briefly restate today's teaching objective and explain the practice tasks

Today we practiced noticing the text features that are going to become the important clues in our detective work. It's important that we are able to name these features and describe how they can help us, because we are going to rely on these features in our future reading. As you're reading today, I want you to circle the different features you come across and label them, just as we did together with this article. Be ready with examples to share at the end of our reading time today. (SL.3.1a)

Practice Students work independently or in small groups to apply today's teaching objective

Students will browse through a variety of informational texts independently. As they browse, students will mark places where they notice a new or helpful text feature, labeling the feature and its purpose. Sticky notes will work well if students are working in books that may not be marked. Students should be ready to share and explain their work at the end of this independent work time.

Wrap Up Check understanding as you guide students to briefly share what they have learned and produced today

Have students share the text features they noticed in their reading. As they do that, be sure to ask them to explain the purpose or function of each text feature and show the class an example of what they are talking about. Some questions you may want to ask are:

- What is the name of that text feature?

- What is the purpose of that text feature?
- How does it help you as a reader?
- Can you show us an example?

 Encourage students to listen carefully to one another so that they can successfully build on one another's thinking by sharing new information or examples, rather than simply repeating the ideas already mentioned. (SL.3.1b, SL.3.1d)

Reading Lesson 3

▼ Teaching Objective

Readers use text features to help determine the main idea and supporting details of informational texts.

▼ Standards Alignment

RI.3.1, RI.3.2, RI.3.5, SL.3.1a–d, SL.3.2, L.3.1, L.3.6

▼ Materials

- Student copies of two different informational articles such as the "Polar Bears Protected by Law" and "The Amazing Humpback Whales" provided in Appendix 3.3 and Appendix 3.4 for modeling and practice, or you may substitute another pair of articles related to a different topic you've chosen to study with your class.)
- Student copies of Main Idea and Supporting Details graphic organizer (Appendix 3.6)
- Two enlarged copies of Main Idea and Supporting Details graphic organizer for modeling—one for each article you will discuss in class today
- Informational Text Features (Clues Researchers Use) list created in yesterday's reading lesson
- Copies of the Milestone Performance Assessment chart titled "Finding Main Idea and Identifying Supporting Details" for you to use in assessing the students' progress

▼ To the Teacher

This lesson represents the first time you will touch on the idea of main idea and supporting details in this lesson set. Today, you will focus on *using* the text features you discussed in Reading Lesson 2 to help determine the main idea and identify key supporting details in an informational piece. Use your students' work from today as an informal assessment. The work students complete in this lesson will give you a glimpse into their existing understanding of main idea and key details, allowing you to scaffold your future teaching in more targeted ways. (Note: In second grade, students were asked to find the main topic of multi-paragraph texts.)

▼ Procedure

Warm Up Gather the class to set the stage for today's learning

Briefly review the Informational Text Features (Clues Researchers Use) list that you created with your class in Reading Lesson 2.

Yesterday we created this amazing list of informational text features. Noticing and understanding these features is really going to help us as we begin our research.

Teach Model what students need to learn and do

Today I want to teach you how to determine the main idea of your reading by reading closely, using the text features as clues. We're going to record our thinking on this chart.

Model going back to the article to find a supporting detail. Think aloud about the location of supporting details (they are not usually found in a topic sentence, but rather in the body of paragraphs).

Main Idea and Supporting Details Graphic Organizer

Title of Article:

MAIN IDEA
This article is mostly about:

SUPPORTING DETAILS

1.

2.

3.

4.

Display to the class the following Main Idea and Supporting Details graphic organizer. **ELL** Provide Comprehensible Input—Organizers. This organizer helps ELLs to see the visual connection between the concepts. If needed, you can offer further visuals to represent the connection between main idea and supporting details such as a table—the main idea as the top and the legs as supporting details. Demonstrate filling it out as you model this process.

Begin by modeling how readers can use the title and headings of one of the sample articles to help them get a big picture of the article's topic and possible main ideas. **ELL** Provide Comprehensible Input—Modeling. Modeling offers a time for ELLs to hear you use language and demonstrate the thought process of thinking about main ideas and supporting details. This model may be the structure that they refer to when thinking through this on their own. Remind students that the purpose of titles and headings is to preview some of the most important information in the text, so they usually serve as good clues to help us determine the main idea.

After reading aloud the article you have chosen, ask yourself, "What is this article mostly about?" Think aloud about how to synthesize the information from different parts of the text to come up with the main idea. Be sure to include how the headings can guide you in the right direction.

Now it's time to strengthen our thinking about the main idea by finding some supporting details from our reading.

Try Guide students to quickly rehearse what they need to learn and do in preparation for practice

There should always be more than one supporting detail. It's time for you to help me find the rest. Can you identify another supporting detail in this article? Turn and talk with a partner.

Give your students a few moments to work together to identify additional supporting details in this first article. **ELL** Enable Language Production—Increasing Interaction. During this time, ELLs have opportunities to clarify language and practice identifying main ideas and supporting details. This is an opportunity to support language by listening in or whispering in to help ELLs describe their thinking to their partners. Listen in to various partnerships and then share with the class the thinking you overheard. Highlight additional supporting facts the class discovered and add them to the graphic organizer.

Clarify Briefly restate today's teaching objective and explain the practice tasks

Today we practiced using the title and headings and other text features to help us determine the main idea and supporting details of an informational article.

Name: Tanks

Title: Polar bears listed as threatened

Main Idea:

The article is mostly about...
to save polar bears.

Supporting Details
1. They could be extinct by 2050
2. Where hunting polar bears is legal will be banned
3. Polar bears were added to the list of threatened species
4. Polar bears will have a safe place in Canada.

Sample chart based on "Polar Bears Listed as Threatened." *National Geographic News,* another article on polar bears.

Milestone Performance Assessment

Finding Main Idea and Support Details

 Use this checklist to assess student work on the Main Idea and Supporting Details graphic organizer.

Standards Alignment: RI.3.1, RI.3.2, RI.3.5

	Achieved	Notes
Identify main ideas.		
Identify supporting details.		
Connect main ideas to supporting details.		

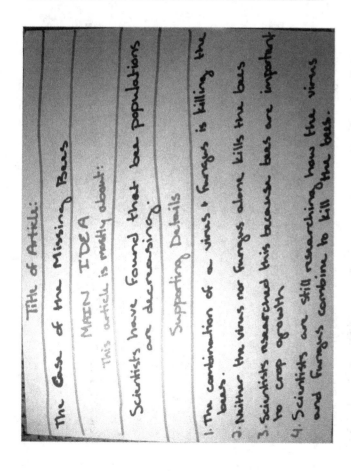

Title of Article:
The Case of the Missing Bees

MAIN IDEA
This article is mostly about:

Scientists have found that bee populations are decreasing.

Supporting Details

1. The combination of a virus & fungus is killing the bees.

2. Neither the virus nor fungus alone kills the bees.

3. Scientists researched this because bees are important to crop growth.

4. Scientists are still researching how the virus and fungus combine to kill the bees.

This technique is going to be really helpful when it comes time to pick the books or articles that will help you the most in your own research.

Instruct students to take a close look at the second article you've chosen for today's lesson. Ask them to read the article during Practice and find the main idea and two or three supporting details. Provide the students with their own copies of the Main Idea and Supporting Detail graphic organizer, to record their thinking.

Practice Students work independently or in small groups to apply today's teaching objective

Students read an informational article and fill out the Main Idea and Supporting Details graphic organizer. Collect this work and use it with the Milestone Performance Assessment for Finding the Main Idea and Support Details, as an informal assessment to determine your students' progress with this skill. **ELL** Assess for Content and Language Understanding—Formative Assessment. The chart can be used to think about the future language support needed, as well as possible partner arrangements to help support their peer interactions in upcoming lessons.

Wrap Up Check understanding as you guide students to briefly share what they have learned and produced today

Gather your class. Ask students to share their thinking with a partner. **ELL** Enable Language Production—Increasing Interaction. Just as you supported in the turn and talk, listen in to see whether the language support aided ELLs in communicating their thinking, providing support as needed through being the "extra partner." As students share their work, record their ideas on another enlarged copy of the Finding the Main Idea and Supporting Details graphic organizer.

The beautiful thing about learning is that no one can take it away from you.

—B. B. King

Reading Lesson 4

▶ Teaching Objective

Readers make informed decisions about which texts will be the most helpful in answering their questions.

▶ Standards Alignment

RI.3.1, RI.3.2, RI.3.5, RI.3.10, W.3.4, W.3.10, SL.3.1a–d, SL.3.2, L.3.6

Close Reading
Opportunity

▶ Materials

- "Zipper's Green Tips" (from the *National Geographic Kids* website) student copies and an enlargement for class discussion
- "Polar Bears Listed as Threatened" (from the *National Geographic Kids* website) student copies and one enlargement
- "Choosing Resources" Decision Sheet (Appendix 3.7)—student copies (with extras, for more than one source per student) and one enlargement
- From Reading Lesson 2, the Features of Informational Text (Clues Researchers Use) list the class filled out
- Student writing materials

▶ To the Teacher

From the start of this lesson set, you've been working with a set of informational texts around a specific topic. (We chose the topic of the environment as an example, but you may be using another topic.) You've led your class in identifying prior knowledge and generating questions for future inquiry. Today, you will model working with the features of informational text to help determine whether a piece of text will be helpful in answering those questions. Overcoming this common stumbling block for third graders is a crucial skill for their future work as researchers. Encourage your class to be critical consumers of text by helping them to understand that not every piece of text they encounter about a given topic will be useful.

▶ Procedure

Warm Up **Gather the class to set the stage for today's learning**

When you start to research a topic like the environment, you'll find a ton of articles, books, and other resources to consider. It's too much for one person to look through! Researchers are busy people—they don't have time to read every single piece of information that comes their way. They have to get good at deciding if a new piece of information is going to help their research before they spend a lot of time reading it. Yesterday we practiced using text features to help us determine the main idea of our informational reading. That work is sure going to come in handy today!

Teach **Model what students need to learn and do**

Today I'm going to teach you how to decide if a piece of informational text is going to help you answer your questions. Remember, we don't have to read every book or article on a topic—we only have to read the ones we are most interested in or the ones that will help us answer our questions. You can make this decision by using the text features to help you predict the main idea and asking yourself, "Will this article help me with my research?"

Briefly review your work from Reading Lesson 3. If your class has completed Writing Lesson 2, remind them of the questions they crafted to narrow their study during that lesson: "Who works to save endangered animals? What can I recycle? How do I compost?" Substitute your own questions if you chose a different topic for the class. Refer the students to the Features of Informational Text (Clues Researchers Use) list from Reading Lesson 2, as you demonstrate. **ELL** Provide Comprehensible Input—Organizers.

Watch me as I skim the text features in this first piece and use that information to make a prediction about what this piece is going to cover.

Choose an article or book. Model reading the title, noticing the headings and skimming through the various text features. Think aloud about your prediction: "Based on the information in these text features, what do I predict this piece will mostly be about?" Then share your decision-making process aloud with the class: "Will this piece help answer my question?" Be sure to model discarding some texts as well as finding some that will suit your needs. Here is one way your modeling could unfold:

Let me take a closer look at the article "Zipper's Green Tips." The title makes me think that this article will be mostly about ways to help save the planet, which could help me answer my question about recycling. Oh, look! The first heading is "Recycle and Reuse," which makes me think this whole section is going to tell me a bit more about what I can recycle. I'm definitely going to take a look at this article when I do my research.

Continue to model this thought process as you make your way through several of the resources you have collected. To make your teaching as visual and concrete as possible, make a big show of sorting your resources into two distinct piles: Sources That Answer My Questions, and Sources That Don't Answer My Questions.

Try Guide students to quickly rehearse what they need to learn and do in preparation for practice

Ask the class to help you decide on a text to read. Guide them through the process of using the text features to help make a prediction of what this piece is mostly going to be about. For example, you might show the class "Polar Bears Listed as Threatened" and tell them to take a look at the features included.

Can you use those text features to help you predict what this piece is going to teach me about? Share your thinking with a partner. **ELL** Enable Language Production—Increasing Interaction. Triad partnerships aid in creating supportive language partnerships and models for ELLs. In a triad, you could partner the ELL with one student who mainly speaks English, and another student who is bilingual in both languages. This situation offers a chance for an exchange between the three students, as well as offering an English discussion model.

Confer with several partnerships as they talk. When you call the students back together, highlight the work of several students, having them explain to the entire class how the text features helped them arrive at their decision.

So, what's our final decision? Will this next piece help me to answer my question? I think I'll record my thoughts on this decision sheet.

Model filling out the "Choosing Resources" Decision Sheet with the class.

Clarify Briefly restate today's teaching objective and explain the practice tasks

When you're searching for the answer to a question, it's important to find texts that will do just that: answer your question. That means that you don't need to read every single piece of information that comes your way, just the ones you believe will help you in your investigation. Today we learned that we can predict what will most likely be the main idea by looking at the text features. Then, we can use that information to help us decide if a piece of text is going to be helpful in answering our questions.

Instruct the class to take out the writing lesson questions they've crafted to narrow their investigation. Tell them to take a look through some of sources they've already looked at, as well as some they haven't had time to check out yet, and use the text features to help them decide which sources are most likely to help them answer their questions, and which sources probably won't be helpful. Students should record their thinking about one text using the "Choosing Resources" Decision Sheet.

Choosing Resources Decision Sheet

Title of source _____

I think this source is mostly about _____

_____

I think that because _____

_____

Are you going to use this source for your research? _____

Why or why not? _____

_____

Students will revisit the sets of informational texts they have on their given topic. Using the various text features, students will decide which texts will most likely be able to help them answer their question(s). If there does not appear to be text to support their investigation, students will need to re-visit their original list of questions.

Students will complete the "Choosing Resources" Decision Sheet for only one resource that they consider.

Students should turn in their "Choosing Resources" Decision Sheet for your consid-eration. Work with the class to evaluate the usefulness of the remaining class-shared texts. Which ones will help answer the class questions?

Reading Lesson 5

▼ **Teaching Objective**

Readers record new information as they read.

Close Reading Opportunity

▼ **Standards Alignment**

RI.3.1, RI.3.2, RI.3.10, W.3.4, W.3.7, W.3.8, W.3.10, SL.3.1a–d, L.3.1, L.3.6

▼ **Materials**

- "Zipper's Green Tips" (from the *National Geographic Kids* website) student copies and an enlargement for class discussion
- Previously read text on the topic your class has chosen to study
- Method for student note taking (see following table for low-tech and high-tech alternatives)

▼ **To the Teacher**

Note taking is a skill that will help your students for years to come. Your students will feel quite grown up as they learn how to take notes and should feel proud of this big step in their academic careers. Throughout our lives we take notes when we have information to remember. We take notes about things that stand out to us when we're reading. Sometimes we

Goal	Low-Tech	High-Tech
Students take notes while they read to record their thinking for sharing with the larger group.	Students take handwritten pencil and paper notes. Consider using several sticky notes or index cards so that students can easily practice sorting their notes into logical categories later in these lesson sets.	There are a variety of high-tech options for student note taking. Consider the following ideas: • Students take their notes using digital Stickies (a program found on Apple computers). This application allows students to color code and visually organize their notes by category by dragging them around on the desktop. • Students use the iPad application Corkulous which allows them to create cork boards that include notes, sticky notes, photos, and to do lists. These corkboards can be easily shared with you or their peers via email. • Students use a note taking program such as Evernote, creating a new notebook for this project.

write down full sentences, other times bullets. Sometimes we write down exact words or quotations; other times we paraphrase into our own words. Helping your students negotiate what type of note to write is a big step in the research process. To make the most of their research, students need to know how to take good notes.

▼ Procedure

Warm Up Gather the class to set the stage for today's learning

Third graders, you have worked so hard to choose a topic that matters to you! And you've begun to read using many different strategies for finding the big ideas and the evidence to prove them. The more we read, the harder it will become to keep track of all the things we've learned.

Teach Model what students need to learn and do

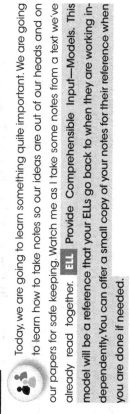 Today, we are going to learn something quite important. We are going to learn how to take notes so our ideas are out of our heads and on our papers for safe keeping. Watch me as I take some notes from a text we've already read together. **ELL** Provide Comprehensible Input—Models. This model will be a reference that your ELLs go back to when they are working independently. You can offer a small copy of your notes for their reference when you are done if needed.

Model for students how to use a heading that indicates the main idea for their notes at the top of the page. Then, use bullets to record evidence that supports the big idea. Model for students when you paraphrase in your own words, and when you want to make sure you have the exact language written down. A good rule of thumb is that when we are recording facts we need accurate language. Subheadings and outlining will be part of our research process in future grades through our lesson sets. Right now you want to keep the note-taking process effective but simple for your third graders. Here's one way your modeling could unfold:

Let's take another look at "Zipper's Green Tips" and take some notes. I want you to watch me as I start my note taking by creating a heading. A heading helps to organize your notes. It's like a title that reminds you what the rest of your notes are going to be all about. Usually, a good heading takes the main idea

and puts it into your own words. The main idea of this article was there are many ways to be more green. I can use that as my heading.

Write "Ways To Be More Green" at the top of your notes.

OK, now I need to take some notes on the supporting details. Remember, a supporting detail is evidence that helps to prove the main idea.

Reread the first section on Recycling and Reusing aloud to the class.

There were a lot of supporting details in that first section. Let's see, this first part teaches me that I can be more green by recycling bottles and cans. Watch me as I add that to our notes.

Add a bullet point and then write, "recycle bottles and cans."

Did you notice how I used this dot? That's called a bullet point and it's one way to show that you're starting to add a new idea to your notes. Then did you see how I just wrote "recycle bottles and cans?" I kept my notes short, I didn't worry about writing in a complete sentence and I didn't copy out of the book.

Continue modeling add more bullet points to your notes based on this first section of the article.

Try Guide students to quickly rehearse what they need to learn and do in preparation for practice

Turn to the class to help with the note taking for the remainder of this article.

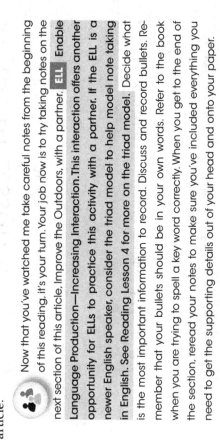 Now that you've watched me take careful notes from the beginning of this reading, it's your turn. Your job now is to try taking notes on the next section of this article, Improve the Outdoors, with a partner. **ELL** Enable Language Production—Increasing Interaction. This interaction offers another opportunity for ELLs to practice this activity with a partner. If the ELL is a newer English speaker, consider the triad model to help model note taking in English. See Reading Lesson 4 for more on the triad model. Decide what is the most important information to record. Discuss and record bullets. Remember that your bullets should be in your own words. Refer to the book when you are trying to spell a key word correctly. When you get to the end of the section, reread your notes to make sure you've included everything you need to get the supporting details out of your head and onto your paper.

Give students several minutes to practice note taking with a partner. Have partners share one note they took from the reading. As students share, record their notes on your larger set of class notes. This is a great opportunity to encourage the class to listen carefully to one another in order to build on each other's ideas, rather than repeat ideas that have already been shared. (SL.3.1b, SL.3.1c)

Here is a list of possible supporting details students could have included in their notes:

• Plant a leafy tree on the south side of your house
• Help to clean up community beaches and parks
• Never litter
• Don't kill spiders—they eat other insects and are important to the food chain
• If you can't keep your pet, make sure it has another good home

Clarify Briefly restate today's teaching objective and explain the practice tasks

Remember, friends, that researchers take careful notes to record the main ideas and the evidence to prove them. Now that we've practiced with a partner I'd like you to choose one of the other readings from your research folder

Reading Lesson 6

▼ **Teaching Objective**

Readers notice and describe cause and effect relationships in informational texts.

Close Reading Opportunity

▼ **Standards Alignment**

RI.3.1, RI.3.2, RI.3.3, RI.3.8, RI.3.10, SL.3.1a–d, SL.3.2, L.3.1, L.3.6

▼ **Materials**

• Student copies of the three-column Finding the Cause and Effect graphic organizer

and practice taking notes. Start with a main idea as your heading and use bullets to record the evidence that proves it.

Practice Students work independently or in small groups to apply today's teaching objective

Students will choose a text from their research folders and practice taking notes using headings, bullets, and a combination of paraphrasing and recording of accurate language. Walk around the room and further support students who you know may have a difficult time deciding what to record or what to leave out of notes.

Wrap Up Check understanding as you guide students to briefly share what they have learned and produced today

Gather your class and review the note-taking process you taught today. Review the class notes you took on "Zipper's Green Tips." Ask your students to help you label the various parts of your notes. For example, circle the heading (Ways To Be More Green) and label it "heading or main idea." Then circle the bullet points and label them "bullets or supporting details."

Then, discuss: "What was easy about taking notes? What was hard?" This will be an important conversation for you to know whom to follow up with and how to make your conferences about note taking more effective.

• Enlarged copy of Finding the Cause and Effect graphic organizer
• Large copy of "Polar Bears Listed as Threatened" (from the National Geographic Kids website)
• Large copy of "Drinking Water: Bottled or from the Tap?" (from the National Geographic Kids website)

▼ **Procedure**

Warm Up Gather the class to set the stage for today's learning

Yesterday we learned that researchers take careful notes about the main ideas and the evidence that support them. That's a very grown-up skill! As we

Polar Bears Listed as Threatened

Main Idea ↔	Cause ↔	Effect
habitat threatened	ice and snow in Arctic is melting too fast as Earth starts to get warmer	polar bears may become endangered species
Saving polar bears depends on people across the world	importing polar bear products from Canada will be banned	polars bears will have safe habitats in Canada

continue our learning and reading in this lesson set, I want you to continue to take notes so that you can save your thinking. Remember, the notes you are taking are going to be very important to your writing work.

Teach Model what students need to learn and do

Today we're going to learn about cause and effect. When we read informational text, one very important strategy is to read for cause and effect. When you discover a cause and effect relationship, you'll definitely want to jot it down in your notes.

Begin by making sure that students understand the meaning of the words *cause* and *effect*. Give simple examples from your own life to make this idea clear (e.g., if you forget to brush your teeth, you might end up with a cavity). **ELL** Frontload the Lesson—Build Background. This is an opportunity for ELLs to comprehend through listening and understanding simple cause and effect scenarios in English. Solicit a few examples of cause and effect relationships from the lives of your students.

Now, model finding a cause and effect relationship in an informational text related to the topic your class is studying. **ELL** Provide Comprehensible Input—Models. Modeling the cause and effect in your shared text is another support for ELLs to deepen their thinking around cause and effect relationships in the second language. Use the main idea of the article as a starting point. Ask yourself, "What is the *cause* of the main idea?" and "What is the *effect* of the main idea?" If you've chosen to study the environment along with us, here is how your modeling could unfold:

Many informational articles and books write about cause and effect relationships. Let's look at the article "Polar Bears Listed as Threatened." We decided that a main idea in that article is that the polar bear's habitat is threatened. What *causes* the polar bear's habitat to be threatened? Well, we learned that the ice in the Arctic is melting too fast as the Earth starts to get warmer. So what's the *effect* of the polar bear's habitat being threatened? They might become an endangered species as more and more of them are unable to survive.

Record your thinking about cause and effect in the Finding the Cause and Effect graphic organizer. **ELL** Provide Comprehensible Input—Organizers. This chart offers a graphic that enables ELLs to see the tie between

these three categories. If needed, you could provide a visual on the headers to support the chart from your group examples from earlier in the lesson.

Finding the Cause and Effect Graphic Organizer

Title of article: _____

Main idea	Cause	Effect

Try Guide students to quickly rehearse what they need to learn and do in preparation for practice

Read aloud the article "Drinking Water: Bottled or From the Tap?" to explore cause and effect. Using a short piece is key because it will not only hold students' attention, but will also help to streamline your teaching, providing students with as much time for independent practice as possible. Ask: *Who can identify a main idea from this article?* (SL.3.2) *Turn and talk to your partner.* **ELL** Enable Language Production—Increasing Interaction. This peer interaction offers a time when your ELs can clarify their thinking in a lower anxiety setting. Take this time to listen in and understand how to best support their language needs. A main idea of this piece is that people in the United States drink more bottled water than any in other nation.

Once your class has arrived at the main idea guide them to answer the following questions: What *causes* the main idea? What is the *effect* of the main idea? Lead the class in a discussion. As students talk, encourage them to listen thoughtfully to one another and build on each other's ideas rather than simply repeating one another. (SL.3.1b, SL.3.1c) Also, this is a good opportunity to encourage students to revisit the article and use the text as evidence in their conversation. (SL.3.2)

Clarify Briefly restate today's teaching objective and explain the practice tasks

When we're reading a piece of informational text, it's important to look for cause and effect relationships. You can do this by identifying a main idea of the text and then asking yourself two simple questions: "What causes the main idea?" and "What are the effects of the main idea?". Today when you're working, I want you to look for this relationship in your reading and use the Finding Cause and Effect graphic organizer to record your thinking.

Practice Students work independently and/or in small groups to apply today's teaching objective

Give each student a copy of the Finding Cause and Effect graphic organizer. As they continue reading and exploring sources, students will choose one piece of text to complete the graphic organizer and illustrate a cause

and effect relationship. Collect student work and use the Milestone Performance Assessment as an informal assessment of your students' understanding of cause and effect relationships in informational text. **ELL** Assess for Content and Language Understanding—Formative Assessment

Milestone Performance Assessment
Finding the Cause and Effect

Use this checklist to assess student ability to identify and understand the relationship between cause and effect.

Standards Alignment: RI.3.1, RI.3.2, RI.3.3, RI.3.8

	Achieved	Notes
Identify causes.		
Identify effects.		
Understand relationship between cause and effect.		

Wrap Up Check understanding as you guide students to briefly share what they have learned and produced today

Call students back together to discuss their work for the day. Ask students if they were successful in identifying cause and effect relationships in their reading.

How did that go? Was there anything that felt hard about finding cause and effect relationships?

Then, solicit a few examples of cause and effect relationships from the class, reminding volunteers of the importance of using text as evidence of their thinking.

Reading Lesson 7

▶ **Teaching Objective**

Readers compare and contrast the important points and key details presented in two texts on the same topic.

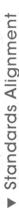

Close Reading Opportunity

▶ **Standards Alignment**

RI.3.1, RI.3.2, RI.3.9, RI.3.10, L.3.1, L.3.6

▶ **Materials**

- Student copies of a Venn diagram
- Enlarged Venn diagram (either on chart paper or an interactive whiteboard)
- "Drinking Water: Bottled or from the Tap?" (from the *National Geographic Kids* website)
- "Zipper's Green Tips" (from the *National Geographic Kids* website)

▶ **Procedure**

Warm Up Gather the class to set the stage for today's learning

I am so proud of all the reading and note taking you have been doing! You all have done a lot of important research to help you in your writing work. Now that you've done so much reading, how many of you have noticed that sometimes different articles and books on the same topic seem to be saying the same thing? Have you ever noticed that sometimes different books and articles on the same topic seem to say completely opposite things?

Teach Model what students need to learn and do

Tell the class that you are going to compare and contrast the information given in two articles on the same topic. Show a Venn diagram to the class and briefly explain how it works. **ELL** Provide Comprehensible Input—Organizers. This organizer will help your ELLs understand how to

see what is similar and different between information. You may need to jot a small note saying "same" or "different" on the outside of Venn. When possible, you can sketch visuals that support the ideas written inside of the diagram. Each circle in the Venn diagram is going to represent a different book or article. The information that is unique to the book or article is recorded in outer parts of the circles. The information that is shared by both books or articles is recorded in the overlapping portion of the two circles.

Model comparing two familiar articles on the same topic. If you're studying the environment along with us, you could use "Drinking Water: Bottled or from the Tap?" and "Zipper's Green Tips." Demonstrate labeling each circle and thinking through the key learning in one article, adding information to the Venn diagram in appropriate spaces. Here is how your modeling could unfold:

I'm going to start by looking at one article and thinking about the main ideas and supporting details. I'll look at the drinking water article first. Well, I remember that one of the main ideas from this article was that people use too many water bottles. Now I need to figure out where to record that main idea. Let me think, was that an idea that was only in this article, or was that an important idea in "Zipper's Green Tips" too? I'm going to double check by looking back at my Zipper article. Model looking back at the "Zipper's Green Tips" to discover that these two articles do indeed share this key idea. They both say the same thing about water bottles, so I'm going to jot that idea in the middle.

Write, "people use too many water bottles" in the center of your Venn diagram.

Model partially completing the Venn diagram, saving a portion of each article for the class to practice working with together. Recap your process explicitly. You might say:

Did you notice what I did? I started by thinking about a main idea from one of the two articles we are comparing. Once I figured that out, I thought about the other article and asked myself, does that article say the same thing? When I realized that both articles do say the same thing, I knew I had to jot that idea in the center of our Venn diagram.

Try Guide students to quickly rehearse what they need to learn and do in preparation for practice

Turn to the class to help you finish comparing these two articles using the Venn diagram to record your thinking. Solicit ideas from the class until you have several items in each part of your Venn diagram. Here's an example of what your Venn diagram could look like at this point in the lesson. (Of course, your Venn diagram will vary based on the suggestions of your students.)

Clarify Briefly restate today's teaching objective and explain the practice task(s)

Today we used a Venn diagram to compare the main ideas and key supporting details in two articles on the same topic, the environment. I have a Venn diagram for each of you to use today. I want you to choose two articles from your research folder and use the Venn diagram to compare and contrast the main ideas and key supporting details. You will need to be prepared to explain your Venn diagram to a partner. (SL.3.1a)

Practice Students work independently and/or in small groups to apply today's teaching objective

Students work independently. Each student chooses two articles to compare and contrast using the Venn diagram. As students work, check in and further support students who need more guided practice.

Wrap Up Check understanding as you guide students to briefly share what they have learned and produced today

Gather students together, asking them to have their own Venn diagrams handy. It's time to share with your students the significance of their work. Explain to your class that focusing on the ideas included in the middle section of your Venn diagram helps you to see which ideas are truly important to your topic. Use the Venn diagram you completed as a class as an example.

If we look at the Venn diagram we worked on together, we can see the idea that people use too many plastic drinking bottles is something significant to consider when studying the environment. You see? The ideas that go in the middle of your diagram represent really important concepts—the idea is so important that two different authors included it in their work.

Ask students to take a look at their own diagrams and ask themselves, "What are the ideas that are truly important to the topic I am studying?" Instruct students to take a moment and explain at least one of those ideas to a partner. This partner work represents a great opportunity to highlight several skills that are key to effective speaking and listening. Remind students how to carefully explain their new understandings in light of your discussion on the importance of Venn diagrams (SL.3.1d).

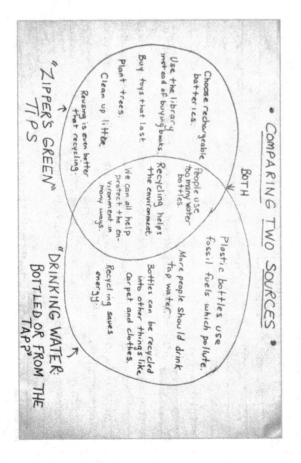

• COMPARING TWO SOURCES •

BOTH

"ZIPPER'S GREEN" TIPS

Choose rechargeable batteries.

Use the library instead of buying books.

Buy toys that last.

Plant trees.

Clean up litter.

Reusing is even better than that recycling.

People use too many water bottles.

Recycling helps the environment.

We can all help protect the environment in many ways.

Plastic bottles use fossil fuels which pollute.

More people should drink tap water.

Bottles can be recycled into other things like carpet and clothes.

Recycling saves energy.

"DRINKING WATER: BOTTLED OR FROM THE TAP?"

Reading Lesson 8

▼ Teaching Objective

Readers notice when they encounter new vocabulary and have a variety of strategies for making meaning.

▼ Standards Alignment

RI 3.1, RI.3.4, RI.3.10, SL.3.1a–d, SL.3.6, L.3.1, L.3.6

▼ Materials

- Chart paper or interactive whiteboard
- Enlarged copy of "The Amazing Humpback Whales" Appendix 3.4 (or if you've chosen to study a different topic with your class, use a new article or short section of a book related to your topic)

▼ To the Teacher

Developing students' academic language is a yearlong endeavor. However, in this lesson, we teach three specific strategies for making meaning when children encounter unfamiliar words. Most likely, these new words may be specific to a content area, or key words that are crucial to understanding a topic they are studying. Here are a few ideas for other ongoing word investigations that highlight the importance (and fun!) of discovering the meaning of new words. **ELL** Identify and Communicate Content and Language Objectives—Academic Vocabulary. With these strategies, your ELLs will grow their academic vocabulary word banks. Encourage them to sketch or provide them with visuals when needed.

- Create a class word jar. As students discover new, interesting, or special words in their reading, they can write these words on a slip of paper to add to the word jar. Once a week (or whenever you have a spare 5 minutes), reach into the word jar and select a new word. Spend time reading, saying, and defining this new word, asking students to "try it out" in different ways. Then display these words in a central place for children to admire and use in their work.

- Post a small word wall of fascinating words. (My grandmother used to call these "25 cent words.") As you read with your class, occasionally pause to notice and admire particularly interesting or fascinating new vocabulary. Practice reading and finding the meaning of these new words as you add them to your wall. If possible, let students craft and record the definitions of these words or add visuals when possible.

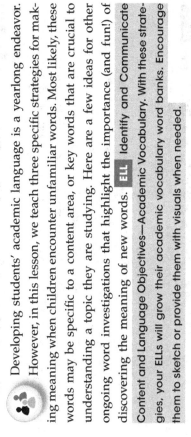

Close Reading Opportunity

▼ Procedure

Warm Up Gather the class to set the stage for today's learning

Strong readers usually understand what they read, but sometimes text looks easier than it is. This happens a lot with informational articles in magazines. An article may be short, with lots of pictures and captions and graphic aids, so you think the information will be easy to understand. Then you may find words or phrases that are super tricky!

Teach Model what students need to learn and do

Explain to your class that looks can be deceiving. Often, an informational article on a topic that is new will include vocabulary that you have never seen before. Earlier, you talked about how many of these words may be in bold or italicized font to indicate their importance.

To completely understand the article, you need to understand what these new words mean. There are several strategies we can use to figure that out. We're going to list them on a graphic organizer today, so you can remember and use them whenever you come across new and tricky vocabulary words in your reading.

Sketch a quick two-column table on your chart paper or interactive whiteboard and title it, "Ways to Discover the Meaning of New Words." Label the left column "New vocabulary" and the right column "Strategy used." **ELL** Provide Comprehensible Input—Organizers. This chart will be a strong anchor chart that your ELLs refer to when encountering new text. Offer visuals to represent strategies when applicable—sketch a dictionary, eyes on a picture, and so on.

Ways to Discover the Meaning of New Words

New vocabulary	Strategy used

Look at the article together. Read aloud from the first paragraph, noting words that the class may not know or examples that feel tricky. Jot down these words for the class to ponder. Introduce, explain, and chart the following four strategies for your class:

- Use context clues. Look for clues that come before or after the tricky word that might help you

- Look for words within words—for example, *starfish* contains the words *star* and *fish*, which can help you get an initial understanding of this new word's meaning.

- Look at the graphic aids on the page—are there any visuals that help explain or provide an image?

- Is there a glossary? If not, consult a dictionary—either a book or online. Or use another online source.

Demonstrate using each of these strategies to discover the meaning of one or two of the words you identified in your initial reading of the article. Be clear that not every strategy will work for every word so students may have to try many strategies. **ELL** Provide Comprehensible Input—Models. Modeling your understanding of new vocabulary will demonstrate ideas and strategies for your ELLs when they are stuck and trying to figure out unknown words.

Try Guide students to quickly rehearse what they need to learn and do in preparation for practice

You watched me use four strategies to uncover the meaning of new words. Let's try using these four strategies right here with another tricky word from this text.

Return to your list of tricky vocabulary from the beginning of this lesson. Select another word for the class to work with. Ask partnerships to practice using these strategies to discover the meaning of this new word. **ELL** Enable Language Production—Increasing Interaction. Take this opportunity to showcase new and novel ways that ELLs are tackling new vocabulary in English. These strategies will aide other ELLs in the class as they are navigating new academic vocabulary. Allow students several minutes to try out the strategy, listening in to each group for interesting tidbits to share with the entire class. As students wrap up their conversations, ask

How did it go? Which strategy helped you discover the meaning of this new word?

Guide the class toward recognizing which strategy seemed to be the most effective, reminding them again that not every strategy will work for every new word. It is important to reinforce the concept that students may have to try several strategies before they are able to successfully determine the meaning of a new vocabulary word.

Clarify Briefly restate today's teaching objective and explain the practice task(s)

We practiced four different strategies for discovering the meaning of new vocabulary we may come across in our reading. Our goal is to truly understand what we read, so it is important to understand the meaning of new words. Your reading challenge today is to continue reading about your topic of interest. As you read, find at least one new vocabulary word that you don't know. Try to use all the strategies we practiced today to uncover your best educated guess for what this word might mean. Be ready to share your word and your thinking at the end of our reading time today.

Practice Students work independently or in small groups to apply today's teaching objective

Students continue to read and research their topic of interest. As they read, students will choose one new vocabulary word from one of their texts. Students will use the four strategies from the chart to uncover the meaning of this new word. Encourage students to try a variety of strategies when they encounter challenging words. Students should be prepared to share their word and their thinking with the class. (SL.3.1a) You may also choose to have your students record their chosen word as well as their new understanding of its meaning.

Wrap Up Check understanding as you guide students to briefly share what they have learned and produced today

Gather your class. Have each student share with a partner their new word and their understanding of its meaning. **ELL** Enable Language Production—Increasing Interaction. ELLs are able to clarify and learn

from their peers during this time in an informal forum. This is an opportunity to whisper in when needed or listen in to understand how to best support their language needs.

When you share your word with your partner, be sure to tell your partner what you think the word means as well as the strategy that helped you the most.

Once partnerships have had a few moments to share their thinking, choose a few students to share their thinking with the entire class.

Reading Lesson 9

▶ Teaching Objective

Readers use the information gained from illustrations to help them better understand a text.

▶ Standards Alignment

RI 3.1, RI 3.7, SL.3.1a–d, L.3.1, L.3.6

▶ Materials

- Chart paper or interactive whiteboard
- Informational article or section from a book with strong visuals

▶ To the Teacher

Encouraging your students to "read" the illustrations or photographs in their informational reading will help support the idea of lingering in these types of texts. Also, this skill may help some of your struggling readers be more successful with texts that interest them but may be out of their reach.

▶ Procedure

Warm Up Gather the class to set the stage for today's learning

Have you noticed that we've only used a few key texts in our research on the environment? We keep returning again and again to these same resources and learning something new and different each time we read them. It's important to be able to linger in an informational text so that you can soak up everything it has to offer. This isn't a race to read more books than someone else!

Teach Model what students need to learn and do

Begin a chart titled, "How to Read Pictures." **ELL** Provide Comprehensible Input—Organizers Your class may have already noticed that the visuals in their informational reading are sometimes detailed illustrations and other times photographs. Share with your class that the images are critical—they are full of information that can add to your understanding of the words. "Today we're going to practice reading the pictures in our informational texts." **ELL** Provide Comprehensible Input—Visuals. This organizer will be a chart that your ELLs refer back to when navigating text. You can visualize the headers with ideas from class reading so that the headers are universal and not just text—e.g., a picture of a classroom for setting and students for people or who was in the picture.

Close Reading Opportunity

Model reading one of the more interesting pictures from your shared text. **ELL** **Provide Comprehensible Input—Models** As you interpret the picture, ask yourself the following four questions, adding each answer to the chart as you go.

Chart: How to Read Pictures

Source: (For a book or magazine, title _____;

date _____, and page no. _____;

for online, URL: _____)

1. Who or what is in the picture?	
2. Where was the picture set? Where did it take place?	
3. What is happening in the picture?	
4. How does this picture help me to better understand the words on the page?	

Try Guide students to quickly rehearse what they need to learn and do in preparation for practice

Select another strong visual image for your class to study. Give students a moment to quietly read the image on their own. Then, pose each of the four questions to your class, soliciting responses from the group. This is an ideal point to hold a class conversation, reinforcing the skill of careful listening and building on others' ideas. (SL.3.1)

> " *The power that makes grass grow, fruit ripen, and guides the bird in flight is in us all.*
> —Angia Yezierska "

Clarify Briefly restate today's teaching objective and explain the practice task(s)

Reiterate to your class the importance of visual images in informational text. Briefly recap the four questions readers ask themselves as they begin to read such images. Instruct students to find a strong image in their reading and use the four questions to delve more deeply into that image. Students should be prepared to share their image as well as their thinking at the end of your lesson today.

Practice Students work independently or in small groups to apply today's teaching objective

Students continue to read independently about their topic of choice using informational texts. Each student will choose a strong image and practice using the four questions to read that image more deeply. Students should be prepared to share their thinking with a partner or with the larger group.

Wrap Up Check understanding as you guide students to briefly share what they have learned and produced today

Ask students to share their image and their thinking about the four questions with a partner. Listen in to several partnerships, choosing one or two groups to share with the larger class.

Reading Lesson 10

▼ Teaching Objective

Read the work of a partner and write a response.

▼ Standards Alignment

RI.3.1, RI.3.6, RI.3.10, W.3.4, W.3.10, SL.3.1a–d, L.3.1, L.3.6

▼ Material

- Enlarged version of "We Learn from Each Other" Response Sheet and copies for students (see Appendix 3.8)

▼ To the Teacher

This final lesson asks students to read and respond to each other's writing. Using the "We Learn from Each Other" Response Sheet, students will determine the main idea and supporting key details of a classmate's work. They will also list the various text features used by their classmate and explain what they learned from one of the illustrations/photographs included. Finally, the students will distinguish their point of view from that of the author. You may choose to collect and save this assignment as evidence of student learning. **ELL** **Assess for Content and Language Understanding—Summative Assessment**

▼ Procedure

Warm Up **Gather the class to set the stage for today's learning**

Compliment students on the work they have done so far.

You have been working hard every day in reading AND writing to research and produce pieces on the topics that interest you most. Today we're going to learn from one another by exchanging our writing with a partner so that we can share all that hard work and exciting learning.

Close Reading Opportunity

Teach **Model what students need to learn and do**

As you're reading your partner's work, I want you to show how much you've learned by filling out this response sheet.

Show the class an enlarged copy of the "We Learn from Each Other" Response Sheet. Model filling out the sheet using the class's shared work on the environment reading (or other reading you have done as a class throughout this lesson set). **ELL** **Provide Comprehensible Input—Models.** Modeling the activity is always a strong support for ELLs; this offers time to see what they are expected to accomplish and time for clarification of the activity if needed. Think aloud and record the main idea and supporting details, list the text features used, and choose one picture to study. Then focus your modeling on the final entry space on this response sheet, for distinguishing the reviewer's point of view from that of the author.

When you're done reading a piece of informational text, it's important to be able to distinguish the author's point of view from your own. For example, it might be clear from the writing that the author thinks people shouldn't drink from plastic water bottles. You might think differently. Maybe you think it's more important to drink enough water and not worry about the bottle. Or maybe you think that as long as you recycle the water bottle, using a plastic one is OK. Or maybe you agree completely with the author. Let's look at this last part of your response sheet. It says, "The author's point of view is _____." In that space, I want you to write what you think the author's opinion is, based on what was included in the writing. After reading this piece on the environment, you might think the author feels it is extremely important to be aware of the ways in which you can help our planet. Let me write that here on our sheet.

Try **Guide students to quickly rehearse what they need to learn and do in preparation for practice**

Now, what is *your* point of view? Do you agree with the author? Or do you have a different opinion? Take a moment to think about this carefully. Then, jot down your point of view using the sentence starter on the response sheet. I agree/disagree with the author's point of view because _____.

Give students a few minutes to complete the work. As students think and jot, move around and check in with several students to get an idea of what they are thinking. You will want to find a few examples to share with the class. Be sure to highlight examples that offer varying opinions.

We Learn from Each Other

1. The main idea of my partner's article is _____

2. One detail I learned is _____

3. My partner used various text features including _____.

4. My favorite illustration/photograph is _____ because _____

I learned _____

5. The author's point of view is _____

6. I agree/disagree with the author's point of view because _____

Clarify Briefly restate today's teaching objective and explain the practice task(s)

We can always learn from one another. Today I want you to show what you learned from your partner as well as what you have learned about reading informational text, by exchanging work with a friend and filling out a response sheet.

Practice Students work independently or in small groups to apply today's teaching objective

Students exchange work with a partner **ELL** **Enable Language Production—Increasing Interaction** and fill out the "We Learn from Each Other" Response Sheet. (Note: You may want to assign partnerships in advance to be sure that partnerships read at a similar level and are therefore easily able to read each other's work.)

Wrap Up Check understanding as you guide students to briefly share what they have learned and produced today

Today we learned about a new topic from one another and showed all that we know about reading informational text. I am so proud of all your hard work!

As a group, discuss and decide where to relocate the charts associated with the work from this lesson set so that students may use them as needed when encountering informational text for the remainder of your school year.

Milestone Performance Assessment

Peer Assessment

Use this checklist to assess student ability to read and respond to the work of their peers.

Standards Alignment: RI.3.1, RI.3.6

	Achieved	Notes
Identify the main idea in a classmate's work.		
Identify the supporting key details in a classmate's work.		
Identify various text features in a classmate's work.		
Explain the significance of an illustration/ photograph in a classmate's work.		

Grade 3

Writing Lessons

The Core I.D.E.A. / Daily Writing Instruction at a Glance table highlights the teaching objectives and standards alignment for all 10 lessons across the four stages (Introduce, Define, Extend, and Assess) of the lesson set. It also indicates which lessons contain special features to support English language learners (ELLs), formative (Milestone) assessments, speaking and listening (S&L) skills, and technology use.

The following Core Ready Writing Rubric is designed to help you record each student's overall understanding across four levels of achievement as it relates to the lesson set goals. We recommend that you use this rubric at the end of the lesson set as a performance-based assessment tool. Use the Milestone Performance Assessments as tools to help you gauge student progress toward these goals, and to reteach and differentiate as needed. See the foundational book, *Be Core Ready: Powerful, Effective Steps to Implementing and Achieving the Common Core State Standards*, for more information about the Core Ready Reading and Writing Rubrics.

The Core I.D.E.A. / Daily Writing Instruction at a Glance

Grade 3   What Matters Most: Research and Analysis in Informational Text

Instructional Stage	Lesson	Teaching Objective	Core Standards	Special Features
Introduce: notice, explore, collect, note, immerse, surround, record, share	1	Researchers follow many specific steps in order to guide their research.	RI.3.10 • W.3.4 • W.3.7 • W.3.10 SL.3.1a-d • SL.3.6 • L.3.1 • L.3.6	ELL Tech S&L
Define: name, identify, outline, clarify, select, plan	2	Researchers narrow their topic by using question words.	RI.3.1 • RI.3.10 • W.3.4 • W.3.7 W.3.10 • SL.3.1a • SL.3.1b SL.3.2 • L.3.6	Close Reading ELL
	3	Informational articles are one way to write up research.	RI.3.1 • RI.3.2 • RI.3.5 • RI.3.10 W.3.4 • W.3.7 • W.3.10 • SL.3.1a-d SL.3.2 • L.3.6	Close Reading ELL S&L
	4	Research notes are organized into logical categories to write an informational article.	W.3.4 • W.3.5 • W.3.7 • W.3.8 W.3.10 • L.3.6	ELL Milestone Assessment
	5	There are many types of leads that begin informational articles.	W.3.2a • W.3.4 • W.3.5 • W.3.10 SL.3.1a-d • SL.3.2 • L.3.1 • L.3.6	ELL S&L
	6	Researchers move from notes to paragraphs.	W.3.2a-c • W.3.4 • W.3.5 • W.3.10 SL.3.6 • L.3.6	ELL Milestone Assessment
	7	Informational articles have effective endings.	W.3.2d • W.3.4 • W.3.5 • W.3.10 SL.3.1a-d • L.3.1 • L.3.6	ELL Milestone Assessment
Extend: try, experiment, attempt, approximate, practice, explain, revise, refine	8	Informational articles combine text and images.	W.3.2 • W.3.4 • W.3.5 • W.3.10 SL.3.1a-d • L.3.1 • L.3.6	Tech
	9	Writers revise for the big ideas and edit for conventions and spelling.	W.3.5 • W.3.10 • SL.3.6 • L.3.1 L.3.2 • L.3.3 • L.3.6	ELL Milestone Assessment S&L
Assess: reflect, conclude, connect, share, recognize, respond	10	Writers reflect on their learning through the Core Questions.	W.3.4 • W.3.10 • SL.3.1a-d SL.3.6 • L.3.1 • L.3.6	Tech

Core Ready Writing Rubric

Grade 3 What Matters Most: Research and Analysis in Informational Text

Lesson Set Goal	Emerging	Approaching	Achieving	Exceeding	Standards Alignment
Take notes to record big ideas and supporting evidence.	Student struggles with locating and recording important or relevant information without extensive support.	With some support, student records main ideas and includes a few supporting details. Student may have some difficulty with organization and determining what is most important.	Student records main ideas and several supporting details. Organizes appropriate information in a logical fashion that reflects what is most important.	Student records main ideas and several supporting details. Notes are highly organized and logical. Student shows strong understanding of what is most important.	RI.3.1 RI.3.10 W.3.4 W.3.7 W.3.8 W.3.10 L.3.6
Write an informational article that includes a headline, lead, and clincher.	Student has little or no success writing the article. Most or all required features are missing.	Student writes article and includes most required features. Some of the components may be more developed or successful than others.	Student writes article and includes all required features. All features serve their basic purpose successfully.	Student writes article and includes all required features. All features are highly successful and serve to make the article more effective.	W.3.2a W.3.2d W.3.4 W.3.7 W.3.10
Produce clear, well-organized, and well-developed informational article.	Student has little or no success writing the article. The information may be significantly disorganized, inaccurate, or incomplete.	Student writes article. Some flaws in organization, completeness, accuracy, or development are present.	Student writes article. Most or all information is clear and organized, accurate, complete, and developed.	Student writes a highly effective article. Information is clear and well organized, accurate, complete, and very well developed.	W.3.2 W.3.7 W.3.10
Write labels and captions for graphics.	Student has little or no success including labels and captions for graphics.	Student demonstrates some understanding of how and why to add labels and captions for graphics. Some of the components are more developed than others.	Student writes effective labels and captions for graphics.	Student writes several very effective labels and captions for graphics. May be remarkably thorough or purposefully concise.	W.3.4 W.3.10
Develop the topic with facts, definitions, details, and use linking words and phrases.	Student makes little or no attempt to develop the topic with facts, definitions, and details. Does not use or inaccurately uses linking words and phrases.	Student demonstrates some evidence of developing the topic with facts, definitions, and details. Uses linking words and phrases inconsistently.	Student consistently develops the topic with facts, definitions, and details and uses linking words and phrases.	Student demonstrates an exceptional understanding of how to develop the topic with facts, definitions, and details and uses linking words and phrases with extraordinary accuracy.	W.3.2b W.3.2c W.3.10
With guidance and support from peers and adults, plan, revise, and edit story, paying close attention to the conventions of standard English and clarity of the story's development.	Student makes little or no attempt to develop and strengthen writing through planning, revising, and editing.	Student attempts to develop and strengthen writing as needed by planning, revising, and editing. Writing may still contain significant errors or lack clarity.	Student develops and strengthens writing as needed by planning, revising, and editing. Some areas of the planning, revision, and editing may be more developed than others.	Student extensively develops and strengthens writing by planning, revising, and editing as needed. Few or no errors or lapses of clarity evident.	W.3.5

Core Ready Writing Rubric, Grade 3, continued

Lesson Set Goal	Emerging	Approaching	Achieving	Exceeding	Standards Alignment
With guidance and support from adults and peers, create a visual presentation of the final story.	Student shows little or no evidence of attempting to create a visual presentation that combines visuals and words to show how the character he or she created provides a mirror and a window for him- or herself. The presentation may or may not be relevant.	Student attempts to create a visual presentation that combines visuals and words to show how the character he or she created provides a mirror and a window for him- or herself. Some components of the presentation may be more relevant and well developed than others.	With some guidance from adults and peers, student successfully creates a visual presentation that combines visuals and words to show how the character he or she created provides a mirror and a window for him- or herself.	With minimal guidance and support from adults and peers, student creates a well-organized visual presentation that combines visuals and words to show how the character he or she created provides a mirror and a window for him- or herself.	W.3.4 W.3.6 SL.3.1a–d SL.3.6 L.3.1 L.3.6
Ask and answer questions to demonstrate understanding of a text, referring explicitly to the text as the basis for the answers.	Student shows little or no evidence of active, purposeful reading or searching the text for specific information and evidence. Student makes little or no attempt to ask or answer questions about the text. Text evidence is minimal or nonexistent.	Student shows some evidence of active, purposeful reading and searching the text for specific information and evidence. Student may be able to ask or answer some questions about the text accurately, but may not provide sufficient textual evidence to support thinking.	Student shows solid evidence of active, purposeful reading and searching the text for specific information and evidence. Student usually asks and answers questions accurately and provides appropriate textual evidence to support thinking.	Student demonstrates exceptional evidence of active, purposeful reading and searching the text for specific information and evidence. Student asks and answers questions with accuracy and provides appropriate, detailed, and thoughtful textual evidence to support thinking.	RI.3.1
By the end of the year, independently and proficiently read and comprehend a variety of informational texts at the high end of the grade 3 text complexity band.	Student shows little or no evidence of reading and comprehending texts appropriate for the grade 3 text complexity band.	Student attempts, with inconsistent success, to independently and proficiently read and comprehend texts appropriate for the grade 3 text complexity band.	Student shows solid evidence of independently and proficiently reading and comprehending texts appropriate for the grade 3 text complexity band.	Student shows solid evidence of independently and proficiently reading and comprehending texts above the grade 3 text complexity year band.	RI.3.10
Write routinely over extended time frames (time for research, reflection, and revision) and shorter time frames (a single sitting or a day or two) for a range of discipline-specific tasks, purposes, and audiences.	Student shows little or no evidence of writing routinely for short or long time frames for a range of discipline-specific tasks, purposes, or audiences.	Student shows some evidence of writing routinely for short and long time frames for a range of discipline-specific tasks, purposes, and audiences.	Student shows solid evidence of writing routinely for short and long time frames for a range of discipline-specific tasks, purposes, and audiences.	Student shows exceptional evidence of consistently and accurately writing for short and long time frames for a range of discipline-specific tasks, purposes, and audiences.	W.3.10

Lesson Set Goal	Emerging	Approaching	Achieving	Exceeding	Standards Alignment
In collaborative discussions, demonstrate evidence of preparation for discussion and exhibit responsibility to the rules and roles of conversation.	In collaborative discussions, student comes unprepared and often disregards the rules and roles of conversation.	In collaborative discussions, student's preparation may be evident but ineffective or inconsistent. May occasionally disregard the rules and roles of conversation.	In collaborative discussions, student prepares adequately and draws on the preparation and other information about the topic to explore ideas under discussion. Usually observes the rules and roles of conversation.	In collaborative discussions, student arrives extremely well prepared for discussions and draws on the preparation and other information about the topic to explore ideas under discussion. Always observes the rules and roles of conversation.	SL.3.1a SL.3.1b
In collaborative discussions, share and develop ideas in a manner that enhances understanding of topic. Contribute and respond to the content of the conversation in a productive and focused manner.	Student shows little or no evidence of engaging in collaborative discussions and makes little or no attempt to ask and answer questions, stay on topic, link comments to the remarks of others, or to explain his or her own ideas and understanding in light of the discussion.	Student shows some evidence of engaging in collaborative discussions and, with marginal success, attempts to ask questions to check understanding of information presented, to stay on topic, link comments to the remarks of others, and explain his or her comments to the remarks of others, and explains his or her own ideas and understanding in light of the discussion.	Student engages in a range of collaborative discussions and asks questions to check understanding of information presented. Stays on topic most of the time and frequently links his or her own ideas and understanding in light of the discussion.	Student effectively and consistently engages in a range of collaborative discussions and asks thoughtful and high-level questions to check understanding of information presented. Always stays on topic and, with great insight and attention to the comments of others, links his or her comments to the remarks of others, and explains his or her own ideas and understanding in light of the discussion.	SL.3.1c SL.3.1d
Speak in complete sentences when appropriate and demonstrate a command of standard English grammar and usage.	Student shows little or no evidence of attempting to speak in complete sentences. Student demonstrates little or no command of standard English grammar and usage.	Student attempts to speak in complete sentences when appropriate and demonstrates some command of standard English grammar and usage.	Student speaks in complete sentences when appropriate and demonstrates a command of standard English grammar and usage.	Student always speaks in complete sentences when appropriate and demonstrates an extraordinary command of the conventions of standard English grammar and usage.	SL.3.6 L.3.1
Demonstrate knowledge of standard English and its conventions.	Student demonstrates little or no knowledge of standard English and its conventions.	Student demonstrates some evidence of knowledge of standard English and its conventions.	Student consistently demonstrates knowledge of standard English and its conventions.	Student demonstrates an exceptional understanding of standard English and its conventions. Use of conventions is sophisticated for grade level and accurate.	L.3.1 L.3.2 L.3.3
Acquire and accurately use grade-appropriate conversational, general academic, and domain-specific vocabulary and phrases.	Student shows little or no evidence of the acquisition or use of grade-appropriate conversational and academic language.	Student shows some evidence of the acquisition and use of grade-appropriate conversational and academic language.	Student shows solid evidence of the acquisition and use of grade-appropriate conversational and academic language.	Student shows a high level of sophistication and precision with the acquisition and use of grade-appropriate conversational and academic language.	L.3.6

Note: See the Core Ready Rubrics chart in the Walk Through for descriptions of category headers.

Writing Lesson 1 • • • • • • • • • •

▶ Teaching Objective

Researchers follow many specific steps in order to guide their research.

▶ Standards Alignment

RI.3.10, W.3.4, W.3.7, W.3.10, SL.3.1a–d, SL.3.6, L.3.1, L.3.6

▶ Materials

- Student Research folders
- Copies of Research Road Map (see Appendix 3.9)

▶ To the Teacher

Today is the start of an exciting set of lessons. Not only will your students conduct research around a topic that matters to them, but over the next several weeks they will grow more confident and capable as independent researchers. This lesson set has great power to help transform students to think of themselves as independent learners and researchers. Today's lesson is about generating excitement for this process. Share an anecdote of a time you had a burning question, and what you did to find the answer. Common questions that students can relate to are "Why is the sky blue?" or "Why does snow fall?" In this lesson, we use the sky example.

▶ Procedure

Warm Up Gather the class to set the stage for today's learning

Gather your class to introduce this new lesson set centered on research. This is an opportunity to begin modeling for them the importance of a burning question, which is where all great research begins.

Third graders, today you begin the very exciting journey of researching a topic that matters to you. Did you know that all great research starts with a burning question, something you just have to find out the answer to, something that sticks in your mind and you keep wondering about? I have burning questions all

the time. Just yesterday I was looking up at the sky and wondered, "Why is the sky blue?" So, I wanted to find some sources to help me find the answer.

Teach Model what students need to learn and do

Model for students steps you have taken as a researcher to provide an anecdote your students can learn from.

Today we're going to talk about the specific steps a researcher takes to find the answers to his or her burning questions.

(In Reading Lesson 1 students will start a K-W-L [K (What I Know) W (What I Want to Know) L (What I Have Learned)] chart. This lesson parallels that instruction but now guides students in what the research process will be from start to finish, giving them a road map for their writing. If you have already conducted Reading Lesson 1 you can refer back to the questions students have begun to generate).

When the question, "Why is the sky blue?" popped in my head, I realized I'd found a topic worthy of research. It was a burning question. I didn't already know the answer to it and I wanted to find out. Then, I needed to find some sources. I asked my family members but they weren't sure. I looked at the books I had at home and couldn't find anything that would help me. Finally, I went to the Internet and did a search using the key question, "Why is the sky blue?". I read about the atmosphere and how blue light is radiated in different directions and gets scattered across the sky. I jotted down some notes in my pocket notebook to share with my family later, and that night I told them all about what I found.

Try Guide students to quickly rehearse what they need to learn and do in preparation for practice

Review with the class the steps you took as a researcher. These should mirror the steps you provide with the Research Road Map to come later in the lesson.

Let's think . . . What steps did I take as a researcher to find the answer to my burning question about why the sky is blue? Turn and talk to a partner sharing some of the steps I took.

Goal	Low-Tech	High-Tech
Students will organize their research materials over the course of the research process.	Provide students with two-pocket portfolio folders, stickies or notecards, copies of handouts.	Students can create a new folder using a digital writing tool. In this folder they will keep notes using digital stickies or another note-taking tool and copies of materials you provide them with digitally.

When students have had a few minutes to share with one another, have partners share out and record their thinking on a chart titled "What Does It Mean to Be a Researcher?" **ELL** Provide Comprehensible Input—Graphic Organizers. This graphic can be visualized by sketching the headers if the group needs this support. During this partner time, you can sit in to offer language support and to promote vocabulary and brainstorming in the group.

Your students' suggestions should include things like:

- Choose topic
- Take notes
- Form questions
- Organize information
- Find resources
- Summarize
- Identify important information
- Put it all together in own words
- Read

Before discussion begins, remind the class of the rules and etiquette of whole class discussions—one voice speaks at a time, listen with care, ask questions when you are unsure of something or you need clarification. (SL.3.1b) Remind students to explain their own ideas and add to the discussion rather than repeat the thoughts of others. (SL.3.1d) Encourage students to speak in complete sentences when sharing their ideas. (SL.3.6)

Clarify Briefly restate today's teaching objective and explain the practice task(s)

Now that the topic of research has been introduced, it's time to orient your students to how they will organize themselves as researchers.

Researchers follow many specific steps to guide their research—to find the answers to their burning questions. To get us ready to start this exciting process we need to organize our materials to help guide us in our steps. Your independent practice today is going to be to label your research folder. On one side is for your notes and copies, the other side is for your drafts. Let's start by labeling the front and inside covers (_____'s Research Folder/Notes/Drafts).

Practice Students work independently and/or in small groups to apply today's teaching objective

Students will take the time to organize their research folders. The first document they receive today will be Research Road Map (see Appendix 3.9), which outlines all of the steps discussed today. **ELL** Provide Comprehensible Input—Graphic Organizer. Displaying the road-map is helpful to demonstrate steps in this process. This will be an important tool throughout the lesson set.

Wrap Up Check understanding as you guide students to briefly share what they have learned and produced today

At the end of class, ask your students to share which step of the research road map they are most excited about.

If you're walking down the right path and you're willing to keep walking, eventually you'll make progress.

—Barack Obama

Writing Lesson 2

▼ Teaching Objective

Researchers narrow their topic by using question words.

▼ Standards Alignment

RI.3.1, RI.3.10, W.3.4, W.3.7, W.3.10, SL.3.1a, SL.3.1b, SL.3.2, L.3.6

Close Reading
Opportunity

▼ Materials

- Student Research folders
- Question Words posted (Who, What, When, Where, Why, How)
- "Young Voices on Climate Change" video (from the *National Geographic Kids* website) or another short video on your topic
- Copies of Research Road Map (see Appendix 3.9)
- Method for student writing

▼ To the Teacher

We've chosen the topic of the environment to guide the lesson set in reading and writing; however, you may opt to change that to something that matches your local curriculum and resources.

▼ Procedure

Warm Up   Gather the class to set the stage for today's learning

Remind your students of the great work they've done as beginning researchers.

We are off to a great start to understanding the important jobs a researcher has. Over the next few weeks, we are going to follow our Research Road Map on the topic of the environment. Let's take a look at the steps you're going to take to research and write your own informational article about an environmental topic you care about.

Review with students the Research Road Map, which should already be in the Research Folders from yesterday.

© Lisa F. Young / Fotolia

Teach   Model what students need to learn and do

Review the first stop on the Research Road Map and direct your students to how you are going to narrow your class topic by using question words.

The first stop on our Research Road Map is to choose a narrowed topic. The environment is a HUGE topic, so we need to narrow it down to something more specific that you want to find out more about. (If the class has started a K-W-L sheet in Reading Lesson 1 already, refer to the kinds of things your students want to know more about.) Do you want to know more about *animals* that might be endangered? *People* who work to help make the earth greener? *Places* that need our help—like the rainforest, wetlands, oceans, and rivers? These are interesting things, right, but still TOO BIG. One tool for narrowing our topics is to use the six question words: *who, what, when, where, why,* and *how* to start our topic. After all, remember that research is about coming up with a burning question. I came up with some narrowed topics that I am interested in learning more about:

- Kids working to save the environment—*Who* are the kids working to save the environment?

Clarify Briefly restate today's teaching objective and explain the practice task(s)

Remind students of the question words that can help them narrow topics they are interested in researching.

Remember that using the question words, *who, what, when, where, why,* and *how* can help you narrow your topic. Today, I want you to brainstorm at least three possible topics you're interested in and then use the six question words to help you narrow down your topic. You can use the ideas you and your classmates came up with on our K-W-L sheet as a starting place. Then, star the one that you are most interested in. Remember to think about what you are *most* curious about.

Practice Students work independently or in small groups to apply today's teaching objective

Students record three possible topics and use the six question words to help them narrow their topic. A suggestion for how they could set up their paper:

Example of Focus Questions Chart

Topic	Focus Question (who, what, where, when, why, how)

Wrap Up Check understanding as you guide students to briefly share what they have learned and produced today

At the end of class, have students share the narrowed topic they are most excited to research. As they do that, record each student's topic for your own reference. Make sure to prioritize conferences with students whose topics seem either too broad or unattainable through print or digital sources.

- Endangered animals
- Recycling
- Composting

Those are still pretty big topics, so I used the six question words to help me narrow them even more.

- *Who* works to save endangered animals?
- *What* can I recycle?
- *How* do I compost?

These are more specific questions that I want to make sure I answer as I research.

Try Guide students to quickly rehearse what they need to learn and do in preparation for practice

There are many wonderful video clips on sites such as *National Geographic Kids*. By viewing a video clip and having students focus on the narrowed topic the story is about, you are providing audio visual support and engaging students in more modalities than when using print texts alone.

Now we are going to watch a video clip about a specific topic on the environment. While you are watching, jot down the narrowed topic this video is teaching us about. Then, we're going to use the question words to help us narrow it even more.

View with students videos from *National Geographic Kids* such as "Young Voices on Climate Change." **ELL** Provide Comprehensible Input—Audiovisual Aides. Videos are a powerful and visual way to display information and support language acquisition around a topic. After the video, stop to ask,

What topic is this video teaching us about?

- The earth getting warmer
- Stronger storms
- Kids working to save the environment

Now let's use the question words to narrow these down even more.

- The earth getting warmer—*Why* is the earth getting warmer?
- Stronger storms—*What* causes stronger storms?

Writing Lesson 3

▼ Teaching Objective

Informational articles are one way to present research.

▼ Standards Alignment

RI.3.1, RI.3.2, RI.3.5, RI.3.10, W.3.4, W.3.7, W.3.10, SL.3.1a–d, SL.3.2, L.3.6

Close Reading
Opportunity

▼ Materials

- Copies of "Polar Bears Listed as Threatened" from *National Geographic News* (online)
- Copies of "Drinking Water: Bottled or from the Tap?" from the *National Geographic Kids* website
- Graphic organizer for Informational Article Techniques (see Appendix 3.16)

▼ To the Teacher

Yesterday, your students chose research topics they are interested in using the six question words to help them narrow their topic. Before moving on to Writing Lesson 3, review your students' choices and consider the resources you have available for their independent research. Informational articles are a fun way to write up research with third graders. Informational articles show insightful coverage of a topic, give detailed information focused on an aspect of the topic, and refer to sources of research but are not encyclopedia reports. Today is all about helping students understand what makes this type of writing special so that they can mirror the techniques they see journalists using when writing up their informational articles.

▼ Procedure

Warm Up Gather the class to set the stage for today's learning

Share some of the research topics your students are interested in.

Last night I read through your research topics and I am now full of burning questions. I can't wait to find out _____

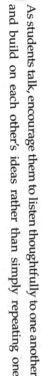

questions). When we find out our answers we are going to put them together in the form of informational articles.

Teach Model what students need to learn and do

Today you are orienting the class to informational articles. Describe what they are and provide a sample for students to learn from.

Informational articles are one way that researchers write up their findings. They are a fun way to tell people what you've learned through writing. Informational articles are like research reports, but instead of just telling us information about the topic, the writers of these kinds of articles make sure the topic is newsworthy and they use different writing techniques to make us want to keep reading. Today, we are going to read some informational articles on two topics that I know you will find interesting—polar bears and how we drink our water. Today, we are going to look for things these writers are doing that we want to try to do in our writing. Let's read "Polar Bears Protected by Law" together.

Read the article. Then, list what students notice about this type of writing. Chart student ideas such as:

- Teaches about a topic
- Includes facts
- Asks question
- Is written in paragraphs
- Includes picture and caption
- Includes headings to show main ideas
- Includes glossary of important or difficult words
- Includes quotes from experts
- Directly addresses the reader ("you")

_____ (cite a few of your students' research

As students talk, encourage them to listen thoughtfully to one another and build on each other's ideas rather than simply repeating one another. (SL.3.1b, SL.3.1c) Also, this is a good opportunity to encourage students to use the text as evidence in their conversation. (SL.3.2)

Try Guide students to quickly rehearse what they need to learn and do in preparation for practice

Wow! This article did so much. Now let's read another research article and use our Informational Article Techniques to see what writing techniques this article uses.

Provide students with copies of "Drinking Water: Bottled or from the Tap?" or another informational article along with copies of the graphic organizer. **ELL** Provide Comprehensible Input—Graphic Organizer. This organizer will help ELLs decode different features and techniques of information text. Consider offering visual examples with the headers to help student understand the meaning of each example—e.g., picture with a heading next to the header 'picture with a heading." Read the first paragraph together and direct students to check off and provide examples of when the article uses various techniques.

Clarify Briefly restate today's teaching objective and explain the practice task(s)

Today you are going to finish reading this article that teaches us about the important things we must think about when we decide whether to drink bottled water or tap water, and fill in the graphic organizer. Remember, not every article will use every technique, so you'll need to read carefully to find the techniques this writer is using.

Practice Students work independently or in small groups to apply today's teaching objective

Students will read and record the writing techniques the author is using in the informational article.

Wrap Up Check understanding as you guide students to briefly share what they have learned and produced today

At the end of class, have students share with a partner or the class what they techniques they noticed and recorded when they were reading and which they are most excited to try out.

Writing Lesson 4

▶ Teaching Objective

Research notes are organized into logical categories to write an informational article.

▶ Standards Alignment

W.3.4, W.3.5, W.3.7, W.3.8, W.3.10, L.3.6

▶ Materials

- Student notes from Practice in Reading Lesson 5
- Teacher-prepared list of notes on "Polar Bears Protected by Law" in Appendix 3.3 (pre-chart 10 to 15 notes from this article spanning the sub-topics suggested in "TEACH" in advance of the lesson)

▶ To the Teacher

This lesson is designed to be taught following Reading Lesson 5, where students are taught to take notes from their sources. Note taking may take students more than one day to complete. This lesson works best when students have enough notes to start grouping them into logical categories. Once students have their notes compiled, they are ready to organize their notes to help them compose the clusters of information within the body of their informational article. In future grades, the categorization of notes will become more complex. For this lesson set, we are introducing the idea of categorization of notes, so it is best to stick to a simple system of naming the category of notes, such as "What bears eat." This grouping and naming process may be challenging for some students, but be assured that the thoughtful struggle they will face will help them to develop a stronger understanding of how informational text is organized.

▼ Procedure

Warm Up | Gather the class to set the stage for today's learning

Remind students of the note-taking work they did in reading class.

I am so impressed by the thoughtful note taking you've done during reading class. Walking around the room, I've learned so much about your topics at-the-ready. I can't wait to learn more! I noticed something interesting about your notes, though, and you may have noticed the same thing. I noticed that some of your notes are about the same topic and that they seem to go together.

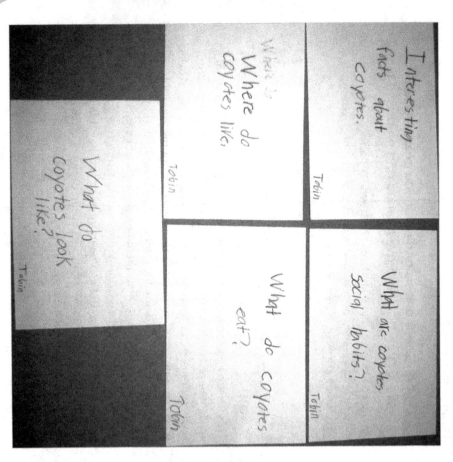

Teach | Model what students need to learn and do

Introduce a categorization system to your students.

In today's writing lesson, we are going to categorize *your notes—put them into groups based on what they are all about. The big idea is your research topic, such as* Why polar bears are protected. *But then there are smaller ideas that seem to go together. We call these clusters of information* subtopics. *Informational nonfiction authors don't just list facts in any order. They group information together by subtopic. Let's take a look at some notes that I took about the article "Polar Bears Protected by Law." What subtopics seem to be coming up in my notes?*

Students should notice that some notes are about:

- Where polar bears live
- Why they are threatened
- How they hunt and what they eat
- What's happening with polar bears now

Great job noticing these subtopics that our notes fit into. Today we are going to group them and give each group a name based on what the notes are about. Watch how I group our notes together by naming.

Try | Guide students to quickly rehearse what they need to learn and do in preparation for practice

Have students sort some of their notes into groups that go together. Then, have students share their thinking with a partner to see if they are on the right track. **ELL** Enable Language Production—Increasing interaction. The use of the sentence starters that follow will help to deepen the level of conversation between students. Listen in to see where you can whisper in to model sentence starters during a lag in partner interaction. Provide them with language for discussing what they notice about each other's work.

Now, open your research folder and look at your notes. Read all of your notes to yourself first. Then, turn and talk to your partner, sharing with him or her some notes that seem to go together. Let your partner know if you agree with what he or she has found. Ask yourselves and each other, "Does it sound like those notes go together?"

Provide your students with some sentence starters for this partner talk:

- "I agree that your notes about _____ go together."
- "I disagree because your notes about _____ and _____ don't seem to fit together."

Clarify Briefly restate today's teaching objective and explain the practice task(s)

Now that you've consulted with a partner about one of your grouping ideas, you are going to finish organizing them into piles or groups. When you are ready, you are going to label them just as I did by giving them a name that explains what they are about.

Practice Students work independently and/or in small groups to apply today's teaching objective

Students continue to group their notes into logical categories and label them according to the system you've modeled.

Wrap Up Check understanding as you guide students to briefly share what they learned and produced today

At the end of class, have students return to their partners to share the rest of their grouping system and provide some feedback on whether they agree with each other's groupings.

 Collect and analyze students' work to monitor whether they are able to accurately organize their notes into logical categories, using the Milestone Performance Assessment "Categorizing Notes" (see also Appendix 3.19). Use this as a quick assessment to determine if your students need additional support with this skill. Based on this assessment, you may

choose to continue this work as a whole group, conduct a small group, or meet with individual students. **ELL** Assess for Content and Language Understanding—Formative Assessment. This is a time to understand the language supports that you can provide to help your ELLs in the upcoming lessons.

Milestone Performance Assessment

Categorizing Notes

Use this checklist to assess student understanding of basic categorization of notes.

Standards Alignment: W.3.4, W.3.5, W.3.7, W.3.8, W.3.10, SL.3.1a–d, SL.3.2, SL.3.6, L.3.1, L.3.6

	Achieved	Notes
Organize notes logically in clusters of similar information.		
Create appropriate labels for groups.		
Discuss notes with a partner and make revisions based on discussion, as needed.		

Writing Lesson 5

▶ **Teaching Objective**

There are many types of leads that begin informational articles.

▶ **Standards Alignment**

W.3.2a, W.3.4, W.3.5, W.3.10, SL.3.1a–d, SL.3.2, L.3.1, L.3.6

▶ **Materials**

- A newspaper or digital projection of a popular news website for kids such as *Time for Kids* or *Scholastic News*

- Copies of informational articles previously read, such as "Polar Bears Protected by Law," "Polar Bears Listed as Threatened," "Zipper's Green Tips," or "Drinking Water Bottled or from the Tap?"
- Charting supplies or interactive whiteboard
- "Extra! Extra!" Headlines and Leads graphic organizer (see Appendix 3.10)

▼ Procedure

Warm Up Gather the class to set the stage for today's learning

Gather your class for some exciting news . . .

"Extra! Extra! Read all about it!' Did you know that newsboys used to shout this in the city streets to grab the attention of people passing by? They were trying to hook readers in to buy the newspaper and find out the must-read stories inside.

Teach Model what students need to learn and do

To demonstrate the power of the headline as the first thing a reader sees, have a newspaper with you or open up on a screen a popular kids' news site such as *Time for Kids* or *Scholastic News*. You want everyone to be able to see the headlines on the page.

When I open up the newspaper (or open up the news online) what is the first thing you see? That's right, the headlines. The headline is the first thing a reader sees when he or she wants to read about the news. The headline is bigger than the rest of the text and in bold letters so that you can't miss it. That's one way that news writers hook us as reader. We see a headline and we become curious about the news story. Now that we've found the headlines, let's read on to found out another way that journalists keep us hooked as readers.

Use the headlines within the newspaper or online news site or refer back to readings you've previously done in this lesson set.

The first sentence in an informational article is called the *lead*. It's what gets us hooked. There are some common ways that writers of informational articles begin their news stories.

Have a chart prepared that includes some common ways informational articles begin include. These will be expanded in future grades, but for third grade texts these are common forms of leads:

- Generalization ("Polar bears are . . .")
- Question ("Did you know . . . ?")
- If or what if ("If you are like many Americans, then . . . / What if we all . . . ?")
- Quotation ("One expert said, '. . .'")

Let's take a look at a few leads together to see the different ways journalists start their informational articles. Using the chart to help us, What kind of lead do you think _____ begins with?

Try Guide students to quickly rehearse what they need to learn and do in preparation for practice

Direct your students to try writing their own headlines and leads for an article they have read together.

Great job finding the different ways that these journalists have written leads to keep our attention as readers. We're going to try writing our own headlines and leads today based on our notes, but first, let's practice together writing some new headlines for an article we know well and already have notes on, "Polar Bears Protected By Law." Our Extra! Extra! Headlines and Leads graphic organizer will help us keep track of our ideas. What would be another great headline for this article?

Jot down student suggestions. They might say something like:

Polar Bears Need Our Help!

Polar Bears in Trouble!

What's Happening to the Polar Bear?

Great headlines, everyone. Now let's create some new leads. This article begins with a generalization, "Polar bears were added to the list of threatened species and will receive special protection under U.S. law." Let's see if we can come up with other types of leads to grab our readers' attention: a question, a quotation, or a what if/if.

Chart ideas with students. They might say something like:

Did you know that polar bears are in trouble?

"Polar bears are likely to become endangered," says _____.

If you were a polar bear you might be struggling to find a safe place to call home.

As students talk, encourage them to listen thoughtfully to one another and build on each other's ideas rather than simply repeating one another. (SL.3.1b, SL.3.1c) Also, this is a good opportunity to encourage students to use the text as evidence for their headlines. (SL.3.2)

Clarify Briefly restate today's teaching objective and explain the practice task(s)

Today, you are going to draft your own headlines and leads on your research topic. Using the "Extra! Extra!" Headlines and Leads

graphic organizer, write down three possible headlines and four possible leads. **ELL** Provide Comprehensible Input—Graphic Organizer Then, star your favorites.

Practice Students work independently or in small groups to apply today's teaching objective

Students will complete the "Extra! Extra!" Headlines and Leads graphic organizer and star their favorites to share with the group.

Wrap Up Check understanding as you guide students to briefly share what they have learned and produced today

At the end of class, have students share the headlines and leads they've starred.

▶ To the Teacher

Now that leads have been established, it's important for students to go back to their notes. Moving from notes to paragraphs can be a challenge for third graders, and modeling how you do that with your collective notes will be important. Learning to cluster information into a paragraph is a critical language skill for third graders. It may take several days for students to create a complete article. This lesson also helps students apply basic paragraphing skills like indenting, writing one sentence after the other, capitalization, and end punctuation.

▶ Procedure

Warm Up Gather the class to set the stage for today's learning

Students should have all of their notes categorized and organized along with their "Extra! Extra!" Headlines and Leads graphic organizer handy.

Didn't the headlines and leads you heard yesterday make you want to learn all about the things we are researching like _____ and _____? (Choose two topics your students are studying.) We are well on our way to sharing important news with each other. What do you think comes next? Let's look at our Research Road Map to find out.

Writing Lesson 6

▶ Teaching Objective

Researchers move from notes to paragraphs.

▶ Standards Alignment

W.3.2a–c, W.3.4, W.3.5, W.3.10, SL.3.6, L.3.6

▶ Materials

- Student notes
- Completed "Extra! Extra!" Headlines and Leads graphic organizer from writing lesson 5
- Group notes on topic such as "Polar Bears Protected by Law"
- Method for student writing
- Charting supplies or interactive whiteboard
- Copy of the Research Road Map from previous lessons
- Milestone Performance Assessment: Creating a Paragraph (see Appendix 3.19)

Teach | Model what students need to learn and do

Model for students how to move from notes to paragraphs.

Today we are going to move from notes to paragraphs. Each of our notes is a single thought, fact, or quote that we want to include. Our notes are grouped, but now we need to turn them into complete sentences and paragraphs that go together. Let's take a look at our organized notes about polar bears—specifically the group of notes about where they live:

- Live in the Arctic where there is ice
- Seals and other sea mammals live there
- Hunt seals and other animals

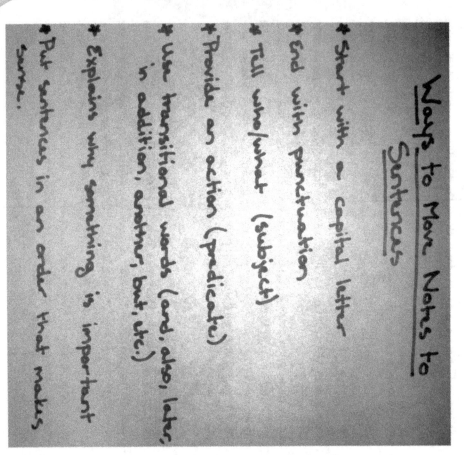

Ways to Move Notes to Sentences

* Start with a capital letter
* End with punctuation
* Tell who/what (subject)
* Provide an action (predicate)
* Use transitional words (and, also, later, in addition, another, but, etc.)
* Explain why something is important
* Put sentences in an order that makes sense.

- Travel, live, and play on ice
- Sea ice is melting

These ideas will make an important paragraph. Watch as I turn the first note into a complete sentence. Since this is going to be the start of a new paragraph I'm going to remember to indent.

▼ Polar bears live in the Arctic where it is cold and icy.

What did I do to make that a complete sentence? Start a chart with student ideas.

Students might say things like:

- Start with a capital letter
- Ending punctuation
- Tells who/what (subject)
- Provides an action (a *predicate*)

Let's try the next note together. Let's turn our second note into a complete sentence. Our second sentence should come right after our first.

- "Animals like seals and other sea mammals live there, too."
- "In addition to polar bears, seals and other sea mammals live there."

Model using transitions.

Let's add to our list of ways to turn notes into complete sentences.

Use transitional words: *and, also, in addition, later, another, but,* and so on.

Try | Guide students to quickly rehearse what they need to learn and do in preparation for practice

Have students try moving sample notes to sentences with a partner.

We have three more ideas here that need to move from notes to sentences. With a partner, jot down an idea for a complete sentence for each of our remaining notes. ELL **Enable Language Production**—Increasing interaction. Peer interactions are strong support for ELLs in practice forming complete sentences. Partnering ELLs with a bilingual partner can aide in sense.

translating thoughts into complete English sentences. Remember, sentences start with a capital letter and end with punctuation.

When students have had time to work together on these three notes, take suggestions for sentences and continue to create a group paragraph.

We've created a whole paragraph here, thanks to your complete sentences. This paragraph is all about where polar bears live and why the melting of the ice is so important. Before we move on to our own notes, what else can we add to our list Ways to Move Notes to Sentences?

Students might say things like:

- Explain why something is important
- Put sentences in an order that makes sense

Clarify Briefly restate today's teaching objective and explain the practice task(s)

Now that we've tried moving our classroom notes to complete sentences, it's time to move your notes to complete sentences. Remember to consult our Moving Notes to Sentences chart to help you. Start with one group of notes to make your first paragraph. When you are ready to move on to a new group of notes, start with a fresh new line and an indent.

Practice Students work independently and/or in small groups to apply today's teaching objective

Students will work to move their notes to complete sentences and paragraphs.

Wrap Up Check understanding as you guide students to briefly share what they have learned and produced today

Have students share one of their complete sentences with their partner or the whole class.

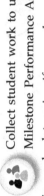 Collect student work to use as a quick assessment using the Milestone Performance Assessment. After looking closely at their work, determine if your class needs additional practice with this work. **ELL** Assess for Content and Language Understanding—Formative Assessment

Milestone Performance Assessment

Creating a Paragraph

 Use this checklist to assess student ability to create a paragraph.

Standards Alignment: W.3.2a–c, W.3.4, W.3.5, W.3.10, SL.3.6, L.3.1, L.3.6

	Achieved	Notes
Use notes to create paragraph content.		
Use punctuation correctly.		
Use transitional phrases.		
Use complete sentences.		
Create a focused, complete paragraph.		

Writing Lesson 7 •••••••••••

▼ Teaching Objective

Informational articles have effective endings.

▼ Standards Alignment

W.3.2d, W.3.4, W.3.5, W.3.10, SL.31a–d, L.31, L.3.6

▼ Materials

- Research Road Map from earlier lessons
- Method of student writing
- Graphic organizer for Clincher: Informational Article (see Appendix 3.17)

▼ To the Teacher

When the body of the article is written it's important to help students develop an effective ending for this type of writing. Some common ending types include:

- Quote: "Any real solution requires action . . . " ("Polar Bears Protected by Law")
- Shocking fact: "The population of the blue-winged bushbird decreases by 75% each decade. Sadly, it's almost too late."
- Summary: "The mission is to keep gorillas in their natural habitat, safe and secure in their own society."
- Appeal to the reader: "Kids can help, too! There are many groups dedicated to saving the humpback whale. Join one today!" ("The Amazing Humpback Whales")

▼ Procedure

Gather the class to set the stage for today's learning

Review with your class the steps they've followed on their Research Road Map. **ELL** Identify and Communicate Content and Language Objective—Check for Understanding. This is an opportunity for ELLs to clarify their thinking and ask for further support in understanding vocabulary, content, and so on. To guide your discussions during this time, do some pre-thinking about ways that there might be confusion around any of these ideas, based on what you have seen so far in their work.

Third graders, I am so impressed by how you've followed our Research Road Map. Let's review the steps we've taken so far.

- Generated topic
- Narrowed topic using question words
- Read to collect information
- Took notes
- Organized notes into groups
- Created headline
- Created lead
- Moved notes to paragraphs

Teach **Model what students need to learn and do**

Introduce how the endings of informational articles are like clinchers. They leave a reader with a responsibility to think and act differently now that he or she is informed.

Today we are going to write *clinchers*, endings that leave the reader with an invitation to do something about the important issues you've been researching. Our articles are informational but they are about things you and many

Organizer. This organizer will offer structural writing support for your ELLs. Then, star your favorite and add it to your informational article.

Practice Students work independently / or in small groups to apply today's teaching objective

Students will be drafting four possible clincher endings and choosing one to add to their informational article.

Wrap Up Check understanding as you guide students to briefly share what they have learned and produced today

Students will share their clincher ending with a partner or the class.

Collect student work to use as a quick assessment, using the Milestone Performance Assessment. After looking closely at their work, determine if your class needs additional practice before moving to the use of images. **ELL** Assess for Content and Language Understanding—Formative Assessment

Milestone Performance Assessment
Creating an Ending

Use this checklist to assess student ability to organize their thoughts into final conclusions.

Standards Alignment: W.3.2d, W.3.4, W.3.5, W.3.10

	Achieved	Notes
Draft a variety of endings.		
Choose an ending that logically concludes content of writing.		

---

other people care about. When people read your article, you want them to pause and think about what they can do to help the environment and make the Earth a greener place for everyone. Writing a clincher ending will help them keep thinking about the important topic you've written about. Just as there are common leads that informational articles start with, there are also some common types of endings to informational articles. The first type of clincher ending is to end with a quote, or something that someone—usually an expert—says. Another way to clinch the ending in this type of writing is to end with a shocking fact. Some writers like to summarize the big idea as their final sentence. Finally, informational articles might appeal to the reader to find out more or get involved.

Note: We have chosen limit the list to four varieties of endings, but if you wish to include other ending techniques, by all means do so.

Try Guide students to quickly rehearse what they need to learn and do in preparation for practice

Look back at articles read in this lesson set and have students share with a partner what they notice about the endings.

Let's look back at some of our favorite articles from this lesson set and how they clinch the ending. With a partner, see if you can label the type of endings that the writers use.

You can have students label with words or different colored stickies. If you are using the articles we've referenced in the lesson set, see the "To the Teacher" section for how they clinch the ending.

Clarify Briefly restate today's teaching objective and explain the practice task(s)

Now that we've moved our notes to sentences and paragraphs, it's time to write our clincher endings. Using the Clincher graphic organizer, draft four ideas for your ending: a quotation, a shocking fact, a summary, and an appeal. **ELL** Provide Comprehensible Input—Graphic

Writing Lesson 8

▼ Teaching Objective

Informational articles combine text and images.

▼ Standards Alignment

W.3.2, W.3.4, W.3.5, W.3.10, SL.3.1a–d, L.3.1, L.3.6

▼ Materials

- Copies of informational articles that combine text and image well, such as articles from *Scholastic News* or *Time For Kids* (both of these publications have rotating online samples that are engaging for students and effective for this lesson)
- Print newspaper or projection of a digital news site
- Student copies of Layout Plan 1 and Layout Plan 2 graphic organizer—see Appendixes 3.11 and 3.12
- Enlarged copy of both layout plans for classroom discussion
- Charting supplies or interactive whiteboard

▼ To the Teacher

Very often, informational articles are a combination of text and image. Today is all about designing the layout of the article and making a Layout

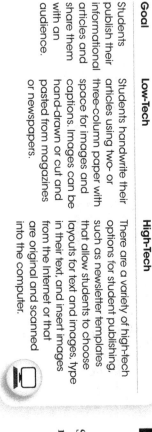

Goal	Low-Tech	High-Tech
Students publish their informational articles and share them with an audience.	Students handwrite their articles using two- or three-column paper with space for images and captions. Images can be hand-drawn or cut and pasted from magazines or newspapers.	There are a variety of high-tech options for student publishing, such as newsletter templates that allow students to choose layouts for text and images, type in their text, and insert images from the Internet or that are original and scanned into the computer.

Plan. Today, introduce your students to the question, "What graphics and text features will you use to enhance your article?" Using examples from magazines and newspapers will help students see how news articles are arranged on the page. Newsletter templates that are available online or through Microsoft Word are wonderful tools if your students will be typing their articles. These templates provide students with a column layout and spaces for their headline and graphics. If students are handwriting their articles, introduce them to how to use a two or three column format and plan boxes for where pictures will go that connect to the text.

▼ Procedure

Warm Up Gather the class to set the stage for today's learning

We know that when we open the newspaper or click on a news site online, we see big, bold headlines, but what else do we see?

Show the print newspaper or projection of a digital news site. Students should respond with things like:

- Pictures/photos
- Writing in columns

© Darrin Henry / Fotolia

HEADLINE:		
Author:	Date:	
Heading:	Picture:	

HEADLINE:		
Author:	Date:	
Heading:	Picture:	Heading:
	Caption:	
Heading:	Picture:	Picture:
Picture:	Heading:	Caption:
Caption:		
Heading:		

- The date
- Headings
- Boxes with additional information
- Maps
- Graphs

Teach Model what students need to learn and do

Emphasize with students the importance of text and images to make informational articles that impact their readers. Provide students with possible layout options.

Informational articles are written to teach readers about important news topics. This happens through a combination of text and images. Today, I am going to share with you two possible layouts of our informational article about polar bears. The layout is important because the pictures, captions, and headings we include will help our readers understand the big ideas. Let's look at our Layout Plan graphic organizer, which has two sides to it, showing us two possible layout designs. Watch as I start to insert some of the material about polar bears that would fit in each layout.

Try Guide students to quickly rehearse what they need to learn and do in preparation for practice

Give students an opportunity to talk with a partner about which layout they are going to choose for their own design.

So, I have two possibilities. Turn and talk to your partner sharing which layout you think will best capture the big ideas about why polar bears are threatened and what led you to your opinion.

Then, have a few students share which layout they preferred, and why. Help focus the conversation on the importance of the big ideas in the article. Finally, have a class vote to determine which layout is most popular.

Clarify Briefly restate today's teaching objective and explain the practice task(s)

Now that we have considered the layout plan for the article on polar bears, it's time for you to decide which layout will work best for your topic. Use the graphic organizer to help you plan your pictures, captions, and headings. There is no wrong answer. Either layout will help capture your readers' attention. It's a matter of choosing which one you are most pleased with. You may want to quickly try out each one and see which layout works best for you.

> It is the commonest of mistakes to consider that the limit of our power of perception is also the limit of all there is to perceive.
>
> —C. W. Leadbeater

Practice	Students work independently or in small groups to apply today's teaching objective

Students will complete the Layout Plan graphic organizer as they prepare to write their final articles.

Writing Lesson 9 •

▼ **Teaching Objective**

Writers revise for the big ideas and edit for conventions and spelling.

▼ **Standards Alignment**

W.3.5, W.3.10, SL.3.6, L.3.1, L.3.2, L.3.3, L.3.6

▼ **Materials**

- Two copies per student of the Milestone Performance Assessment: Research Wrap Up (see Appendix 3.19)
- Copies for students of Revising and Editing Segments from "The Amazing Humpback Whales" (see Appendix 3.14)

▼ **To the Teacher**

With the article written and the graphics designed, it's time to help students with the revision process. For third graders this is not always the most exciting part of the research process. They often think, "We're done! We did it!" Helping them realize the importance of revision is essential not only for this lesson set but for their writing lives moving forward. Today, model for your students how you revise for a journalistic voice and edit for conventions of standard English. This lesson may be best served over two days—one day for revision and one day for editing of conventions. Since this piece of writing requires a particular focus for

conventions, the Research Wrap-Up Checklist from Appendix 3.13 will serve as an important tool for students to independently account for the big ideas of their articles as well as the conventions that will be most critical to this piece of writing consistent with the third grade Common Core State Standards. **ELL** Provide Comprehensible Input—Graphic Organizers/Outlines. This organizer will offer structural writing support for your ELLs.

▼ **Procedure**

Warm Up	Gather the class to set the stage for today's learning

Review with students the Research Road Map from earlier lessons.

You have accomplished a lot, news writers, over the course of this lesson set. Let's look at our Research Road Map to see where we are today. We started by choosing our topics, and worked our way through all these tasks. Now, we're ready to reread our articles to check that we've done our best job of explaining the big ideas of our topic and why it should matter to our readers. We also want to be sure we followed the rules of English so that our readers can focus on those big ideas.

Teach	Model what students need to learn and do

Provide students with copies of Revising and Editing Segments from "The Amazing Humpback Whales" (Appendix 3.14), which contains selected (modified) segments that require editing and revision. Purposeful errors in the organization and conventions of the article will require diligence on the part of your students. The "Humpback Article Revision and Editing Key"

Wrap Up	Check understanding as you guide students to briefly share what they have learned and produced today

Have students share their work, which layout they chose, and why.

Milestone Performance Assessment

Research Wrap Up

Use this checklist to assess student ability to complete their research.

Standards Alignment: W.3.2a–d, W.3.4, W.3.5, W.3.10, SL.3.6, L.3.1, L.3.6

	Achieved	Notes
Include a lead that hooks the reader.		
Connect all information in each paragraph to the main idea of the paragraph.		
Use headings that match the content of the paragraph.		
Put the ideas in each paragraph in a sequence that makes sense.		
Use linking words and phrases (e.g., also, another, and, more, but) to connect ideas.		
Include a clincher ending (a quotation, a shocking fact, a summary, an appeal).		

will be convenient for you in helping them find all instances that require correction. As you distribute the segments to be revised, you might say something like the following:

I have parts of an article here by a writer who was on the right path but got lost somewhere along the way. Our job is to get that writer back on the road and polish the writing so it is more understandable to readers. Luckily, we have a Research Wrap-Up Checklist that can help us do just that.

As you distribute the checklist, continue with your orientation to today's task:

The Research Wrap-Up Checklist reminds us of some important features of informational articles that we want to include, in order to make our big ideas clear to our readers. It also helps us check that we've followed the conventions of formal English. We'll read through the Research Wrap-Up Checklist so that we know what to watch for. Then, we're going to read what the author drafted and correct what seems missing or confused. Finally, we are going to revisit the Research Wrap-Up Checklist and check off each item after making sure it's complete. Let's set that checklist aside for a few minutes while we read the first paragraph together and see how we can help this writer. You'll notice some ways to help right away.

Try Guide students to quickly rehearse what they need to learn and do in preparation for practice

Direct students to continue using the checklist with a partner.

Now, finish reading the other segments of the article on your own, making corrections as you go. Then, with your partner, use the Research Wrap-Up Checklist to do a final sweep, making sure each item has been met. This process takes time. Remember to read through each sentence carefully as you go through your Research Wrap-Up Checklist.

Clarify Briefly restate today's teaching objective and explain the practice task(s)

Today, you are going to read through your article looking to make sure the big ideas are clear and that you have followed the rules of English. Then, you are going to use the Research Wrap-Up Checklist to carefully go through each sentence, making sure all of the items are complete.

(continued)

COPS Editing Checklist*

	Achieved	Notes
Correct **c**apitalization.		
Correct **o**rder and usage of words.		
Correct **p**unctuation.		
Correct **s**pelling.		

*We recommend that you focus your assessment lens in these areas. Select and assess a few skills you have previously taught or that have emerged as areas of need in your ongoing assessment of student writing.

Practice Students work independently or in small groups to apply today's teaching objective

Students will reread their articles using the Milestone Performance Assessment: Research Wrap Up.

Writing Lesson 10

▼ Teaching Objective

Writers reflect on their learning through the Core Questions.

▼ Standards Alignment

W.3.4, W.3.10, SL.3.1a–d, SL.3.6, L.3.1, L.3.6

▼ Materials

- Student informational articles
- Core Questions for Writing (posted or student copies provided):
  - What does it mean to conduct research?
  - What can I learn from reading informational articles to help me write my own?
  - How do I translate my research into an informational article?
  - What are the steps I should follow in the research process to determine the big ideas and form my own opinions?

▼ To the Teacher

When the newsletters are completed, copied and distributed, it's time to reflect on what was learned from this lesson set. Today is all about reflection—an important part of the lesson set process both for students as individuals and for the class as a collective. Helping students pause and think

Wrap Up Check understanding as you guide students to briefly share what they have learned and produced today

Have students share one change they made to their informational article by using the Research Wrap-Up Checklist.

Collect student work to use as an assessment. Use the Milestone Performance Assessment to assess each student's work. After looking closely at their work, determine if your class needs additional time for revision and editing before moving on to reflection. **ELL** Assess for Content and Language Understanding—Formative Assessment. This will be a key time to understand how to best support your ELLs with language and structure to guide them in completion of this lesson set.

Once you have reviewed student submissions, provide an opportunity for your students to share their news articles with one another. You may opt to have them read their articles aloud or distribute them as newsletters to the classmates and other classes in paper or electronic form. Remind students that when sharing their articles they need to speak clearly at an understandable pace. (SL.3.4)

about what they've learned and what they've enjoyed can have long-lasting effects. This is something you may also want to discuss with families when they visit your classroom or through newsletters or other communication you send home. Some structures to build reflection into the teaching day and into home life include:

• Taking the time to think about three things you enjoyed about the day

• Jotting down your favorite moment of the day

• Sharing with a classmate or family member something new that you learned that day

These are all ways of building reflective habits into our students' lives. Today's lesson is meant to be celebratory and help students build those important reflection skills. Emphasize with students that research is ongoing and that they will continue to have questions about this topic and many others, and now they have some tools for finding the answers all on their own!

▶ Procedure

Warm Up   Gather the class to set the stage for today's learning

Congratulate the class on a job well done as researchers and journalists.

Congratulations, writers, on your informational article success! Not only have you researched topics that matter to you, but you have written newsworthy articles that have captured the attention of the school. It's been quite a journey. We packed our bags and hit the road of research and luckily we had a road map to help us along the way.

Teach   Model what students need to learn and do

Emphasize with students the importance of reflection as a time to consider what they have learned over the course of the lesson set.

Today is about reflecting on our road trip as researchers. Our Core Questions for these lessons capture the big ideas I wanted you to think about and focus on as you researched and wrote up your findings. Now, I want to hear from you. This is an opportunity for you to share with me what you learned about research and writing in this genre. Let's choose a Core Question together to write a reflection as a class on what we learned.

Poll the class for which Core Question they would like to write about together and compose a paragraph together using sentence starters depending on the question chosen. One example is:

In this lesson set we learned many things about researching and writing informational articles. First, we learned _____. In addition, we learned _____. We also learned _____. Most of all, we enjoyed _____ because _____. Now I will remember to _____ when I have a burning question.

Try   Guide students to quickly rehearse what they need to learn and do in preparation for practice

Now choose another Core Question. Before you start writing, turn and talk to your partner sharing how you plan to answer the question.

Provide students with conversational starters such as:

• What does it mean to conduct research? To me, conducting research means _____. It also means _____.

• What are the steps I should follow in the research process to determine the big ideas and form my own opinions? The first step in the research process is _____.

• How do I translate my research into an informational article? Moving from research to writing up an article involves many steps. First, _____.

• What can I learn from reading informational articles to help me write my own? I learned a lot about writing informational articles. One thing I learned was _____.

These are helpful to have posted in the room or provided to individual students who may benefit from having these as a guide for discussion and writing.

Clarify   Briefly restate today's teaching objective and explain the practice task(s)

Now you're ready to write your reflection. I can't wait to hear about what you've learned about research and writing in this exciting genre. Remember that when writing your reflections you want to follow the rules we've learned about paragraphing. Those include indenting your first sentence, using end punctuation, and starting each sentence with a capital letter. Also remember the transitional words that can help you move from one sentence to the next like *first, next, then,* and *finally.*

Practice   Students work independently or in small groups to apply today's teaching objective

Students will write personal reflections in response to one of the Core Questions. These are important writing pieces to include in your students' writing portfolios along with their informational articles.

> " To penetrate and dissipate these clouds of darkness, the general mind must be strengthened by education.
>
> — Thomas Jefferson

Wrap Up   Check understanding as you guide students to briefly share what they have learned and produced today

Have students share their reflections with the class, a partner, or electronically in a blog.

Goal	Low-Tech	High-Tech
Students will reflect through writing on what they learned about research and writing informational articles.	Students write their responses in notebooks or on paper to be collected by the teacher or shared with classmates.	Students write their responses on a class blog allowing class members to read and comment on one another's reflections.

Language Companion Lesson

This lesson is best taught at nearly any point during the lesson set. Remind and guide students to apply what they learn in this lesson during all stages of the writing process.

▼ Teaching Objective

Singular antecedents require singular pronouns. Plural antecedents require plural pronouns.

▼ Standards Alignment

*L.3.1f (The asterisk is used by the Common Core State Standards Initiative to indicate topics that students find especially difficult to master, which therefore need to be presented and reinforced multiple times across the school years.)

▼ Materials

- Enlarged Third-Person Personal Pronoun Word Bank (p. 70)
- Enlarged Pronoun Antecedent Reference Chart (p. 71)
- Note cards, two for each student, one marked *singular*, one marked *plural*
- Pronoun Antecedent Review (Appendix 3.18)

▼ To the Teacher

Third grade is the earliest grade that "pronoun–antecedent agreement" appears in the Common Core State Standards. It is accompanied by an asterisk, which the authors include when standards are "particularly likely to require continued attention in higher grades as they are applied to increasingly sophisticated writing and speaking." No kidding! This clearly is a challenging concept with which many adults struggle when speaking and writing. In this lesson, we introduce students to the concept in a way that allows third graders to begin to build a foundation. Additional study will certainly be needed to reinforce this learning and add new layers of complexity.

A basic ability to identify nouns and discriminate between easier singular and plural nouns is very helpful for this lesson. Previous formal study

of pronouns and the concepts of singular and plural would be helpful but is not essential for this lesson.

The "Teacher" segment of this lesson should be split into two or more parts depending on your time and the attention span of your students. We numbered major sections below.

▼ Procedure

Warm Up **Gather the class to set the stage for today's learning**

Distribute plural and singular word cards to all students. Define singular and plural.

Singular: One   Plural: More Than One

Ask students to raise their cards to identify the following examples as singular or plural. Mix up the examples as you go.

Singular examples	Plural examples
Dog	Trees
My class	Students
She	Children
Our teacher	Them
Everyone	Schools
Tree	Both

You may have to explain some of the trickier ones. Singular indefinite pronouns (*everyone, each, somebody*) can be challenging. *Everyone* sounds like it should be plural, but it is always treated as singular. Mastery of the especially tough ones is certainly not expected yet. Assure students that this is confusing for everyone, but with practice, it all starts to make sense . . . *really!*

Teach **Model what students need to learn and do**

❶ Introduce/review pronouns. Display the following sentences to the class.

- ▲ 1—Jose ate Jose's dinner.
- ▲ 2—Jose ate his dinner.

Assuming that there is only one Jose, which sentence sounds the best? Why? Sentence 1 sounds strange. We don't usually repeat the same person's name in one sentence. Normally, we would replace Jose with his, a pronoun. We use pronouns to replace a noun so we don't have to keep repeating the noun, because that sounds awkward. Here is another example: "The tree lost its leaves." What is the pronoun? (its) What noun does the pronoun stand in for? (tree) Right. We would never say, "The tree lost the tree's leaves." We use a pronoun to stand in for tree.

Provide another example: The girl drew a picture of herself. Ask the same questions.

2 Introduce antecedents.

In these sentences, we found the pronouns—his, its, herself. Pronouns stand in for nouns—Jose, tree, girl. There is a name for the word that a pronoun replaces—an antecedent. Jose, tree, and girl are called "antecedents" in these examples.

▼ Jose ate his dinner.

▼ The tree lost its leaves.

▼ The girl drew a picture of herself.

Here is one more sentence:

▼ The teacher ate her apple.

What is the pronoun or the word that stands in for a noun? (her) What antecedent does the pronoun (her) replace? (teacher)

Practice with additional examples, if needed.

▼ The babies sang to themselves. (antecedent: babies; pronoun: themselves)

▼ Mr. Jenkins loves his new bike. (antecedent: Mr. Jenkins, pronoun: his)

3 Introduce pronoun-antecedent agreement. Display the following six sentences to the class. Read each sentence. Have the students show a thumbs-up if they think the sentence is grammatically correct, thumbs-down if incorrect. Note: These are meant to be tricky. They probably all sound pretty good, as they are commonly heard in everyday conversation. Chances are that many of the children will think they all sound OK.

▼ The girls were looking for their books. (correct)

▼ The dog ate his dinner. (correct)

▼ The family wants to see their new house. (incorrect)

▼ Somebody wants to read their book. (incorrect)

▼ Few remembered their lunchbox. (correct)

▼ No one can find themselves in the photo. (incorrect)

Reveal which are correct and incorrect. It's OK and expected that the students be a little confused at this point. Explain that the reason some are correct and some are incorrect has to do with pronouns and antecedents.

In order to use correct English, we have to learn how to make sure that our antecedents agree with our pronouns. What about the word agree? Whatever does that mean? How can words agree with each other? Let's move on and see.

Recall the singular and plural exercise at the beginning of the lesson. Have the students pick up their singular/plural cards again. Say the antecedents aloud. Have students identify them as singular or plural with their cards. Label the antecedents.

▼ The girls (plural); The dog (singular); Somebody (singular); No one (singular); Few (plural)

It is a rule in English that if the antecedent is singular, its pronoun should be also. Likewise, if the antecedent is plural, its pronoun has to be plural. That is what it means when we say they have to agree. Here is a chart that may help you to keep track of singular and plural personal pronouns.

Proceed to work through the examples that follow, modeling how to use the chart as a reference.

Third-Person Personal Pronoun Bank

Singular	Plural
he, him, his, himself, she, her, hers, herself, it, its, itself	they, them, their, theirs, themselves

I'm going to present you with some sentences where the antecedents and pronouns may not match. Let's see if you can find them.

Pronoun Antecedent Reference Chart

Singular Antecedents	Plural Antecedents
each, either, neither anybody, anyone, anything everybody, everyone, everything nobody, no one, nothing somebody, someone, something	both, several, few, many, all

▲ The girls were looking for their books. (correct)

Girls is plural, and so is their.

▲ The dog ate his dinner. (correct)

Dog is singular. So is his.

▲ The team wants to win their game. (incorrect)

Team is singular. Their is plural. Change their to its. Try additional examples such as:

▲ The brothers need (his/their) library cards.

▲ The student earned (their/her) diploma.

❹ **Continue to work on pronoun–antecedent agreement with irregular indefinite pronouns.**

Now I want to introduce some antecedents that are common, yet they confuse people when it comes to agreement. Words like everybody, everyone, everything sound plural, but they are actually singular. They require a singular pronoun. Here is a trick for how to remember: every**body** is singular. Every**one**—one is singular. Every**thing**—thing is singular.

▲ Everybody needs to bring his science book to class tomorrow. (correct)

But must we use his? After all, there are girls in the class, too. In this sentence you could say his or her, but another way to handle a tricky situation like this is to keep the same idea but revise the wording so it doesn't sound so awkward. For example, it might not sound so strange if I were to say:

▲ "I want each of you to bring your science book to class with you tomorrow."

Another confusion comes up when we don't know if the word someone refers to a boy or a girl. It is tempting to use their to replace the antecedent, but that would be incorrect.

▲ Someone forgot to put away their gym clothes. (incorrect)

▲ Someone forgot to put away his or her gym clothes. (correct, but a bit awkward)

You could get around the problem by rewriting the sentence.

▲ I see that someone's gym clothes need to be put away.

Here is another example. How would you fix this?

▲ Somebody wants to read their book. (incorrect)

Somebody is singular. Their is plural. Change their to his or her, or find a way to reword the sentence in a way you like better. Depending on the situation, it might be

▲ Somebody wants to read that book! Or

▲ Somebody has a special book to read. Or

▲ I know someone who wants to read a book.

(The possibilities might be endless!)

How about a real stumper:

▲ No one can find themselves in the photo. (incorrect)

No one is singular. Themselves is plural. Change themselves to himself or herself. Good luck rewording this sentence to avoid the awkwardness altogether! Let's end with an easier one.

▲ Few remembered their lunchbox. (correct)

Few and their are both plural, so this sentence is correct.

❺ **Practice in small groups.** Engage students in creating new sentences using both singular and plural antecedents and the matching type of pronoun. Note that this is more likely to transfer to real writing skills for students than is a task of completing worksheets where students simply have to choose the correct words. The Pronoun Antecedent Reference chart (see Appendix 3.18), will help students with this task. Due to the level of challenge of this new concept, we suggest that this practice take place in small groups.

6 For enrichment follow up, discuss options when choosing gender-specific pronouns such as *him, her,* and *him and her* followed by singular indefinite pronoun antecedents. There are some interesting nuances involved when balancing being grammatically correct, gender-sensitive, and not overly wordy.

▼ Someone needs to clear off <u>his</u> lunch table and throw out <u>his</u> trash.

▼ Someone needs to clear off <u>her</u> lunch table and throw out <u>her</u> trash.

▼ Someone needs to clear off <u>his or her</u> lunch table and throw out <u>his or her</u> trash. (awkward)

▼ Whoever sat at that messy table needs to pick up the trash and throw it away!

Wrap Up

Our work with pronoun–antecedent agreement will be useful to you whenever you are speaking or writing in formal, correct English. Let's keep our charts in the room to help us when we need them.

> *Only the person who is relaxed can create, and to that mind ideas flow like lightning.*
>
> —Cicero

GLOSSARY

article: a piece of nonfiction writing on a particular subject, as in a magazine.

caption: the words that describe a picture or graph in a magazine, book, or newspaper.

diagram: a drawing or plan that shows the parts of something or how the parts work together.

evidence: something that gives proof of or a reason to believe something.

fact: something said or known to be true.

glossary: a list of unusual or difficult words and their meanings.

hypotheses: a prediction or educated guess that can be tested and can be used to guide further study.

index: an alphabetical list of subjects, names, or other information in a book, with page numbers given for each item.

informational text: text designed to convey factual information, rather than tell or advance a narrative.

Informational text may employ techniques such as lists, comparing/contrasting, or demonstrating cause/effect, and may be accompanied by graphs or charts.

lay out (v): to spread or arrange for viewing or consideration.

layout (n): an arrangement, design, or plan as shown either by laying its components out in a drawing or model, or by the structure itself on its actual site.

main idea: the central purpose or gist of a passage; the primary message expressed by a passage. The main idea of a paragraph may be explicitly stated in a topic sentence.

nonfiction: written works that are not fiction.

opinion: what one thinks about something or somebody; viewpoint. An opinion is not necessarily based on facts. Feelings and experiences usually help a person form an opinion.

outline: a line showing the outside edge of a figure or object.

paraphrase: a restatement of a passage or text in somewhat different words so as to simplify or clarify.

quote: to repeat the exact words used by someone else.

research: the serious study and collecting of information about something.

supporting detail: facts or pieces of text that support the main ideas.

table of contents: an organized arrangement of information laid out in rows and columns.

tables: an organized arrangement of information laid out in rows and columns.

template: a pattern used as a guide or outline for cutting, drawing, or inserting generic information.

 PD TOOLKIT™

Accompanying *Core Ready for Grades 3–5*, there is an online resource site with media tools that, together with the text, provides you with the tools you need to implement the lesson sets.

The PDToolkit for Pam Allyn's *Core Ready Series* is available free for 12 months after you use the password that comes with the box set for each grade band. After that, you can purchase access for an additional 12 months. If you did not purchase the box set, you can purchase a 12-month subscription at **http://pdtoolkit.pearson.com**. Be sure to explore and download the resources available at the website. Currently the following resources are available:

- Pearson Children's and Young Adult Literature Database
- Videos
- PowerPoint Presentations
- Student Artifacts
- Photos and Visual Media
- Handouts, Forms, and Posters to supplement your Core-aligned lesson plans
- Lessons and Homework Assignments
- Close Reading Guides and Samples
- Children's Core Literature Recommendations

In the future, we will continue to add additional resources. To learn more, please visit. **http://pdtoolkit.pearson.com**.

Grade 4

What Happened and Why: Studying Cause and Effect through Events in History

Introduction

We often use cause and effect to understand natural phenomena or human behavior. Authors, too, rely on the structure of cause and effect to explain, show order, change order, change character behavior, and create plot. As they study what happened and why in history, this lesson set will help introduce fourth graders to this important text structure that is often found in science and social studies texts.

Cause and effect is one type of text structure authors use to convey meaning. Text structure refers to the ways that authors organize information in a text. Teaching students to recognize the underlying structure of subject area texts can help students focus attention on key concepts and relationships, anticipate what's to come, and monitor their comprehension as they read. As readers interact with text to make meaning, their comprehension is aided when they organize their thinking in a manner similar to that used by the author. When students are having difficulty comprehending subject area texts, we can aid them with the meaning-making process by helping them recognize the organizational structure of what they are reading and making them aware of the cues they can use to alert them to particular text structures.

Beginning in fourth grade, students are expected to navigate more complex content area texts. These texts can be challenging to readers to understand for many reasons, including abstract concepts, unknown academic words, and unfamiliar topics. Readers benefit from explicit instruction on how to anticipate where information is located in the text to make predictions about content (Duke & Pearson, 2002). In addition, readers benefit from explicit instruction on text structure as

a strategy to help them figure out the meaning and clear up confusions they may have (Tovani, 2000). Once students understand that text structures exist and what the major ones are, they can use strategies such as graphic organizers and signal words to help them structure the text of their own writing.

Helping students understand common structures in writing is a hallmark of grade 4, and this lesson set provides a critical introduction to one type of text structure— providing a knowledge base students will build on in the grades to follow. Building from grades K–3, students in grades 4 apply knowledge of decoding to negotiate multisyllabic words, which in turn increases their fluency and confidence when reading new and unfamiliar material.

Why This Lesson Set?

In this lesson set, students will:

- Read closely to recognize cause and effect relationships between events in history

- Recognize and use words and phrases that signal cause and effect relationships

- Summarize cause and effect relationships through speaking and writing

- Examine multiple accounts of the same event, take notes, and use their findings to create fact-based historical fiction diary entries that contain cause and effect relationships from a specific time period

In support of the reading standards, students are taught in this lesson set to ask questions of one another to deepen their understanding of the big ideas and supporting details that prove them. Students will have many opportunities to read aloud fluently and offer appropriate elaboration on the ideas of classmates by building on what has been said before. By focusing on the text structure of cause and effect, students will develop a deeper understanding of how content area texts are structured and what strategies they can employ to make meaning.

Through the writing process students will practice using text structure as a way to organize their ideas around a topic. In addition, the importance of paragraphing to cluster information will be emphasized, as well as variety of sentence types to help hook readers and then guide them to what matters most in the article.

Common Core State Standards Alignment

Reading Standards

RI.4.1 Refer to details and examples in a text when explaining what the text says explicitly and when drawing inferences from the text.

RI.4.2 Determine the main idea of a text and explain how it is supported by key details; summarize the text.

RI.4.3 Explain events, procedures, ideas, or concepts in a historical, scientific, or technical text, including what happened and why, based on specific information in the text.

RI.4.5 Describe the overall structure (e.g., chronology, comparison, cause/effect, problem/solution) of events, ideas, concepts, or information in a text or part of a text.

RI.4.6 Compare and contrast a firsthand and secondhand account of the same event or topic; describe the differences in focus and the information provided.

RI.4.7 Interpret information presented visually, orally, or quantitatively (e.g., in charts, graphs, diagrams, timelines, animations, or interactive elements on Web pages) and explain how the information contributes to an understanding of the text in which it appears.

RI.4.8 Explain how an author uses reasons and evidence to support particular points in a text.

RI.4.9 Integrate information from two texts on the same topic in order

to write or speak about the subject knowledgeably.

RI.4.10 By the end of the year, read and comprehend informational texts in the grades 4-5 text complexity band proficiently, with scaffolding as needed at the high end of the range.

Writing Standards

W.4.2 Write informative/explanatory texts to examine a topic and convey ideas and information clearly.

a. Introduce a topic clearly and group related information in paragraphs and sections; include formatting (e.g., headings), illustrations, and multimedia when useful to aiding comprehension.

b. Develop the topic with facts, definitions, concrete details, quotations, or other information and examples related to the topic.

c. Link ideas within categories of information using words and phrases (e.g., *another, for example, also, because*).

d. Use precise language and domain-specific vocabulary to inform about or explain the topic.

e. Provide a concluding statement or section related to the information or explanation presented.

W.4.4 Produce clear and coherent writing in which the development and organization are appropriate to task, purpose, and audience.

W.4.5 With guidance and support from peers and adults, develop and

strengthen writing as needed by planning, revising, and editing.

W.4.6 With some guidance and support from adults, use technology, including the Internet, to produce and publish writing as well as to interact and collaborate with others; demonstrate sufficient command of keyboarding skills to type a minimum of one page in a single sitting.

W.4.7 Conduct short research projects that build knowledge through investigation of different aspects of a topic.

W.4.10 Write routinely over extended time frames (time for research, reflection, and revision) and shorter time frames (a single sitting or a day or two) for a range of discipline-specific tasks, purposes, and audiences.

Speaking and Listening Standards

SL.4.1 Engage effectively in a range of collaborative discussions (one-on-one, in groups, and teacher-led) with diverse partners on grade 4 topics and texts, building on others' ideas and expressing their own clearly.

a. Come to discussions prepared, having read or studied required material; explicitly draw on that preparation and other information known about the topic to explore ideas under discussion.

b. Follow agreed-upon rules for discussions and carry out assigned roles.

c. Pose and respond to specific questions to clarify or follow up on information, and make comments that contribute to the discussion and link to the remarks of others.

d. Review the key ideas expressed and explain their own ideas and understanding in light of the discussion.

SL.4.2 Paraphrase portions of a text read-aloud or information presented in diverse media and formats, including visually, quantitatively, and orally.

SL.4.3 Identify the reasons and evidence a speaker provides to support particular points.

SL.4.4 Report on a topic or text, tell a story, or recount an experience in an organized manner, using appropriate facts and relevant, descriptive details to support main ideas or themes; speak clearly at an understandable pace.

SL.4.6 Differentiate between contexts that call for formal English (e.g., presenting ideas) and situations where informal discourse is appropriate (e.g., small-group discussion); use formal English when appropriate to task and situation.

Language Standards

L.4.1 Demonstrate command of the conventions of standard English grammar and usage when writing or speaking.

a. Use relative pronouns (who, whose, whom, which, that) and relative adverbs (where, when, why).

b. Form and use the progressive (e.g., I was walking; I am walking; I will be walking) verb tenses.

c. Use modal auxiliaries (e.g., can, may, must) to convey various conditions.

d. Order adjectives within sentences according to conventional patterns (e.g., a small red bag rather than a red small bag).

e. Form and use prepositional phrases.

f. Produce complete sentences, recognizing and correcting inappropriate fragments and run-ons.

g. Correctly use frequently confused words (e.g., to, too, two; there, their).

L.4.2 Demonstrate command of the conventions of standard English capitalization, punctuation, and spelling when writing.

a. Use correct capitalization.

b. Use commas and quotation marks to mark direct speech and quotations from a text.

c. Use a comma before a coordinating conjunction in a compound sentence.

d. Spell grade-appropriate words correctly, consulting references as needed.

L.4.3 Use knowledge of language and its conventions when writing, speaking, reading, or listening.

a. Choose words and phrases to convey ideas precisely.

b. Choose punctuation for effect.

c. Differentiate between contexts that call for formal English (e.g., presenting ideas) and situations where informal discourse is appropriate (e.g., small-group discussion).

L.4.6 Acquire and use accurately grade-appropriate general academic and domain-specific words and phrases, including those that signal precise actions, emotions, or states of being (e.g., quizzed, whined, stammered) and that are basic to a particular topic (e.g., wildlife, conservation, and endangered when discussing animal preservation).

Essential Skill Lenses (PARCC Framework)

As part of its proposal to the U.S. Department of Education, the multi-state Partnership for Assessment of Readiness for College and Careers (PARCC) has developed model content frameworks for English Language Arts to serve as a bridge between the Common Core State Standards and the PARCC assessments in development at the time of this publication. In the grade 3 to 5 lesson sets, we expect students to engage in reading and writing through eight PARCC specified skill lenses that are rooted in the standards. The following table details how each skill lens is addressed across the lesson set.

	Reading	Writing
Cite Evidence	Students cite the text as evidence throughout this lesson set. In particular, students use text as evidence to identify the cause and effect text structure.	Students cite specific evidence when writing about events that happened and why, using the structure of cause and effect.
Analyze Content	Students carefully analyze complex content area texts to identify cause and effect and in some cases multiple causes and effects.	Students analyze what they have read with careful attention to cause and effect.
Study and Apply Grammar and Usage	Emphasis will be placed on conventional elements frequently found in historical texts, such as effective paragraphing, to cluster information, and production of simple, compound, and complex sentences.	When writing their own cause and effect diary entries, students apply grammar lessons from reading, in particular, how to create a multi-paragraph essay and how to vary sentences for effect.
Study and Apply Vocabulary	Specific academic language is included with this lesson set. It is expected that students be exposed to and successfully incorporate these terms into their speaking and writing during this study.	Students are expected to choose precise language to strengthen their writing.

	Reading	Writing
Conduct Discussions	Rules and behaviors that foster productive conversation are a crucial element of this study.	Students continuously engage in conversations about what they see as the causes and subsequent effects of key events in history texts.
Report Findings	Students share their analysis of cause and effect relationships in texts on a daily basis with partners and in whole-class discussions.	By creating cause and effect posters and diary entries, students will individually and collectively report on their findings.
Phonics and Word Recognition	We recommend that teachers plan opportunities for students to build Reading Foundational Skills by exploring grade-level appropriate skills in the context of the Core Texts from each lesson set and applying this knowledge to their independent reading.	We recommend that teachers encourage students to apply Reading Foundational Skills in the context of their daily writing.
Fluency and Stamina	Fluency and stamina are emphasized throughout the lesson set. Content area texts can easily be scaffolded to provide students with short texts, building up to longer texts as the lesson set progresses. This will help students build greater fluency and stamina within this genre.	There are many opportunities for short, quick writes as well as longer, more extended writing with their independently written articles. When reading their diary entries aloud, students will be encouraged to read accurately, with an appropriate pace, and with expression.

Core Questions

These questions should remain at the core of your teaching. Refer back to them often, encouraging your class to share their thinking as it evolves.

- What strategies can I use to identify major events in a text and why they occurred? (asking questions, identifying signal words, and using graphic organizers)

- What can I learn from how writers use the text structure of cause and effect?

- What does it mean to conduct research?

- What are the steps I should follow in the research process to identify cause and effect relationships?

- How do I translate my research into a diary entry from the point of view of a fictionalized or real figure from history?

> 66
>
> *Before the effect one believes in other causes than after the effect.*
>
> —Friedrich Nietzsche
>
> 99

Ready to Get Started?

Let's tap into our students' quest to know why things happen. Fourth graders are history detectives eager to know what happened in the past and why events that they've heard about happened at all. Fourth graders are also at an age that they now realize there are parts of history that are rather ugly, where people treated each other unkindly, where the progress of one group meant the destruction of another. This lesson set is not only an opportunity to teach students an important text structure that will help them navigate nonfiction and narrative nonfiction texts with greater success, but it is also an opportunity to introduce important historical moments to students. When tailoring this lesson set to meet your students' needs you will want to consider what history topics are a part of your social studies curriculum and use pivotal moments from one historical time period to guide your study. For the purposes of this shared curriculum, we'll be focusing on moments from history where people showed kindness despite hardship, struggle, and tragedy; where people worked toward peace; and where the goodness of sometimes a single person caused more goodness to spread. By studying history from this perspective we hope this lesson set helps students tap into their power to make a difference.

Lesson Set Goals

Within this lesson set, there are many goals we as teachers want to help our students reach.

Reading Goals

- Explain what happened and why (effect, cause) in historical texts and discuss the cause and effect relationship using transitional words and phrases. (RI.4.1, RI.4.3, RI.4.5, RI.4.6, RI.4.8, RI.4.10, W4.2c, W.4.4, W.4.10, SL.4.1a–d, SL.4.3, SL.4.6, L.4.1, L.4.6)

- Identify cause and effect structure in historical texts using signal words and other strategies. (RI.4.1, RI.4.3, RI.4.5, RI.4.7, RI.4.10)

- Summarize a historical text with an emphasis on cause and effect. (RI.4.1, RI.4.5, RI.4.6, RI.4.10, W.4.2a–d, W.4.4, W.4.6, W.4.10, SL.4.2)

- Report on findings through a clear and organized book poster or book trailer. (RI.4.1, RI.4.10, W.4.10, SL.4.4, L.4.1, L.4.6)

- Refer to details and examples in a text when explaining what the text says explicitly and when drawing inferences from the text. (RI.4.1)

- By the end of the year, read and comprehend a variety of informational texts at the high end of the grade 4 text complexity band independently and proficiently. (RI.4.10)

- Write routinely over extended time frames (time for research, reflection, and revision) and shorter time frames (a single sitting or a day or two) for a range of discipline-specific tasks, purposes, and audiences. (W.4.10)

- In collaborative discussions, demonstrate evidence of preparation for discussion and exhibit responsibility to the rules and roles of conversation. (SL.4.1a, SL.4.1b)

- In collaborative discussions, share and develop ideas in a manner that enhances understanding of topic. Contribute and respond to the content of the conversation in a productive and focused manner. (SL.4.1c, SL.4.1d)

- Demonstrate knowledge of standard English and its conventions. (L.4.1, L.4.2, L.4.3)

- Acquire and use accurately grade-appropriate conversational, general academic, and domain-specific vocabulary and phrases. (L.4.6)

Writing Goals

- Take and logically organize notes to record the causes and effects of a moment from history in preparation for writing. (RI.4.1, RI.4.2, RI.4.9, RI.4.10, W.4.4, W.4.7, W.4.10, SL.4.2, L.4.6)

- Write a diary entry that examines a historical period with an introduction that introduces a topic clearly, groups related information in paragraphs and sections, and includes a concluding statement or section related to the information or explanation presented. (W.4.2a, W.4.2e; W.4.4, W.4.7, W.4.10, L.4.6)

- Develop the topic with facts, concrete details, or other information and examples related to the topic. (RI.4.1, RI.4.2, RI.4.5, RI.4.9, RI.4.10, W.4.2b, W.4.4, W.4.10, L.4.6)

- Link ideas within categories of information using words and phrases (e.g., *another, for example, also, because*). (RI.4.1, RI.4.4, RI.4.10, W.4.2c, W.4.10, SL.4.4, L.4.6)

- With guidance and support from peers and adults, develop and strengthen writing as needed by planning, revising, and editing. (W.4.5)

- By the end of the year, read and comprehend a variety of informational texts at the high end of the grade 4 text complexity band independently and proficiently. (RI.4.10)

- Write routinely over extended time frames (time for research, reflection, and revision) and shorter time frames (a single sitting or a day or two) for a range of discipline-specific tasks, purposes, and audiences. (W.4.10)

- In collaborative discussions, demonstrate evidence of preparation for discussion and exhibit responsibility to the rules and roles of conversation. (SL.4.1a, SL.4.1b)

Choosing Core Texts

- In collaborative discussions, share and develop ideas in a manner that enhances understanding of topic. Contribute and respond to the content of the conversation in a productive and focused manner. (SL.4.1c, SL.4.1d)
- Demonstrate knowledge of standard English and its conventions. (L.4.1, L.4.2, L.4.3)
- Acquire and use accurately grade-appropriate conversational, general academic, and domain-specific vocabulary and phrases. (L.4.6)

The texts you choose for this lesson set will depend on the history curriculum within your local district. However, there are many excellent narrative and narrative nonfiction texts that provide a wonderful foundation in the text structure of cause and effect for students.

Picture Books to Introduce Cause and Effect

Across the Stream by Mirra Ginsburg

Alexander and the Terrible, Horrible, No Good, Very Bad Day by Judith Viorst

Don't Slam the Door! by Dori Chaconas

If You Give a Moose a Muffin by Laura Numeroff

If You Give a Mouse a Cookie by Laura Numeroff

If You Give a Pig a Pancake by Laura Numeroff

If You Take a Mouse to the Movies by Laura Numeroff

Sylvester and the Magic Pebble by William Steig

Where the Wild Things Are by Maurice Sendak

Picture Book to Introduce the Metaphor of Text Structure

Word Builder by Ann Whitford Paul

Independent Reading/Small-Group Reading Possibilities in American History

Defining Moments: Overcoming Challenges series

Great Moments in American History series

History News series

Selections from *A History of Us* series by Joy Hakim

Native American Experience

Brother Eagle Sister Sky: A Message from Chief Seattle by Susan Jeffers

Encounter by Jane Yolen

American Revolution

When Washington Crossed the Delaware: A Wintertime Story for Young Patriots by Lynne Cheney

Chinese History

Kubla Khan: The Emperor of Everything by Kathleen Krull

The Silk Route: 7,000 Miles of History by John S. Major

Civil War

"The Gettysburg Address" by Abraham Lincoln

Harriet Beecher Stowe and the Beecher Preachers by Jean Fritz

Just a Few Words, Mr. Lincoln by Jean Fritz

Pink and Say by Patricia Polacco

Sojourner Truth: Ain't I a Woman? by Patricia C. McKissack

Slavery

Henry's Freedom Box by Ellen Levine and Kadir Nelson

Desegregation/Racial Discrimination

The Story of Ruby Bridges by Robert Coles

Time for Kids article "Sitting Down to Take a Stand" by Suzanne Zimbler

We Are the Ship: The Story of Negro League Baseball by Kadir Nelson

Japanese Internment Camps/WWII

Baseball Saved Us by Ken Mochizuki

Disease

Dr. Jenner and the Speckled Monster: The Discovery of the Smallpox Vaccine by Albert Marrin

Outbreak! Plagues That Changed History by Bryn Barnard

Stories of Peace around the World

14 Cows for America by Carmen Agra Deedy

Beatrice's Goat by Page McBrier

One Hen—How One Small Loan Made a Big Difference by Katie Smith Milway

Seeds of Change by Jen Cullerton Johnson

Time for Kids article "Obama Wins Nobel Peace Prize" by Jonathan Rosenbloom

Wangari's Trees of Peace: A True Story from Africa by Jeanette Winter

Helpful Websites

I.N.K. (Interesting Nonfiction for Kids)

Time for Kids

A Note about Addressing Reading Standard 10: Range of Reading and Level of Text Complexity

This lesson set provides all students with opportunities to work with texts deemed appropriate for their grade level as well as texts at their specific reading level. Through shared experiences and focused instruction, all students engage with and comprehend a wide range of texts within their grade level complexity band. We suggest a variety of high-quality complex texts to use within the whole-group lessons and recommend a variety of additional titles under Choosing Core Texts to extend and enrich instruction. During independent practice and in small-group collaborations, however, research strongly

suggests that all students need to work with texts they can read with a high level of accuracy and comprehension (i.e., at their developmentally appropriate reading level), in order to significantly improve their reading (Allington, 2012; Ehri, Dreyer, Flugman, & Gross, 2007). Depending on individual needs and skills, a student's reading level may be above, within, or below the grade-level band. Students must be given the opportunity to read at their independent levels to build stamina and fluency and to read beyond their levels in texts of high interest, to build comprehension and cultivate habits of high energy for challenging texts.

Teacher's Notes

Fourth graders need help understanding how the word *structure* applies to texts. Once they understand the metaphor it will be easier for them to recognize when authors are using text structures to convey a particular meaning. *Word Builder* is a great read-aloud to help students understand that writers use words to build their pieces of writing and that words can be grouped into particular structures.

It is important that fourth graders develop an understanding of real-world cause and effect relationships. Students who leave the primary grades with a solid grasp of cause and effect in everyday life will find more success when confronted with the cause/effect text structures used in expository writing and textbooks. This lesson set begins with this connection in mind, so you will see foundational texts that will help students identify cause and effect relationships in their own lives before diving into identifying cause and effect in moments in history.

Additionally, this lesson set requires research. The following steps are an important road map for your research with students:

• Immersion in topic

• Asking questions (in this lesson set: What Happened? and Why?)

• Narrowing the topic

• Creating key words

• Locating sources

- Locating information within sources
- Recording information—note taking
- Organizing information
- Coming to conclusions
- Presenting information

The following materials will help you organize the research process for students:

- Student research folders
- Ready to Review baskets for submission
- Reminder charts

Core Message to Students

Before the first lesson, use this as a shared reading or read-aloud to set the stage and engage students in discussion about your upcoming study. See Appendix 4.1 for an enlarged version to reproduce and share with students.

Everything happens for a reason! This means that there are causes for all actions and effects of all actions. You forget to brush your teeth, you might end up with a cavity. If you don't pick up your room, you can't find your book in the morning. Who else can think of a good example of cause and effect from their own lives? As readers we should always be thinking, "Why did this happen?" or "What caused this?" This is especially important when reading about things that happened in history.

66

Cause and effect are two sides of one fact.

—Ralph Waldo Emerson

99

Questions for Close Reading

The Core Ready lessons include many rich opportunities to engage students in close reading of text that requires them to ask and answer questions, draw conclusions, and use specific text evidence to support their thinking (Reading Anchor Standard 1). These opportunities are marked with a close reading icon. You may wish to extend these experiences using our recommended Core Texts or with texts of your choosing. Use the following questions as a resource to guide students through close reading experiences in any informational text.

- Identify an important event in the text. Why is it important?
- Identify an important event in the text. What caused the important event to happen?
- Identify an important event in the text. What happened as a result of this event?
- What words in the text signal cause and effect relationships?
- Describe a cause and effect relationship that is found in the text.
- What evidence does the text provide that one event caused another? Are there any other possible causes suggested in the text?
- Are there events in the text that have more than one cause? More than one effect?

Building Academic Language

Included here is a list of academic language to build your students' comprehension of the focus of this lesson set and facilitate their ability to talk and write about what they learn. Rather than introduce all the words and phrases at once, systematically add them to a learning wall as your teaching unfolds. See the glossary at the end of this chapter for definitions of the words. Also listed are sentence frames that may be included on a sentence wall (Carrier and Tatum, 2006), a research-proven strategy for English language learners (Lewis, 1993; Nattinger, 1980), or as a handout to scaffold student use of the content words. Some students, especially English language learners, may need explicit practice using the sentence frames. Encourage all students to use these words and phrases in their conversations and writing.

Recognition

At the end of the lesson set, it is important to recognize the hard work your students have put into their learning and the care with which they have spoken to and listened to their peers. At the end of the reading lesson set, students will create cause and effect books. At the end of the writing lesson set, students will create a class newspaper from the historical time period you have chosen to focus on throughout the lesson set.

Assessment

Assessment in this lesson set is both ongoing and culminating, meaning that as teachers we are constantly kid-watching and observing how students make meaning and how they are interpreting new material. Throughout this lesson set, look for performance-based assessments, called Milestone Performance Assessments, each marked with an assessment icon. Milestone Performance Assessments are opportunities to notice and record data on standards-aligned indicators during the course of the lesson set. Use the results of these assessments to determine how well students are progressing toward the goals of the lesson set. Adjust the pace of your teaching and plan instructional support as needed.

Also, we encourage you to use the Reading and Writing Rubrics, also marked with an assessment icon, with each lesson set to evaluate overall student performance on the standards aligned lesson set goals. In this lesson set, the finalized posters and diary entries are important pieces of performance assessment that can be analyzed and then placed in a portfolio of student work.

In addition, we have provided a Speaking and Listening Performance Checklist (Appendix 4.15) that provides observable Core Standards–aligned indicators to assess student performance as speakers and listeners. There are multiple opportunities in every Core Ready lesson set to make such observations. Use the checklist in its entirety to gather performance data over time or choose appropriate indicators to create a customized checklist to match a specific learning experience.

Core Words

because	since
cause	so
consequently	therefore
effect	thus
history	why
nevertheless	

Core Phrases

- _____ is the reason that _____.
- Because of the fact that _____.
- Due to the fact that _____.
- If _____, then _____.
- As a result of _____.
- Because of this _____.
- _____ happened because _____.
- I think this because _____ (textual evidence to support your thinking).
- The reason for _____ is _____.

Core Support for Diverse Learners

This lesson set was created with the needs of a wide variety of learners in mind. Throughout the day-by-day lessons, you'll find examples of visual supports, graphic organizers, highlighted speaking and listening opportunities, and research-driven English language learner supports aimed at scaffolding instruction for all learners. Also, we urge you to consider the following areas of challenge with which your students may need guided support. The following sections are written to spotlight important considerations as you move through the lesson sets.

Reading

Choosing texts that are at students' reading levels is essential for their reading success and reading identity. When finding texts, make sure you have various levels represented in your classroom collection. All or some of your students may benefit from repeated exposure to a lesson's teaching objective over several days. This can be accomplished with the whole class or in small-group settings.

Closely monitor your students who are reading below grade level to determine whether they are reading with accuracy, fluency, and stamina to support comprehension. Encourage students to use context to confirm or self-correct word recognition and understanding and to reread when necessary. Refer to the Common Core Foundational Skills Standards—both at the grade 4 level as well as earlier grade standards—for direct, explicit foundational skills support that your students reading below grade level may need.

Informational texts can often have unfamiliar words that will require teacher support to decode and understand. While our Core Words provide overarching informational text vocabulary, it is essential to preview the informational texts that readers who are below grade level are independently reading during this lesson set. Consider providing your fourth graders with highlighters so that they can record words that they know and words that are unfamiliar. For many students, this may mean words that they do not know the meaning of; however, students working to decode multi-syllabic words should be encouraged to highlight or record words that they are unsure of. In this way, you can provide ongoing support for them as developing readers while building independence. In addition, students reading below grade level or students who

struggle with organization of ideas may need a great deal of help with their independent research. You may want to pair students with a research partner.

As you continue your work with students, use observational notes and reading assessment data to create two to three specific short-term goals for your students with diverse needs. For example, as stated above, these goals may be related to increasing word accuracy, building vocabulary, improving fluency, building stamina, or enhancing comprehension. Throughout this lesson set, tailor your individualized and small-group instruction set so that it addresses and evaluates student progress toward these goals.

Writing

Inspired writers are motivated writers. Allowing students to choose the topic of their writing is critical for their ultimate success and their positive development of identity as a writer. When immersing your students in a new genre, form, or purpose for writing, emphasize the meaning and function this particular type of writing may have in their own lives. Many of your students will also benefit from exposure to strong mentor texts, examples of your own writing, as well as the experience of sharing their own work—both the final product and the work in process.

Many of your students will significantly benefit from the opportunity to sketch the information they've found from informational texts before adding words. This is especially helpful for visual learners and students who need to "sketch to stretch." Even your most proficient writers can benefit from this step, but many of your resistant writers will feel more comfortable with getting their ideas on paper through drawing first. Giving students some sentence starters (see the Core Words and Core Phrases) can vastly help them focus on their ideas and have the stamina to get their thoughts on paper.

- One important fact about _____ is _____.
- Another important fact is _____.

 _____ is important because _____.

As your students move from determining their ideas for their diary entries and begin telling a logical sequence of events, provide your students with a variety of templates that are fourth grade appropriate. For students with fine motor control issues, providing students with a variety of writing templates that have handwriting lines with a dotted line in the middle can offer support, as letter formation may require significant energy for some writers. Also consider having some students electronically publish their diary entries if that is a medium more conducive to their writing success.

We want our fourth graders to communicate the important ideas about historical events to an audience, and supporting them as developing writers is essential. In addition to providing students with topic choice and the opportunity to draw prior to writing, we can provide further scaffolding by having students orally rehearse their diary entries to us or to a peer. For some students, the oral rehearsal will provide a springboard to writing. Others will have greater success dictating their diary entries to you.

As with the reading lessons, your students may benefit from several days on a single lesson's teaching objective. This can be done with the whole class or in small-group settings.

English Language Learners

Although it is always our goal as teachers to get to know all of our students deeply both in and out of the classroom setting, this work is perhaps more critical when considering our English language learners. Honoring families' cultural traditions and experiences is important for getting to know your students and working with them in meaningful ways.

English language learners are learning about historical events alongside native English speakers in your classroom, but they are also simultaneously learning English. For English language learners, it is essential to simultaneously develop their ability to easily hold conversations about their reading and writing and build their academic language base. Goldenberg (2010) defines "academic English" as the more abstract, complex, and challenging language that permits us to participate successfully in mainstream classroom instruction. English language learners will over time be responsible for understanding and producing academic English both orally and in writing. However, language acquisition is a process and English language learners range in their development of English language proficiency. Consider your students along a spectrum of language acquisition, from students new to this country to those who are proficient conversationally to those who have native-like proficiency.

Refer to the English language learner icons throughout this lesson set for ways to shelter instruction for English Language Learners. These elements will help English language learners participate successfully in the whole-group lesson and support the development of their language skills. While these moments during instruction are designed to support English language learners, many schools are adding a separate ELD (English language development) block targeted at oral English language development to further support their students in language acquisition.

Establishing routines will be essential for all learners but will be especially important for English language learners needing consistent opportunities to process the information required to conduct research. Frequently monitor students who need extra support. Condense the main ideas and key concepts from readings for students who need adaptations. In addition, emphasize and repeat the steps required for research for students who need repeated practice. Consider forming small groups of students and conducting small-group research rather than independent projects for those students who need more scaffolding. Work closely with colleagues to find sources at all levels.

Students with growing English proficiency will benefit from a history word wall, which will build vocabulary (refer to the Core Words and Core Phrases). A sentence word wall that gives sentence starters to help with conversation will also offer students another layer of support. Some students may benefit from having their own personalized copies of these words to keep in their reading or writing notebooks for quick reference. Visual aids will further support students and guide them on what words are important to this study and what they mean.

Some students will benefit from several days on the same teaching objective. Consider gathering small groups of readers or writers for repeated instruction or using one-on-one conferences as an opportunity to revisit teaching objectives.

Complementary Core Methods

Read-Aloud

Take this opportunity to share a wide variety of nonfiction texts during read-aloud, both narrative and informational. Make sure to include texts that vary in length, topic, and presentation style. Use your knowledge of students' interests to select texts that will inspire and excite your class. When appropriate, use your read-aloud as another chance for students to practice one or two of the following skills:

- Making a prediction about a text's potential content by skimming the text features

- Determining the main idea and key details of a text

- Asking and answering questions about a text, using portions of the text as evidence in your responses

- Identifying and exploring the meaning of new vocabulary

- Generating a list of key words to use in a search for additional information on the same topic

Shared Reading

Shared reading provides a wonderful opportunity to conduct a mini-study on a topic of general interest for the class. In particular, it can also provide the chance to further link social studies content to the work you are doing in this lesson set. Think about selecting a range of short texts that match your current lesson set of study in social studies. Use shared reading to reinforce the idea of reading to learn (versus learning to read). Here are some prompts you may want to use in your conversations about these texts:

- What is the event? What were the causes?

- After reading this text, what questions do we still have about our topic?

- What new vocabulary did we take away from this text? How can we use this new vocabulary?

- Let's summarize what we just learned in our own words . . .

Shared reading can also be a great place to specifically highlight the linking words found within a shared text and discuss how they connect ideas within a specific category of information.

Shared Writing

Shared Writing also provides an opportunity to link to your work in social studies. Use this time to:

- Create shared lists of prior knowledge around a content area topic of study

- Generate key words to use in an Internet search

- Jot notes about a shared reading

- Organize notes into logical categories

- Compose questions about a topic for further investigation

- Craft answers to shared questions

- Revise shared writing to link ideas together, creating more complex sentences words and phrases such as *also, another, and, more, but*

Core Connections at Home

Invite families to spend time in their local library or online at home researching a historical topic of shared interest—possibly a historical topic tied to their own cultural background.

Have students share their final book posters/trailers and diary entries with their families during a special recognition. Ask families to write a letter to their child sharing what they learned from their presentations. Display these letters alongside students' final presentations.

Grade 4

Reading Lessons

The "Core I.D.E.A. / Daily Reading Instruction at a Glance" table on the next page highlights the teaching objectives and standards alignment for all ten lessons across the four stages of the lesson set (Introduce, Define, Extend, and Assess). It also indicates which lessons contain special features to support English language learners as well as technology, speaking and listening, and formative ("Milestone") assessments.

The Core Ready Reading Rubric that follows next is designed to help you record each student's overall understanding across four levels of achievement as it relates to the lesson set goals. We recommend that you use this rubric at the end of the lesson set as a performance-based assessment tool. Use the Milestone Performance Assessments and checklists as tools to help you gauge student progress toward these goals, and reteach and differentiate as needed. See the foundational book, *Be Core Ready: Powerful, Effective Steps to Implementing and Achieving the Common Core State Standards,* for more information about the Core Ready Reading and Writing Rubrics.

The Core I.D.E.A. / Daily Reading Instruction at a Glance

Grade 4   What Happened and Why: Studying Cause and Effect through Events in History

Instructional Stages

Introduce: notice, explore, collect, note, immerse, surround, record, share

Define: name, identify, outline, clarify, select, plan

Extend: try, experiment, attempt, approximate, practice, explain, revise, refine

Assess: reflect, conclude, connect, share, recognize, respond

Lesson	Teaching Objective	Core Standards	Special Features
1	Readers can identify text structures.	RI.4.1 • RI.4.5 • RI.4.10 • W.4.4 • SL.4.1a • SL.4.1b • L.4.1	Close Reading ELL
2	Asking what happened (effect) and why (cause) helps readers identify cause and effect.	RI.4.1 • RI.4.3 • RI.4.5 • RI.4.8 • RI.4.10 • SL.4.1c • SL.4.1d • L.4.6	Close Reading ELL
3	Signal words help readers identify cause and effect.	RI.4.1 • RI.4.3 • RI.4.5 • RI.4.8 • RI.4.10 • W.4.2c • SL.4.1a • SL.4.1b • L.4.6	Close Reading ELL
4	Readers notice multiple effects and causes.	RI.4.1 • RI.4.3 • RI.4.5 • RI.4.8 • RI.4.10 • SL.4.1a • SL.4.1b • SL.4.2 • L.4.6	Close Reading ELL Milestone Assessment S&L
5	Readers can create timelines to identify causes and effects in history.	RI.4.1 • RI.4.3 • RI.4.5 • RI.4.7 • RI.4.10 • W.4.10 • SL.4.1a-d • L.4.1 • L.4.6	Close Reading ELL Milestone Assessment Tech
6	Readers can talk about cause and effect relationships using transitional words and phrases.	RI.4.3 • RI.4.5 • RI.4.10 • SL.4.1a-d • SL.4.6 • L.4.1 • L.4.6	ELL S&L
7	Readers can write summaries that explain the cause and effect.	RI.4.1 • RI.4.5 • RI.4.9 • RI.4.10 • W.4.2a-d • W.4.4 • W.4.6 • W.4.10 • SL.4.1a • SL.4.1b • SL.4.2 • L.4.6	Close Reading ELL Milestone Assessment
8	Readers can create cause and effect posters or book trailers to retell a historical moment graphically.	RI.4.1 • RI.4.9 • RI.4.10 • W.4.4 • W.4.6 • W.4.10 • SL.4.1a-d • L.4.1	Close Reading ELL Milestone Assessment Tech
9	Readers can ask each other questions about what happened and why in texts they read.	RI.4.2 • RI.4.3 • RI.4.5 • RI.4.10 • SL.4.1a-d • SL.4.2 • SL.4.3 • L.4.1 • L.4.6	Close Reading ELL S&L
10	Readers reflect on their learning by responding to Core Questions.	RI.4.1 • RI.4.10 • W.4.4 • W.4.10 • SL.4.1a-d • L.4.1 • L.4.6	Close Reading ELL Milestone Assessment Tech

Core Ready Reading Rubric

Grade 4   Core Ready Reading and Writing Rubrics

Lesson Set Goal	Emerging	Approaching	Achieving	Exceeding	Standards Alignment
Explain what happened and why (effect, cause) in historical texts and discuss the cause and effect relationship using transitional words and phrases.	Student demonstrates minimal ability to explain what happened and why (effect, cause) in historical texts. Does not use or improperly uses transitional words and phrases when discussing the cause and effect relationship.	Student attempts, with some success, to explain what happened and why (effect, cause) in historical texts. Attempts to use some transitional words and phrases when discussing the cause and effect relationship. Some inaccuracies may be present. May be incomplete.	Student explains what happened and why (effect, cause) in historical texts and effectively uses transitional words and phrases to discuss the cause and effect relationship.	Student provides an in-depth and insightful explanation for what happened and why (effect, cause) in historical texts and is highly accurate and successful at using transitional words and phrases to discuss the cause and effect relationship.	RI.4.1 RI.4.3 RI.4.5 RI.4.6 RI.4.8 RI.4.10 W.2c W.4.4 W.4.10 SL.4.1a–d SL.4.3 SL.4.6 L.4.1 L.4.6
Identify cause and effect structure in historical texts using signal words and other strategies.	Student may show a very limited grasp of how to identify the cause and effect structure in historical texts using signal words and other strategies, but needs significant support to be successful.	Student shows some understanding of how to identify cause and effect structure in historical texts using signal words and other strategies. Some inaccuracies may be present. May be incomplete.	Student successfully identifies cause and effect structure in historical texts using signal words and other strategies. Accurate and complete.	Student is highly successful in identifying cause and effect structure in historical texts using signal words and other strategies. May grasp subtle or challenging relationships.	RI.4.1 RI.4.3 RI.4.5 RI.4.7 RI.4.10
Refer to details and examples in a text when explaining what the text says explicitly and when drawing inferences from the text.	Student shows little or no evidence of active, purposeful reading or searching the text for specific information and evidence. Student makes little or no attempt to provide details and examples when explaining what the text says explicitly and is unable to draw inferences from the text.	Student shows some evidence of active, purposeful reading and searching the text for specific information and evidence. Student may provide some details and examples, with marginal accuracy, when explaining what the text says explicitly and when drawing inferences from the text.	Student shows solid evidence of active, purposeful reading and searching the text for specific information and evidence. Student usually provides appropriate details and examples when explaining what the text says explicitly and when drawing inferences from the text.	Student demonstrates exceptional evidence of active, purposeful reading and searching the text for specific information and evidence. Student provides accurate, explicit, and thoughtful details and examples when explaining what the text says explicitly and when drawing inferences from the text.	RI.4.1 RI.4.2 RI.4.3 RI.4.4 RI.4.10 SL.4.1a–d L.4.1 L.4.6
Summarize a historical text with an emphasis on cause and effect.	Student shows little or no evidence of successfully summarizing a historical text with an emphasis on cause and effect.	Student attempts to summarize a historical text with an emphasis on cause and effect. Summaries may have some inaccuracies or lack complete clarity.	Student summarizes a historical text with an emphasis on cause and effect. Summaries are mostly clear, accurate, and succinct.	Student generates excellent summaries of historical texts with an emphasis on cause and effect. Summaries are very clear, accurate, and succinct.	RI.4.1 RI.4.5 RI.4.6 RI.4.10 W.4.2a–d W.4.4 W.4.6 W.4.10 SL.4.2

Lesson Set Goal	Emerging	Approaching	Achieving	Exceeding	Standards Alignment
Report on findings through a clear and organized book poster or book trailer.	Student struggles to produce a clear and organized book poster or trailer that reports findings. Key elements are undeveloped or missing.	Student attempts to report findings through a book poster or trailer. May lack some clarity and organization.	Student reports findings through a clear and organized book poster or trailer.	Student reports findings through a highly effective, clear, and well-organized book poster or trailer.	RI.4.1 RI.4.10 W.4.10 S.L.4.4 L.4.1 L.4.6
Refer to details and examples in a text when explaining what the text says explicitly and when drawing inferences from the text.	Student shows little or no evidence of actively and purposefully reading or searching the text for specific information and evidence.	Student attempts to actively and purposefully read or search the text for specific information and evidence. Incorporates some details and examples, with marginal accuracy, when explaining what the text says explicitly and when drawing inferences from the text.	Student shows solid evidence of actively and purposefully reading or searching the text for specific information and evidence. Consistently provides accurate and effective details and examples when explaining what the text says explicitly and when drawing inferences from the text.	Student demonstrates an exceptional ability to actively and purposefully read or search the text for specific information and evidence. Provides accurate, explicit, and thoughtful details and examples when explaining what the text says explicitly and when drawing inferences from the text.	RI.4.1
By the end of the year, proficiently read and comprehend informational texts in the grades 4–5 text complexity band, with scaffolding as needed at the high end of the range.	Student shows little or no evidence of reading and comprehending texts appropriate for the grade 4 text complexity band.	Student shows inconsistent evidence of independently and proficiently reading and comprehending texts appropriate for the grade 4 text complexity band.	Student shows solid evidence of independently and proficiently reading and comprehending texts appropriate for the grade 4 text complexity band. Needs scaffolding at the grade 5 level.	Student shows solid evidence of independently and proficiently reading and comprehending texts above the grade 4 text complexity band.	RI.4.10
Write routinely over extended time frames (time for research, reflection, and revision) and shorter time frames (a single sitting or a day or two) for a range of discipline-specific tasks, purposes, and audiences.	Student shows little or no evidence of writing routinely for short or long time frames for a range of discipline-specific tasks, purposes, and audiences.	Student shows some evidence of writing routinely for short and long time frames for a range of discipline-specific tasks, purposes, and audiences.	Student shows solid evidence of writing routinely for short and long time frames for a range of discipline-specific tasks, purposes, and audiences.	Student shows exceptional evidence of consistently and accurately writing for short and long time frames for a range of discipline-specific tasks, purposes, and audiences.	W.4.10

Lesson Set Goal	Emerging	Approaching	Achieving	Exceeding	Standards Alignment
In collaborative discussions, demonstrate evidence of preparation for discussion and exhibit responsibility to the rules and roles of conversation.	In collaborative discussions, student comes unprepared and often disregards the rules and roles of conversation.	In collaborative discussions, student's preparation may be evident but ineffective or inconsistent. May occasionally disregard the rules and roles of conversation.	In collaborative discussions, student prepares adequately and draws on the preparation and other information about the topic to explore ideas under discussion. Usually observes the rules and roles of conversation.	In collaborative discussions, student arrives extremely well prepared for discussions and draws on the preparation and other information about the topic to explore ideas under discussion. Always observes the rules and roles of conversation.	SL.4.1a SL.4.1b
In collaborative discussions, share and develop ideas in a manner that enhances understanding of topic. Contribute and respond to the content of the conversation in a productive and focused manner.	Student shows little or no evidence of engaging in collaborative discussions and makes little or no attempt to ask and answer questions, stay on topic, link comments to the remarks of others, or to explain his or her own ideas and understanding in light of the discussion.	Student shows some evidence of engaging in collaborative discussions and, with marginal success, attempts to ask questions to check understanding of information presented, to stay on topic, link comments to the remarks of others, and explain his or her own ideas and understanding in light of the discussion.	Student engages in a range of collaborative discussions and asks questions to check understanding of information presented. Stays on topic most of the time and frequently links his or her comments to the remarks of others, and explains his or her own ideas and understanding in light of the discussion.	Student effectively and consistently engages in a range of collaborative discussions and asks high-level questions to check understanding of information presented. Always stays on topic and, with great insight and attention to the comments of others, links his or her comments to the remarks of others, and explains his or her own ideas and understanding in light of the discussion.	SL.4.1c SL.4.1d
Demonstrate knowledge of standard English and its conventions.	Student demonstrates little or no knowledge of standard English and its conventions.	Student demonstrates some evidence of knowledge of standard English and its conventions.	Student consistently demonstrates knowledge of standard English and its conventions.	Student demonstrates an exceptional understanding of standard English and its conventions. Use of conventions is sophisticated for grade level and accurate.	L.4.1 L.4.2 L.4.3
Acquire and accurately use grade-appropriate conversational, general academic, and domain-specific vocabulary and phrases.	Student shows little or no evidence of acquisition and use of grade-appropriate conversational and academic language.	Student shows some evidence of the acquisition and use of grade-appropriate conversational and academic language.	Student shows solid evidence of the acquisition and use of grade-appropriate conversational and academic language.	Student shows a high level of sophistication and precision with the acquisition and use of grade-appropriate conversational and academic language.	L.4.6

Note: See the Core Ready Rubrics chart in the Walk Through for descriptions of category headers.

Reading Lesson 1

▼ Teaching Objective

Readers can identify text structures.

Close Reading Opportunity

▼ Standards Alignment

RI.4.1, RI.4.5, RI.4.10, W.4.4, W.4.10, SL.4.1a, SL.4.1b, L.4.1, L.4.6

▼ Materials

- *Word Builder* by Ann Whitford Paul
- Read-aloud text that illustrates cause and effect such as *Across the Stream* by Mirra Ginsburg; any of the Laura Numeroff series: *If You Take a Mouse to the Movies, If You Give a Mouse a Cookie, If You Give a Pig a Pancake; If You Give a Moose a Muffin, If You Give a Mouse a Cookie, If You Give a Pig a Pancake;* Maurice Sendak's *Where the Wild Things Are; Alexander and the Terrible, Horrible, No Good, Very Bad Day* by Judith Viorst; *Sylvester and the Magic Pebble* by William Steig; *Don't Slam the Door!* by Dori Chaconas
- Structures Writers Use to Organize Their Writing, Appendix 4.3

▼ To the Teacher

Fourth graders are ready to be history detectives, to think deeply about what has happened in the past and why events happened. Today you will be launching your reading lesson set focused around the strategies readers use to identify the causes and effects of historical events. More specifically, over the next few weeks you will guide your class to practice a variety of skills including asking and answering questions about a topic, using the text as evidence, identifying what happened and why, and making meaning with new vocabulary words. This first lesson introduces students to the idea that writers use structures to help them communicate their ideas more effectively. By taking the time to explore the metaphor of how the word structure applies to texts, students will better be able to consider cause and effect as a specific text structure that writers use in historical texts.

©Andy Dean/Fotolia

▼ Procedure

Warm Up Gather the class to set the stage for today's learning

Gather your students and introduce the idea that writers use structures to build their ideas.

Did you know that writers use structures to help them make their ideas stronger? You might be wondering, Hmmm . . . I know structures are the things builders make, what does that have to do with writing? Well, what would a sentence be without words? What would words be without letters? Just as if you were constructing a building, you must build your words and sentences and paragraphs and think about how they go together.

Teach Model what students need to learn and do

First, read aloud the picture book *Word Builder*. The illustrations and simple sentences will help introduce students to the metaphor that writers use structures to help them craft their writing. Then, explain to students that

Try Guide students to quickly rehearse what they need to learn and do in preparation for practice

Read aloud for students a fictional text that will help them identify cause and effect, which will be the text structure focused on for the remainder of the lesson set. *If You Give a Mouse a Cookie* is a classic children's picture book that will allow you to stop after just a few pages to have students turn and talk with a partner to discuss: What type of text structure is this? How do you know?

Clarify Briefly restate today's teaching objective and explain the practice task(s)

In your independent reading today you are going to ask yourself, What type of text structure is this? How do I know?

Practice Students work independently or in small groups to apply today's teaching objective

Students will be reading independently and marking places where they see writers using a text structure to better communicate their ideas: cause/effect; problem/solution; compare/contrast.

Wrap Up Check understanding as you guide students to briefly share what they have learned and produced today

Have students share with the class or a partner one place they marked and explain what type of text structure they identified. The big question to come back to is "How did they know?" This will help prepare them for lessons to come.

Close Reading Opportunity

▶ **Materials**

- Sample historical nonfiction text displayed so it can be read and highlighted with the class (see Appendix 4.2)
- Charting supplies or interactive whiteboard
- Highlighting tools (two different colors for each partnership)
- What Happened and Why chart

---

writers use structures so that readers can build a better understanding of the text. Have a chart prepared called "Some Text Structures Writers Use to Organize Their Writing."

Cause-Effect	Cause is why something happened. Effect is what happened.
Problem-Solution	Tells about a problem. Then, gives a solution or more than one solution
Compare-Contrast	Shows how two or more things are alike and different.

©Benjamin Mercer/Fotolia; ©cantor pannatto/Fotolia; ©travis manley/Fotolia

Share with students simple sentences that illustrate these three different text structures, such as:

▲ The tree fell down because it was a windy day.

▲ The boy spilled his milk at lunch. His friend helped him clean it up.

▲ My sister and I are both tall but her hair is long and mine is short.

Have students help you identify what types of structures these sample sentences illustrate. **ELL** Provide Comprehensible Input—Visuals. Simple visuals and graphics on your charts help anchor ideas to visual learners and ELLs.

Reading Lesson 2

▶ **Teaching Objective**

Asking what happened (effect) and why (cause) helps readers identify cause and effect.

▶ **Standards Alignment**

RI.4.1, RI.4.3, RI.4.5, RI.4.8, RI.4.10, SL.4.1c, SL.4.1d, L.4.6

▼ To the Teacher

This lesson is designed to help students ask the questions "What happened?" and "Why?" as a way of identifying cause and effect structures in writing. This lesson also guides students to start by identifying the effect and then looking for the causes.

▼ Procedure

Warm Up   Gather the class to set the stage for today's learning

Yesterday, we learned that authors organize their writing and this is called text structure. One of the text structures we will learn more about today is cause and effect. The purpose of cause and effect writing is to tell the reader what event happened and the reasons why it happened.

Tell a story from your own life that illustrates the cause and effect relationship such as:

My daughter was so sleepy this morning, she almost missed her bus. I thought, "Why is she so tired this morning?" I remembered that last night she stayed up late reading a book. It was a classic cause and effect relationship. What happened? She was tired. What made this happen? She stayed up too late reading.

Begin a two-column chart and record this cause and effect. Label this T-chart "What Happened and Why?" **ELL** Provide Comprehensible Input—Organizers. This kind of organizer helps ELs to categorize their thoughts in a visual way. You can also consider using your visuals from the chart in Reading Lesson 1 in the headers (or have them create their own cause and effect visuals) to tie a visual to the thinking.

What Happened and Why?

Effect—What Happened?	Cause—Why?

Then show photos that illustrate an effect (muddy child, burnt toast, fallen tree). Have students speculate as to the causes. Add on to the chart. Explain that part of the job of readers is to notice cause and effect relationships. This

helps us understand our reading better. Recommend that students change the order of this to "Effect and Cause," because as readers it is often easier to find the effect first, then the cause.

Teach   Model what students need to learn and do

Today you are going to learn how you can find cause and effect relationships in what you read, especially in texts that explain something about history.

Before you begin to read aloud the sample history text about Irena Sendler from the appendix or another article that includes cause and effect relationships, introduce it to the students along the lines of the following: Recommend that students change the order of this to "Effect and Cause" because as readers it is often easier to find the effect first, then the cause. Explain that it helps to look for something important that happens in the text (an *effect*). Then ask "What made this happen (the *cause*)?" Emphasize that in reality a cause always comes before an effect, but it does not always come in that order in the text.

When we read stories about history, to help us better understand when one event causes another to happen we can look for the author's use of a particular structure called cause and effect. The effect is what happens. The causes are why it happens. Let's read together a short passage about a very brave woman who helped save the lives of thousands of children. While we're reading, you will notice that the author makes sure to explain why this woman was able to save so many lives.

Read with students the first few paragraphs of the first sample historical nonfiction text.

"Irena Sendler was 29 years old when her city, Warsaw, in Poland, was occupied by the Nazis. Because of this, everything changed. Life was suddenly dangerous for the city's Jewish families because they were all forced into an area of the city called the Warsaw Ghetto. Irena was Catholic, but she could still get in trouble easily. If she wanted to survive then the smart thing would be to keep her head down and try not to be noticed. Irena did not do this. Instead, she smuggled Jewish children out of the Warsaw Ghetto to safety. This required a great deal of courage. If Irena were caught, she would be in terrible danger.

What Happened and Why?

Effect—What Happened?	Cause—Why?
Irena Sendler saved 2,500 children during the Nazi invasion of Warsaw, Poland.	• She smuggled Jewish children out of the Warsaw Ghetto to safety. • Irena was brave. • She worked with about 30 other volunteers. • Sometimes children were driven out in ambulances. • Sometimes children were disguised as packages or put in potato sacks. • Children often escaped through underground corridors.

Yet, Irena was brave. By the end of the war, she had saved the lives of about 2,500 children."

Use a highlighting tool to color-code the effect one color (By the end of the war, she had saved the lives of about 2,500 children) and the causes another. (She smuggled Jewish children out of the Warsaw Ghetto to safety. . . . Irena was brave.)

Watch me as I highlight the effect, or what happened, in one color and the causes, or why it happened, in another.

Try Guide students to quickly rehearse what they need to learn and do in preparation for practice

Continue reading the article together. Explain to students that the article goes on to explain more ways that Irena was able to save so many children's lives. These are further causes. They answer the question "Why was Irena able to save so many children's lives?"

"She worked with about thirty other volunteers, mostly women. Sometimes the children were driven out in ambulances; one driver brought a dog with him whose barking distracted the soldiers. Sometimes they were disguised as packages, or put in potato sacks. They often traveled an escape route through underground corridors in an old courthouse at the edge of the ghetto." OK, friends, now it's your turn. Does anyone recognize any more causes in this article by asking themselves, "Why"?

Wait for most students to indicate they are ready. **ELL** Enable Language Production—Listening and Speaking.

Turn and share what you noticed with a partner. **ELL** Enable Language Production—Increase Interaction. During the partner share you can listen in to help support and scaffold speaking through whispering in and providing sentence structures to convey their thinking if needed.

Listen in to various partnerships, jotting down interesting and relevant responses to share with the larger group. Call the group back together. Add on to the Cause and Effect chart. Emphasize how you are going to start with identifying the effect and then list the causes.

Clarify Briefly restate today's teaching objective and explain the practice task(s)

Direct students to read their own independent reading books with attention to noticing any "effect and cause" moments in the text.

Practice Students work independently or in small groups to apply today's teaching objective

Students will be reading in their own independent text selections, noting any "effect and cause" moments by asking themselves "what happened?" and "why?".

Wrap Up Check understanding as you guide students to briefly share what they have learned and produced today

Have students share an "effect and cause" moment from their own independent reading selection.

Every cause produces more than one effect.

—Herbert Spencer

Reading Lesson 3

▼ **Teaching Objective**

Signal words help readers identify cause and effect.

▼ **Standards Alignment**

RI.4.1, RI.4.3, RI.4.5, RI.4.8, RI.4.10, W.4.2c, SL.4.1a, SL.4.1b, L.4.6

Close Reading Opportunity

▼ **Materials**

- *Baseball Saved Us* by Ken Mochizuki, or another narrative nonfiction read-aloud
- Cause and Effect Signal Words chart
- Copies of the sample text
- Highlighting tools (two different colors for each partnership)

▼ **To the Teacher**

Baseball Saved Us is about a boy named Shorty and his family who, along with thousands of Japanese Americans, are sent to an internment camp after the attack on Pearl Harbor. Shorty and his father decide to build a baseball diamond and form a league in order to boost the spirits of the internees. The baseball storyline can help students make sense of this complex chapter in American history.

One challenge with the cause and effect text structure is the time factor. For instance, if authors organize text using the sequence text structure, they may use the signal words: *first, second, next, finally,* etc. For cause and effect, some of the signal words are: *because, as a result of, therefore.* Unlike a sequence text structure where events happen in order, one of the challenges with cause and effect is that authors may not present information in the order in which events occurred. Sometimes, the author presents the *cause* first and in other instances, the *effect* may be first. Here is an example:

▼
- As a result of the heavy rain, the roof got a leak.
- The roof got a leak as a result of the heavy rain.

When readers are familiar with the signal words, they are better able to identify what the cause is and what the effect is. For instance, a cause signal word often indicates that the cause is stated nearby. Explain that signal words are clues, and as readers students must be detectives to find the cause, which is often stated nearby.

▼ **Procedure**

Warm Up **Gather the class to set the stage for today's learning**

Yesterday, we learned to ask ourselves, "What happened?" and "Why?" to determine cause and effect in writing about history. These questions help us as readers. Another strategy to use to help determine cause and effect is to look for clues authors give us that help us identify cause and effect moments.

Teach **Model what students need to learn and do**

Introduce to students the Cause and Effect Signal Words chart.

I have on this chart some signal words that help us as readers identify moments in the text where causes are explained.

Cause and Effect Signal Words

as a result	if . . . then	therefore
because	in order that	thus
consequently	nevertheless	why
due to the fact	since	
	so	
	the reason for	

I'm going to read aloud the first page from a book that explains an important and difficult moment in American history. As I'm reading, listen for any of these signal words that can help explain what happened to our main character Shorty and his family. **ELL** **Identify and Communicate Content and Language Objectives—Language Form and Function.** Signal words that connect ideas can be tricky for your second language learners. This chart will help them see a bank of these words for them to use to extend and justify their thinking. You can also consider giving them sentence examples that put the signal words in context. This chart could even be on an index card for quick reference during partner talk.

Read aloud for students the first page from *Baseball Saved Us* by Ken Mochizuki. Following the first page, pause and ask students if they heard any of the signal words that can help them identify cause and effect. Your students should identify that the Dad character said, "Because" and then explains why they are in a Japanese internment camp.

When Dad says "Because," it's giving us the signal that he is going to explain why Shorty and his family are in the camp. Signal words help us as readers identify why things have happened.

Try **Guide students to quickly rehearse what they need to learn and do in preparation for practice**

Give each student an anchor card, review the signal words, and explain how one way to identify cause and effect is by circling the signal word and underlining the cause. Example 1: "I had a stomachache because I ate too many cookies." Example 2: "Since I woke up late, I missed the school bus."

Return to the sample history text in the appendix. Use this to have students zoom in on the signal words. Just as they did with your sample sentences, have students circle signal words and underline the cause.

Now you are going to continue to circle the signal words and underline the cause with a text we've read before. This time you are going to read for how these signal words help identify the causes to an event.

Clarify **Briefly restate today's teaching objective and explain the practice task(s)**

Students will be reading their own independent text selections, noting any clue words that help identify cause and effect moments in the text.

Practice **Students work independently or in small groups to apply today's teaching objective**

Students will be reading independently, marking places where they see signal words from the Signal Words chart and underlining the cause.

Wrap Up **Check understanding as you guide students to briefly share what they have learned and produced today**

Have students share a moment in the text where they marked a signal word. In addition, have students share what the cause is.

Most people get ahead during the time that others waste.

—Henry Ford

Reading Lesson 4

▶ Teaching Objective

Readers notice multiple effects and causes.

▶ Standards Alignment

RI.4.1, RI.4.3, RI.4.5, RI.4.8, RI.4.10, SL.4.1a, SL.4.1b, SL.4.2, L.4.6

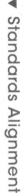

Close Reading
Opportunity

- Mugumo trees
- Ancestors
- Spirit
- Landscape

▶ Materials

- A narrative nonfiction history text such as *Seeds of Change* by Jen Cullerton Johnson
- What Happened and Why chart begun in Reading Lesson 2, plus blank copies for students to use in their independent work

▶ To the Teacher

There are many wonderful narrative nonfiction texts that illustrate the power of an individual to help the lives of others. Your social studies curriculum can guide your text selection. Our core texts suggestions can also supplement your curriculum by providing a foundation for not only discussing cause and effect but also how individuals can make a difference in the world. *Seeds of Change* is published by Lee and Low Press. On their website they have a book talk with the author, Jen Cullerton Johnson, and the illustrator, Sonia Lynn Sadler, that provides insight into why they created the book and the message they want children to take away.

▶ Procedure

Warm Up Gather the class to set the stage for today's learning

Gather your class for today's teaching. Orient them to the text you've chosen as a narrative nonfiction read-aloud. If you choose *Seeds of Change*, introduce the vocabulary your students may need to better identify and understand the cause and effect relationships that are the heart of the story:

Teach Model what students need to learn and do

So far in this lesson set, we learned that cause and effect is one type of text structure that writers of history use to better explain what happened and why it happened. We also learned that signal words can help us identify cause and effect more easily.

Today, we are going to read a story from recent history about a woman from another part of the world whose actions made a big difference. In this story there are many things that happen and many reasons why they happen. Some stories that document moments in history have multiple effects, or things that happen, and multiple causes or reasons why they happen. This can be tricky to keep track of. While I'm reading I'm going to pause and have us think about what happened and why it happened.

Read the first half of the text and pause at the introduction of the Green Belt Movement. Model for students that the movement discussed is an effect and that there are identifiable causes that led to the creation of this movement.

What Happened, and Why?

Effect—What Happened?	Cause—Why?
Green Belt Movement began.	• Women planted rows of trees. • Wangari Maathai started with one tree and encouraged other women to join her.

Try Guide students to quickly rehearse what they need to learn and do in preparation for practice

As I'm reading I want you to add to your own Cause and Effect chart noting other events that happen thanks to Wangari's work, and why they were able to happen.

Milestone Performance Assessment

Finding Cause and Effect

Use this checklist to assess student work on the What Happened and Why chart.

Standards Alignment: RI.4.1, RI.4.3, RI.4.5, RI.4.8

	Achieved	Notes
Identify effects cited in the text.		
Identify causes corresponding to the effects.		

Wrap Up Check understanding as you guide students to briefly share what they have learned and produced today.

Have students share an effect and multiple causes if they have identified them today.

▶ **Materials**

- Timeline Organizer (see Appendix 4.4)

▶ **To the Teacher**

When there is an increased amount of text, finding the cause and effect can be complicated. Creating timelines can help students look back at the text

---

Give students an opportunity to paraphrase the story at different points in your reading. (SL.4.2) This will help them keep track of the events and how one event in Wangari's life caused future events to happen.

Clarify Briefly restate today's teaching objective and explain the practice task(s)

In your independent reading today, you are going to continue looking for cause and effect relationships to add to your chart. Remember, sometimes there are multiple effects and multiple causes. Keep asking yourself, "What happened and why?"

Practice Students work independently or in small groups to apply today's teaching objective

Students will read independently, adding on to their Cause and Effect charts, and noting multiple causes and effects when possible.

ELL Assess for Content and Language Understanding—Formative Assessment. This is an opportunity to examine their language usage and see how to best scaffold upcoming lessons to extend and support their learning in English.

Collect this work and use it as an informal assessment to determine your students' progress with this skill.

Reading Lesson 5

▶ **Teaching Objective**

Readers can create timelines to explain causes and effects in history.

Close Reading Opportunity

▶ **Standards Alignment**

RI.4.1, RI.4.3, RI.4.5, RI.4.7, RI.4.10, W.4.10, SL.4.1a–d, L.4.1, L.4.6

to identify what caused events to happen. This will call for careful, close reading to identify the sequence of events that cause a chain reaction in history. The readings so far are great texts to use for identifying how one event leads to another in history.

▼ Procedure

Warm Up | Gather the class to set the stage for today's learning

Use this Warm Up as an opportunity to review with students the texts you've read so far.

So far in this lesson set we've read three important texts about historical events. One about a courageous woman who helped save thousands of children from the Nazis in World War II. We also read about a boy and his father in a Japanese internment camp and how they created a baseball league that gave them pride and unity in the camp. Finally, we read about a woman who planted trees in her home country of Kenya and started the Green Belt Movement, which inspired people all over the country to plant trees and preserve their homeland. As we've learned, we can keep track of important historical events through the lens of cause and effect. Oftentimes, a chain reaction occurs. One event causes another, which causes another.

Teach | Model what students need to learn and do

Introduce the Timeline Organizer and model how to use it with a book you've read so far with a clear chronology of events over time.

To keep track of how cause and effect unfolds over time, we can use a timeline. A timeline shows us how things happen over time. Let's look back at the book we read yesterday, *Seeds of Change*, to see how Wangari's life was like a chain reaction, where one event caused a future event to happen. One strategy for locating the causes of events is to work your way backwards. Then, you start with the end. So, let's start with Wangari winning the Nobel Peace Prize as the final box in our timeline and then look back in the text for what immediately caused this to happen.

Try | Guide students to quickly rehearse what they need to learn and do in preparation for practice

Now that we've started this timeline together by identifying a final effect and reading for causes, you're going to complete it on your own/with a

partner. I'm going to reread select sections of the text aloud. (You can also provide copies of selected passages for students to reread on their own.)

Guide students to add events to the timeline and discuss cause and effect relationships between them.

Clarify | Briefly restate today's teaching objective and explain the practice task(s)

In your independent practice today, complete a Timeline Organizer for your independent reading book. You'll want to begin with the end, or identify the final event and then work backwards to identify what caused it to happen over time. Continue to ask yourself what caused this to happen. Then you can look for other events (effects) and what caused them to happen (causes). Below your timeline, describe at least one cause and effect relationship in a few sentences or more.

Practice | Students work independently or in small groups to apply today's teaching objective

Students will complete a Timeline Organizer for their own independent reading book on which they list multiple events in their text and look for cause and effect relationships. **ELL** Provide Comprehensible Input—Organizers. A timeline organizer is another strong graphic for your ELLs. If needed, you can preteach the concept of a timeline in a small group, using their lives as an example.

Goal	Low-Tech	High-Tech
Students will create timelines to illustrate cause and effect of historical events.	Students can use the Timeline Organizer to plot what happened in sequential order.	Students can create digital, interactive timelines using tools such as: Dippity, Timetoast, or Viewzi. These tools allow anyone to insert events in order and create dynamic, eye-popping timelines.

Wrap Up Check understanding as you guide students to briefly share what they have learned and produced today

Have students share a few cause/effect relationships from their timelines and why they chose those events. Collect this work and use it as an informal assessment to determine your students' understanding of causal relationships and how events happen over time. **ELL** Assess for Content and Language Understanding—Formative Assessment.

Milestone Performance Assessment

Cause and Effect across Time

Use this checklist to assess student work on Timeline Organizer.

Standards Alignment: RI.4.1, RI.4.3, RI.4.5, RI.4.7

	Achieved	Notes
Identify when events occur in a story on the timeline.		
Identify cause and effect relationships on the timeline.		

Reading Lesson 6

▶ Teaching Objective

Readers can talk about cause and effect relationships in texts by using transitional words and phrases.

▶ Standards Alignment

RI.4.3, RI.4.5, RI.4.10, SL.4.1a–d, SL.4.6, L.4.1, L.4.6

▶ Materials

- Read-alouds used so far, such as *Seeds of Change* and *Baseball Saved Us*
- Cause and Effect Talking Points chart produced by the teacher for this lesson

▶ To the Teacher

This lesson is an opportunity to teach your students how to talk to one another about the cause and effect relationships they see in the texts they've read so far. Modeling for students the language they need to discuss complex texts will help ensure that they are more capable of using the language of cause and effect in their discussions.

▶ Procedure

Warm Up Gather the class to set the stage for today's learning

Yesterday we learned about how authors use signal words to help us identify cause and effect moments in the texts we read. Did you know there are signal words we can use with each other when we are discussing the causes and effects of the historical moments we've been reading about.

CAUSE and Effect,
using
transitional words and phrases

- Why would people from Japanese descent be taken to special camps here in America during WWII?

Since the Japanese attacked Pearl Harbor, the American government felt it could not trust Japanese Americans.

- Why did the American Japanese people need baseball in their camp?

Being that the American Japanese people were away from their jobs, they needed a positive activity to keep them busy.

- How did baseball help mend segregation for Japanese Americans?

Seeing that the Japanese Americans loved their country's favorite past time brought people together.

---

would people from Japanese descent be taken to special camps here in America during World War II? These are complicated questions about history and talking about them can help us better understand.

Just as we had signal words charted to help us identify special words in our reading, we have some phrases that can help us talk about the causes and effects in history we've been reading about.

Share with students the Cause and Effect Talking Points chart. Review all of the phrases and provide sample sentences. Emphasize with students that these discussions are informal but that these phrases will help keep their discussion centered on cause and effect. (SL.4.6)

Cause and Effect Talking Points Chart

Cause	for the reason that, being that, in view of, because of the fact, seeing that, due to the fact that, since
Effect	as a result of, because of this, as a consequence, so much so that, therefore, thus

Let's take one of my questions about a story we've read so far and work together to talk about an answer using our Cause and Effect Talking Points chart. One of my questions was "Why would anyone be opposed to Wangari's planting of trees?" Let's use our talking points to help us craft an answer. Watch as I choose a phrase that helps me better explain this effect: Many political figures and people in business profited from the way the land was before. As a result of Wangari's trees and the Green Belt Movement, the land was changing, so these people were opposed to Wangari's efforts. This statement helps explain more about why people were upset. ELL Enable Language Production—Listening and Speaking. Think about the stage of language acquisition that your ELL is in when modeling the talking points. You can give more novice English speakers simpler and more extended sentence prompts. (e.g., "I think that _____ because _____.")

Teach | Model what students need to learn and do

Today I will teach you some important words to use in conversations with one another about the events in history we've been reading about. There have been some complicated ideas we've been reading about. You might have been wondering why would anyone be opposed to Wangari's planting of trees? Why

---

Try | Guide students to quickly rehearse what they need to learn and do in preparation for practice

Have students use phrases from the Cause and Effect Talking Points chart to generate other answers to the same question. Have students share the phrase they used to form their ideas.

far this lesson set. Listen in on these partnerships to see who is using the phrases successfully.

Wrap Up Check understanding as you guide students to briefly share what they have learned and produced today

Have students share one thing they discussed or one phrase they used from the Cause and Effect Talking Points chart.

> *It is our choices that show what we truly are, far more than our abilities.*
>
> —J. K. Rowling

Clarify Briefly restate today's teaching objective and explain the practice task(s)

Now it's time for students to either continue discussing that text or another one you've read as a group. The independent practice is continuing the conversation. Once students have discussed your questions, encourage them to form their own and use the talking points to respond to one another's inquiries.

In your independent practice today, you are going to talk to one another about these complex texts. You may continue your conversation by posing questions you have about *Seeds of Change* and responding to one another, or think about another text such as *Baseball Saved Us* and "Why would people of Japanese descent be taken to special camps here in America during World War II?"

Practice Students work independently or in small groups to apply today's teaching objective

Students will continue to use the Cause and Effect Talking Points chart to ask and answer questions about the complex historical texts you've read so

Reading Lesson 7

▶ Teaching Objective

Readers can write summaries that explain the cause and effect.

▶ Standards Alignment

RI.4.1, RI.4.5, RI.4.9, RI.4.10, W.4.2a–d, W.4.4, W.4.6, W.4.10, SL.4.1a, SL.4.1b, SL.4.2, L.4.6

▶ Materials

- Graphic organizers completed from Reading Lessons 4 and 5
- Copies of Summary Plan Sheet from Appendix 4.5

Close Reading Opportunity

▶ To the Teacher

This lesson builds on previous lessons by having students use their graphic organizers to generate a summary of the historical text they've been reading independently. At this point, we are asking students to put their ideas in writing by creating summaries that explain the causes and effects of historical events. Learning to summarize what they've read is an important skill for fourth graders. This lesson is designed to give students the language they need to provide a topic sentence that introduces the historical event, supporting details that explain the causes and further effects, and a concluding sentence.

▶ Procedure

Warm Up Gather the class to set the stage for today's learning

For this Warm Up, we use metaphors like an Oreo or hamburger to help students remember all of the parts of a paragraph that they need to write a complete summary. This is introduced in third grade in this book series and continues through fifth grade to give students a common language around the structure of a paragraph. The cookies or buns are like the topic sentence and concluding sentence, and the filling or burger ingredients are like the details.

Did you know that Oreo cookies and paragraphs have a lot in common? What are the parts of an Oreo cookie? There is a top cookie, a bottom cookie, and the filling in the middle. If we were missing any of those ingredients it wouldn't be an Oreo. Like Oreo cookies, paragraphs have a topic sentence in the beginning, a concluding sentence at the end, and details in the middle. Our topic sentence is like the top cookie. The details are like the creamy filling. The concluding sentence is like the bottom cookie.

Teach   Model what students need to learn and do

Remind students of the graphic organizers they created in Reading Lessons 4 and 5. Those will help provide the details they'll need to write their summary paragraphs.

Today, we are going to write paragraphs that summarize the historical events we've been reading about and the causes and effects of those events. Let's review a sample summary I've written about *Baseball Saves Us* that focuses on the causes and effects of the Japanese internment camp on our main character, Shorty.

In the book *Baseball Saved Us*, the characters are in a Japanese internment camp during World War II. They were placed in the camp because they were of Japanese descent and America was fighting Japan during the war. As a result, the American government was unfairly suspicious of anyone Japanese. One of the effects of the camp experience was that Shorty's father started a baseball league. This gave Shorty and the others something to focus on that gave them pride. When he returned from the camp Shorty experienced a lot of continued discrimination because he was Japanese. In the end, he showed the other kids that he was a great baseball player.

What are some of the things I did to create my summary?

- Topic sentence: introduced book title and historical event
- Details: explained causes of an important event (WWII, suspicious of Japanese Americans)
- Details: explained further effects (the baseball league is formed)
- Conclusion: explained the end of the story
- Used transitional phrases like *As a result* and *In the end*

Try   Guide students to quickly rehearse what they need to learn and do in preparation for practice

Now it's your turn to try. Using your graphic organizer from our previous lesson, I want you to take notes on what you will include in your topic sentence, details, and conclusion. **ELL** Provide Comprehensible Input—Organizers. This organizer can help ELLs see the connections between their thinking and justifying their reasoning. You can scaffold in by helping extend ideas/sentences based on language proficiency by checking in on the organizer.

Summary Plan Sheet

Plan Your Topic Sentence: Include the book title and the main event that happened in your text.	
Details about Causes: What caused this event to happen?	
Details about Effects: What things happened as a result of the main event?	
Conclusion: What finally happened in the end?	

Clarify   Briefly restate today's teaching objective and explain the practice task(s)

In your independent practice today, I want you to use your notes to generate a summary about the historical text you've been reading. Remember to start with a topic sentence, provide details that explain the causes and effects, and include a conclusion that explains the end of the story.

Practice Students work independently or in small groups to apply today's teaching objective

Students will create summaries that introduce the historical event, its causes, further effects, and how the story ends.

Wrap Up Check understanding as you guide students to briefly share what they have learned and produced today

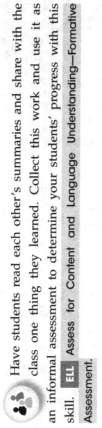 Have students read each other's summaries and share with the class one thing they learned. Collect this work and use it as an informal assessment to determine your students' progress with this skill. **ELL** Assess for Content and Language Understanding—Formative Assessment.

Milestone Performance Assessment

Summaries

Use this checklist to assess student summaries of effect and cause relationships.

Standards Alignment: W.4.2a–d, W.4.4, W.4.6, W.4.10, SL.4.2

	Achieved	Notes
Plan a topic sentence with main event.		
Plan supporting details about causes.		
Plan supporting details about effects.		
Plan a conclusion.		

Reading Lesson 8

▶ Teaching Objective

Readers can create cause and effect posters or book trailers to retell a historical moment graphically.

Close Reading Opportunity

▶ Standards Alignment

RI.4.1, RI.4.9, RI.4.10, W.4.4, W.4.6, W.4.10, SL.4.1a–d, L.4.1, L.4.6

▶ Materials

- Posters or digital tools such as *Animoto* or *iMovie* for animated book trailers
- Poster/Trailer Plan Sheet (see Appendix 4.6)

▶ To the Teacher

Today's lesson is an opportunity for your students to think about how they want to present their findings from their independent reading graphically with the class. Their graphic organizers and summaries will be useful resources for them to consult as they think about the images and text they want to use to share the causes and effects of the historical moments they read about. If you choose to create book trailers with your students, there are many wonderful digital resources online for viewing powerful existing trailers such as *Book Trailers for Readers, Kidlit Book Trailers, Book Trailers for All,* and *YouTube.*

Whether you are creating posters or book trailers, this lesson will help students storyboard their ideas to convey the major causes and effects they read about. In creating book trailers with your fourth graders, think about whether you want them to collect still images, create captions, and possibly add their own voice or music.

▼ Procedure

Warm Up Gather the class to set the stage for today's learning

Gather your students to congratulate them on their great reading and writing about reading so far in this lesson set. They have closely analyzed texts about complex historical events and have written summaries that explain the causes and effects of historical events. Now they have the chance to consider how to effectively use images and text to share their findings with one another.

Congratulations, fourth graders, on your close reading of complex historical events. You've read carefully noticing the causes and effects of important historical events. Your summaries taught me so much about why these events occurred and what exactly happened. Now it's time for you to share your findings with one another by creating book posters/trailers. Book posters/trailers are a way for publishers to grab the attention of potential readers and encourage them to read the book. Do you think others should read your book? Why? Do you think others will pick up your book and read it? If you want lots of people to read it, you need to promote it!

©Jacek Chabraszewski/Fotolia

succinct text to match the images. Provide your students with examples here by searching for book posters online or on the book trailer sites recommended. Then ask,

What grabbed your attention? Did it make you want to read the book? What did the author tell about the story? What did the author leave out? Why do you think the author didn't explain everything?

For this lesson set, your students will want to capture the heart of the historical event they read about, the causes and effects. Choosing a single detailed image (in the case of posters) or series of images (for book trailers) is the place to start. Then, you want to help your students generate text to match.

Today, I will show you how we can plan and then create our own book posters/trailers. The first step is focusing on the most important event of your story. What powerful image could you use to represent this event? What caused this event to happen? What image could represent that?

Now let's plan our text. We want our posters/trailers to say something about the causes and effects we read about.

Teach Model what students need to learn and do

When people create book posters/trailers, they need to capture the heart of the story through a single detailed image or series of images as well as

🎯 See Appendix 4.6 to formulate a plan.

ELL Provide Comprehensible Input—Organizers & Visuals. Visuals are a strong, nonverbal pathway for ELLs to communicate their thinking. If students are not able to use words in the organizer to describe, have them start by sketching a visual, then help them in bulleting the words that describe what they are thinking. They can use GoogleTranslate to start brainstorming in their native language, then translate this thinking to English. Or they can use Google Images to find images that match their thinking in either language.

Try Guide students to quickly rehearse what they need to learn and do in preparation for practice

Have students complete the book poster/trailer planning sheet on their own and then share it with a partner. Direct partners to share a compliment and at least one suggestion. Post these guiding questions for their conversation:

- Does the image capture the viewers' attention?
- Does each image do a good job representing an event?
- Is the text clear and succinct?
- Can you determine the causes and effects?

Clarify Briefly restate today's teaching objective and explain the practice task(s)

In your independent practice today you are going to move from your planning to the creation of your poster or trailer. Make sure the heart of your work is capturing the causes and effects of the historical event you read about. That can be achieved through the images or the text.

Goal	Low-Tech	High-Tech
Students will present the causes and effects from their reading in graphic form.	Students can create posters that show the cause and effect relationships from their reading.	Students can create book trailers using digital images and text to explain the cause and effect relationships from their reading using tools such as Animoto or iMovie.

Practice Students work independently or in small groups to apply today's teaching objective

Students will move from the planning stage to creating their posters/trailers. This may take several sessions for students to

complete. If you are creating book trailers you may consider a follow-up lesson on the use of music or sound to build suspense and further excitement for reading the book. Collect this work and use it as an informal assessment to determine your students' progress with this skill. **ELL** Assess for Content and Language Understanding—Formative Assessment.

Milestone Performance Assessment

Creating a Poster/Trailer

Use this checklist to assess student ability to effectively use images to convey a historical idea.
Standards Alignment: W.4.4, W.4.6, W.4.10

	Achieved	Notes
Find suitable images to represent each historical event.		
Craft a poster/trailer that clearly illustrates cause and effect relationships.		

Wrap Up Check understanding as you guide students to briefly share what they have learned and produced today

Ask students to share how they decided on the image(s) and text for their work.

Reading Lesson 9

▼ Teaching Objective

Readers can ask each other questions about what happened and why in texts they read.

▼ Standards Alignment

RI.4.1, RI.4.2, RI.4.3, RI.4.5, RI.4.10, SL.4.1a–d, SL.4.2, SL.4.3, L.4.1, L.4.6

Close Reading
Opportunity

▼ Materials

- Sample book poster or trailer selected by the teacher from online sources or elsewhere
- The Inquiring Minds Ask Questions list
- Student book posters or trailers

▼ To the Teacher

Now that your students have read complex historical texts, written about events and their causes, and created visual displays that show their thinking, it's time for them to ask questions of one another for deeper understanding of the historical moments that have centered their reading. This will help students determine if they want to read texts that their fellow classmates have been reading and generate enthusiasm for narrative nonfiction reading to continue when this lesson set is complete.

▼ Procedure

Warm Up   Gather the class to set the stage for today's learning

Remind your students of the good work they've done as history detectives through asking what happened and why, and how they have worked hard to present their findings to one another . . . and that their exciting work continues.

History detectives, you've worked hard to read stories about history that leave us with more questions than answers. You know that historians often start their wonderings by asking, "What happened?" and "Why?" but the questioning doesn't stop there. Now that you've completed your book posters/trailers, it's time for us to share them with one another and ask questions of one another to find out more.

Teach   Model what students need to learn and do

Share with students a book trailer about a historical text such as Scholastic's *Ruby Bridges Goes to School*. While watching, pause to model the kinds of questions you are asking to probe what the cause and effect relationships were and think about the decisions the creator made in developing the book trailer. As a low-tech option use one of your students' book poster/trailer to model the questioning.   **ELL**   Frontload the Lesson—Build Background. For students who need verbal support, consider previewing and practicing these question prompts so that they have understanding and fluency before using them in the whole group and with their partners.

While we're watching this book trailer about an important historical event, listen for how I ask questions about what I'm wondering. Notice the kinds of questions I'm asking as I dig deeper into what happened and why. Here are some samples.

Inquiring Minds Ask Questions

- What was the most important event?
- What caused it to happen?
- What were the resulting effects?
- What happened in the end?
- What images did the creator include?
- How did the creator decide to include these images?
- What was the most powerful part of the poster/trailer?

tions your classmates ask you about the book, but today the questions are even more important than the answers.

Practice Students work independently or in small groups to apply today's teaching objective

Students will ask inquiring questions as their classmates share their book posters/trailers. Encourage everyone to ask at least one question out loud over the course of the sharing.

Wrap Up Check understanding as you guide students to briefly share what they have learned and produced today

Have students turn and tell a partner another question they had that they were unable to ask out loud today.

> Educating the mind without educating the heart is no education at all.
>
> —Aristotle

Try Guide students to quickly rehearse what they need to learn and do in preparation for practice

First, have students paraphrase what they viewed (SL.4.2), then have students generate their own inquiring questions about the shared product and record them in writing. Have students jot them down or turn and talk to a partner before sharing them aloud with the group. This will hold everyone accountable if you do not have time for everyone to share aloud with the whole class. **ELL** Enable Language Production—Listening & Speaking, Increasing Interaction. In order to help facilitate speaking and communication, you can pair speakers together based on language and proficiency. For example, you could partner a Spanish speaker with someone who speaks Spanish and English to model language, as well as offer the option to use native language if needed.

Clarify Briefly restate today's teaching objective and explain the practice task(s)

Emphasize with students that today they are going to identify the reasons and evidence that a classmate gives to explain the cause and effect relationships in the books they read and that they are then going to add on to their comments by posing questions. (SL.4.3)

Today you are going to listen to your classmates share their book posters or trailers. Your job is to ask questions of one another to dig deeper into what happened and why, and the decisions that the creator made when developing this product. You may not know the answers to all of the ques-

Reading Lesson 10

▶ **Teaching Objective**

Readers reflect on their learning by responding to Core Questions (you can find the Core Questions on page 78).

▶ **Standards Alignment**

RI.4.1, RI.4.10, W.4.4, W.4.10, SL.4.1a–d, L.4.1, L.4.6

▶ **Materials**

- Charting supplies or an interactive whiteboard
- Method for students to create a written reflection

▶ **To the Teacher**

Reflection is a crucial element to this work. It provides students with the necessary time to think about and articulate their own learning as well as develop and express their identity as readers and writers. Helping students pause and think about what they've learned and what they've enjoyed can have long-lasting effects. This is something you may also want to discuss with families when they visit your classroom or through newsletters or other communication you send home. Emphasize with students that reading about history and thinking about the past is a lifelong process and that they will continue to have questions about moments from history, but now they have some tools for reading like a history detective, asking the questions "What happened?" and "Why?" to find answers all on their own.

▶ **Procedure**

Warm Up | **Gather the class to set the stage for today's learning**

I am so impressed by all of the learning you've done around complex historical readings and the causes and effects of moments from history. Plus, we've learned a lot about how to discuss complicated events in history and

Close Reading Opportunity

what caused them using strong language and supporting our thinking with relevant reasons and evidence. I'm really proud of all of you!

Teach | **Model what students need to learn and do**

Today I want us to take some time and reflect on everything we've learned about reading about moments in history. One thing we worked on was identifying multiple causes and effects and how to discuss these issues with each other. Now that we've finished this work with book posters/trailers, I want us to think a bit about where else we think we can use the skills we've learned.

Try | **Guide students to quickly rehearse what they need to learn and do in preparation for practice**

Lead the class in a discussion around this question. As the discussion unfolds, begin to craft a shared response to the question. **ELL** Provide Comprehensible Input—Models. Ideally, your class response should name other contexts for students to transfer this learning. Some might be watching the news, considering environmental issues, doing a science lab, and reading stories.

Clarify | **Briefly restate today's teaching objective and explain the practice task(s)**

It's important to take some time to reflect on your learning at the end of a lesson set. This helps make what you learn stay in your brain so you can use it later! I want to know what you have learned about yourself as a reader through this process. Today, you are going to write a response to your choice of one of our Core Questions (the Core Questions are on page 78).

Post the questions in a central location for students to refer back to as they work.

Practice | **Students work independently or in small groups to apply today's teaching objective**

Students individually craft responses to the Core Questions posed. **ELL** Enable Language Production—Reading and Writing.

texts they have read to support their thinking. Collect student work to assess their understanding of historical nonfiction. Let this information help you determine where students need additional guidance or support.

Milestone Performance Assessment

Reflection

Use this checklist to assess student written reflection on the text.

Standards Alignment: RI.4.1, W.4.4, W.4.10

	Achieved	Notes
Craft responses to Core Questions posed.		
Use details from the text to support their ideas and thinking.		

Goal	Low-Tech	High-Tech
Students craft a written response to one or two reflection questions.	Students answer the questions using pencil and paper. Students share their responses orally. You could choose key snippets of conversation to write up and create a reflection bulletin board.	Students draft a response on a Word document, practicing their keyboarding skills. They can share this document with you by dragging it into a shared folder on Dropbox or via email. In addition, students can post their reflections to a class blog to share with their peers. As homework, students could comment thoughtfully on the reflections of two (or more) of their classmates.

Wrap Up Check understanding as you guide students to briefly share what they have learned and produced today

After students have had sufficient time to complete their responses, call the class together to share their ideas. Lead a discussion centered on student responses to these questions. Encourage students to use details from the

Writing Lessons

The Core I.D.E.A. / Daily Writing Instruction At a Glance table on the next page highlights the teaching objectives and standards alignment for all 10 writing lessons across the four stages of the lesson set (Introduce, Define, Extend, and Assess). It also indicates which lessons contain special features to support ELLs, technology, speaking and listening, and formative ("Milestone") assessments.

The Core Ready Writing Rubric that follows next is designed to help you record each student's overall understanding across four levels of achievement as it relates to the lesson set goals. We recommend that you use this rubric at the end of the lesson set as a performance-based assessment tool. Use the Milestone Performance Assessments and checklists as tools to help you gauge student progress toward these goals, and reteach and differentiate as needed. See the foundational book, *Be Core Ready: Powerful, Effective Steps to Implementing and Achieving the Common Core State Standards*, for more information about the Core Ready Reading and Writing Rubrics.

Grade 4

The Core I.D.E.A. / Daily Writing Instruction at a Glance

Grade 4   What Happened and Why: Studying Cause and Effect through Events in History

Instructional Stages	Lesson	Teaching Objective	Core Standards	Special Features
Introduce: notice, explore, collect, note, immerse, surround, record, share	1	Writers conduct research from historical "headlines."	RI.4.1 • RI.4.2 • RI.4.6 • RI.4.10 • W.4.4 W.4.7 • W.4.10 • SL.4.1a • SL.4.1b • L.4.6	Close Reading ELL Tech
Define: name, identify, outline, clarify, select, plan	2	Researchers of history ask what happened and why.	RI.4.1 • RI.4.5 • RI.4.10 • W.4.4 • W.4.7 W.4.10 • SL.4.1a–d • L.4.1 • L.4.6	Close Reading
	3	Researchers take notes to better understand the time period.	RI.4.1 • RI.4.2 • RI.4.6 • RI.4.9 • RI.4.10 W.4.4 • W.4.7 • W.4.10 • SL.4.1a–d • L.4.6	Close Reading ELL Milestone Assessment S&L Tech
	4	Researchers organize their notes and come to their own conclusions.	RI.4.9 • RI.4.10 • W.4.4 • W.4.7 • W.4.10 SL.4.1a–d • L.4.1 • L.4.6	ELL Milestone Assessment
Extend: try, experiment, attempt, approximate, practice, explain, revise, refine	5	Writers plan diary entries that spotlight a historical "headline."	W.4.4 • W.4.7 • W.4.10 • SL.4.1a–d SL.4.2 • L.4.1 • L.4.6	ELL Milestone Assessment S&L Tech
	6	Writers include factual information from the time period.	RI.4.1 • RI.4.6 • RI.4.10 • W.4.2a • W.4.2b W.4.2d • W.4.4 • W.4.6 • W.4.10 • SL.4.6 L.4.6	Close Reading ELL Milestone Assessment
	7	Writers use the five senses to vividly describe the event.	RI.4.10 • W.4.2b • W.4.4 • W.4.6 • W.4.10 L.4.6	ELL
	8	Writers use signal words to help readers identify cause and effect.	RI.4.10 • W.4.2c • W.4.4 • W.4.6 • W.4.10 SL.4.1a–d • L.4.1 • L.4.2 • L.4.3 • L.4.6	
	9	Writers revise for cause and effect and edit for conventions of standard English.	W.4.5 • W.4.6 • W.4.10 • SL.4.6 • L.4.1 L.4.2 • L.4.3 • L.4.6	ELL Milestone Assessment
Assess: reflect, conclude, connect, share, recognize, respond	10	Writers present their diary entries and reflect on what they've learned about research and writing.	W.4.10 • SL.4.1a–d • SL.4.4 • L.4.1 • L.4.6	S&L

Grade 4 Core Ready Writing Rubric

Lesson Set Goal	Emerging	Approaching	Achieving	Exceeding	Standards Alignment
Take and logically organize notes to record the causes and effects of a moment from history in preparation for writing.	Student shows little or no evidence of success in taking and organizing notes to record the causes and effects of a moment from history in preparation for writing.	Student shows some evidence of taking and logically organizing notes to record the causes and effects of a moment from history in preparation for writing.	Student takes and logically organizes notes to record the causes and effects of a moment from history in preparation for writing.	Student takes highly effective notes in a very organized and clear manner to record the causes and effects of a moment from history in preparation for writing.	RI.4.1 RI.4.2 RI.4.9 RI.4.10 W.4.4 W.4.7 W.4.10 SL.4.2 L.4.6
Write a diary entry that examines a historical period with an introduction that introduces a topic, clearly, groups related information in paragraphs and sections, and includes a concluding statement or section related to the information or explanation presented.	Student struggles to write a diary entry that examines a historical period. Required elements are ineffective, incomplete, or missing. Major inaccuracies may be present.	Student attempts to write a diary entry that examines a historical period. Some required elements may be missing or underdeveloped. Some inaccuracies may be present.	Student writes a diary entry that examines a historical period with all required elements present. All elements are basically effective, but development of some elements may be uneven. Any inaccuracies are minor.	Student writes an organized and thorough diary entry that examines a historical period in which all required elements are present, well developed, and highly effective.	W.4.2a W.4.2e W.4.4 W.4.6 W.4.7 W.4.10 L.4.6
Develop the topic with facts, concrete details, or other information and examples related to the topic.	Student demonstrates little or no success in developing the topic with facts, concrete details, or other information and examples related to the topic.	Student demonstrates some evidence of developing the topic with facts, concrete details, or other information and examples related to the topic.	Student successfully develops the topic with facts, concrete details, or other information and examples related to the topic.	Student demonstrates an exceptional understanding of how to develop the topic with facts, concrete details, and other relevant information and examples related to the topic.	RI.4.1 RI.4.2 RI.4.5 RI.4.9 RI.4.10 W.4.2b W.4.4 W.4.10 L.4.6
Link ideas within categories of information using words and phrases (e.g., another, also, for example, because)	Student shows little or no evidence of linking ideas within categories of information using words and phrases.	Student has some success linking ideas within categories of information using words and phrases. May use some words and phrases incorrectly or rely on only very basic ones.	Student successfully attempts to link ideas within categories of information using a variety of words and phrases.	Student displays exceptional ability to link ideas within categories of information using a wide variety of words and phrases. Makes use of some advanced words and phrases.	RI.4.1 RI.4.4 RI.4.10 W.4.2c W.4.10 SL.4.4 L.4.6

Lesson Set Goal	Emerging	Approaching	Achieving	Exceeding	Standards Alignment
With guidance and support from peers and adults, develop and strengthen writing as needed by planning, revising, and editing.	Student makes little or no attempt to develop and strengthen writing through planning, revising, and editing.	Student attempts to develop and strengthen writing as needed by planning, revising, and editing. Writing may still contain significant errors or lack clarity.	Student develops and strengthens writing as needed by planning, revising, and editing. Some areas of the planning, revision, and editing may be more developed than others.	Student extensively develops and strengthens writing by planning, revising, and editing as needed. Few or no errors or lapses of clarity evident.	W.4.5
Refer to details and examples in a text when explaining what the text says explicitly and when drawing inferences from the text.	Student shows little or no evidence of active, purposeful reading or searching the text for specific information and evidence. Student makes little or no attempt to provide details and examples when explaining what the text says explicitly. Is unable to draw inferences from the text.	Student shows some evidence of active, purposeful reading and searching the text for specific information and evidence. Student may provide some details and examples, with marginal accuracy, when explaining what the text says explicitly and when drawing inferences from the text.	Student shows solid evidence of active, purposeful reading and searching the text for specific information and evidence. Student usually provides appropriate details and examples when explaining what the text says explicitly and when drawing inferences from the text.	Student demonstrates exceptional evidence of active, purposeful reading and searching the text for specific information and evidence. Student provides accurate, explicit and thoughtful details and examples when explaining what the text says explicitly and when drawing inferences from the text.	RI.4.1
By the end of the year, proficiently read and comprehend a variety of informational texts in the grades 4–5 text complexity band, with scaffolding as needed at the high end of the range.	Student shows little or no evidence of reading and comprehending texts appropriate for the grade 4 text complexity band at this point of the school year.	Student shows inconsistent evidence of independently and proficiently reading and comprehending texts appropriate for the grade 4 text complexity band at this point of the school year.	Student shows solid evidence of independently and proficiently reading and comprehending texts appropriate for the grade 4 text complexity band.	Student shows solid evidence of independently and proficiently reading and comprehending texts above the grade 4 text complexity band.	RI.4.10
Write routinely over extended time frames (time for research, reflection, and revision) and shorter time frames (a single sitting or a day or two) for a range of discipline-specific tasks, purposes, and audiences.	Student shows little or no evidence of writing routinely for short or long time frames for a range of discipline-specific tasks, purposes, and audiences.	Student shows some evidence of writing routinely for short and long time frames for a range of discipline-specific tasks, purposes, and audiences.	Student shows solid evidence of writing routinely for short and long time frames for a range of discipline-specific tasks, purposes, and audiences.	Student shows exceptional evidence of consistently and accurately writing for short and long time frames for a range of discipline-specific tasks, purposes, and audiences.	W.4.10

Lesson Set Goal	Emerging	Approaching	Achieving	Exceeding	Standards Alignment
In collaborative discussions, demonstrate evidence of preparation for discussion and exhibit responsibility to the rules and roles of conversation.	In collaborative discussions, student comes unprepared and often disregards the rules and roles of conversation.	In collaborative discussions, student's preparation may be evident but ineffective or inconsistent. May occasionally disregard the topic to explore ideas under discussion. Usually observes the rules and roles of conversation.	In collaborative discussions, student prepares adequately and draws on the preparation and other information about the topic to explore ideas under discussion. Usually observes the rules and roles of conversation.	In collaborative discussions, student arrives extremely well prepared for discussions and draws on the preparation and other information about the topic to explore ideas under discussion. Always observes the rules and roles of conversation.	SL.4.1a SL.4.1b
In collaborative discussions, share and develop ideas in a manner that enhances understanding of topic. Contribute and respond to the content of the conversation in a productive and focused manner.	Student shows little or no evidence of engaging in collaborative discussions and makes little or no attempt to ask and answer questions, stay on topic, link comments to the remarks of others, or to explain his or her own ideas and understanding in light of the discussion.	Student shows some evidence of engaging in collaborative discussions and, with marginal success, attempts to ask questions to check understanding of information presented, to stay on topic, link comments to the remarks of others, and explain his and her own ideas and understanding in light of the discussion.	Student engages in a range of collaborative discussions and asks questions to check understanding of information presented. Stays on topic most of the time, frequently links his or her comments to the remarks of others, and explains his or her own ideas and understanding in light of the discussion.	Student effectively and consistently engages in a range of collaborative discussions and asks high-level questions to check understanding of information presented. Always stays on topic and, with great insight and attention to the comments of others, links his or her own comments to the remarks of others, and explains his or her ideas and understanding in light of the discussion.	SL.4.1c SL.4.1d
Demonstrate knowledge of standard English and its conventions.	Student demonstrates little or no knowledge of standard English and its conventions.	Student demonstrates some evidence of knowledge of standard English and its conventions.	Student consistently demonstrates knowledge of standard English and its conventions.	Student demonstrates an exceptional understanding of standard English and its conventions. Use of conventions is sophisticated for grade level and accurate.	L.4.1 L.4.2 L.4.3
Acquire and accurately use grade-appropriate conversational, general academic, and domain-specific vocabulary and phrases.	Student shows little or no evidence of the acquisition or use of grade-appropriate conversational and academic language.	Student shows some evidence of the acquisition and use of grade-appropriate conversational and academic language.	Student shows solid evidence of the acquisition and use of grade-appropriate conversational and academic language.	Student shows a high level of sophistication and precision when using grade-appropriate conversational and academic language.	L.4.6

Note: See the Core Ready Rubrics chart in the Walk Through for descriptions of category headers.

Writing Lesson 1

▶ Teaching Objective

Writers conduct research from historical "headlines."

Close Reading Opportunity

▶ Standards Alignment

RI.4.1, RI.4.2, RI.4.6, RI.4.10, W.4.4, W.4.7, W.4.10, SL.4.1a, SL.4.1b, L.4.6

▶ Materials

- Student research folders
- Copies of headlines and articles from time periods/topics you'd like students to choose from
- Copies of Historical Headlines Leave Me Wondering (see Appendix 4.7)

▶ To the Teacher

Today is the start of an exciting set of lessons. Not only will your students conduct research around a topic that matters to them, but over the next several weeks they will grow more confident and capable as independent researchers. This lesson set has great power to help transform students to think of themselves as independent learners and researchers. Today's lesson is about generating anticipation for this process.

▶ Procedure

Warm Up Gather the class to set the stage for today's learning

Gather your class to introduce this new lesson set centered on historical research. Headlines from recent or past history are one way to get students interested in the research they're about to embark on.

Fourth graders, today you begin the very exciting journey of researching a historical topic that matters to you. Did you know that moments from history can be found in the headlines newspapers create to grab their readers' attention

to the news of the day? Let's take a look at some headlines from history to think about historical topics you want to research and dig more deeply into to find out what happened and why.

Teach Model what students need to learn and do

Gather headlines and articles for students from either the newspaper or Internet based on the history topics you'd like them to choose from. Some of our favorites are from Time for Kids and include:

"Sitting Down to Take a Stand"

"A Double War"

"Obama Wins Nobel Peace Prize"

"Working for Peace"

"World Leaders Unite"

All of these articles capture our imagination and make me wonder, "What happened?" and "Why?" Some of these topics are about things that happened in the past that are difficult to understand because people did not treat each other with dignity or justice. Other topics are about hopeful moments in history.

Try Guide students to quickly rehearse what they need to learn and do in preparation for practice

Direct students to review headlines from history to determine topics they want to know more about.

Today you are going to review the headlines and articles I've gathered to determine a research topic for yourself. Choose the topic that you wonder the most about. This will become the topic in history you will research over the next few weeks. You will gather information, take notes, organize your ideas, and finally share with the class a diary entry as if you were living in that moment. Choose the topic that makes you most curious and leaves you with the question, What was it like to live at this time?

Clarify Briefly restate today's teaching objective and explain the practice task(s)

As you are reading these headlines and articles today, you are going to list your top three choices for your research topic. Underneath, explain why these are topics you most want to research. Make sure you explain what you are wondering about and what you hope to learn about living during this moment in time.

Practice Students work independently or in small groups to apply today's teaching objective

Students will read a sampling of historical headlines and news articles to determine research interests. To help explain their thinking, students will complete a Historic Headlines Leave Me Wondering sheet. Review these to determine topics your students will research. Consider the levels of texts you have available for each topic and how many students you want to research each topic.

Wrap Up Check understanding as you guide students to briefly share what they have learned and produced today

Have students share one of their top research choices and why they are interested in digging deeper into this topic. The articles should be the first item in your students' research folders, which they will use for collecting notes and organizing their write-ups. **ELL** Enable Language

---

Production—Reading & Writing: When gathering information, a low-tech option is providing bilingual dictionaries to help students transfer language to understand headlines. As a high-tech option, consider translation sites that translate a whole webpage to aide in language transfer and comprehension.

Goal	Low-Tech	High-Tech
Students will organize their research materials over the course of the research process.	Provide students with two-pocket portfolio folders, stickies or notecards, and copies of handouts.	Students can create a New Folder using a digital writing tool. In this folder they will keep notes using digital stickies or another note-taking tool and copies of materials you provide them with digitally.

> "The task of the modern educator is not to cut down jungles, but to irrigate deserts.
>
> —C. S. Lewis

Writing Lesson 2

▼ **Teaching Objective**

Researchers of history ask what happened and why.

🔍 Close Reading Opportunity

▼ **Standards Alignment**

RI.4.1, RI.4.5, RI.4.10, W.4.4, W.4.7, W.4.10, SL.4.1a–d, L.4.1, L.4.6

▼ **Materials**

- *We Are the Ship: The Story of Negro League Baseball* by Kadir Nelson
- Student research folders
- Research Road Map (see Appendix 4.8)
- Selection of informational texts for students to use in their research

▼ To the Teacher

Today is the first day your students will immerse themselves in the topic they've chosen. We encourage you to choose a class topic that you will use as a model throughout the research cycle. By modeling the reading, thinking, and writing strategies the lesson set focuses on, you'll be setting your students up for success in the weeks to come as independent researchers. This lesson mirrors Reading Lesson 2, which introduces the strategy of asking "What happened?" and "Why?" to identify cause and effect structures. In this lesson, the emphasis is on students using these questions to frame their research. In this writing lesson set, they are reading for information as well as for how these events shaped human lives so that they are able to imagine the perspective of someone who experienced it firsthand.

▼ Procedure

Warm Up Gather the class to set the stage for today's learning

Open today's lesson by reminding your students that they are history detectives and that their reading is now going to be focused on research to answer particular questions and understand what happened and why with greater understanding.

Our journey as history detectives has begun. We've chosen topics we're excited about and we're ready to dig into reading about these topics to understand these historic events more deeply. To place ourselves in the shoes of the people who lived through these historic events we can ask ourselves questions to understand what caused the events to occur and how they shaped human lives.

Teach Model what students need to learn and do

Introduce "What happened?" and "Why?" as framing questions for research about history. Refer to the Research Road Map as a guide.

Researchers who wonder about history often read with particular questions in mind. They ask themselves "What happened?" and "Why?" so that they can understand the causes of events and how human lives were affected. These questions also help researchers stay focused on the topic they want to learn more about. Today we are going to read with those questions in mind to understand the causes of the historic event we are studying. Let's take a look at our Research Road Map together to see where we are in our quest for understanding. So far, we've chosen topics. Now we are going to read with questions in mind. This will help us narrow our topic. Before you dive into your own topics we are going to study the story of Negro League Baseball together as a class.

You may want to choose a topic that aligns with your social studies curriculum. Our Core Texts offer suggestions for a wide range of history topics. If you teach using a different example, model your approach on the following description. Read the first few pages on the beginnings of the league. Then, model for students how to ask yourself "What happened?" and "Why?" in order to form a more specific question you want to find the answer to. "What happened to African-American baseball players?" and "Why did they form the Negro League baseball league?"

Try Guide students to quickly rehearse what they need to learn and do in preparation for practice

Display or give students access to page 9 of *We Are the Ship: The Story of Negro League Baseball*. This passage explains Andrew "Rube" Foster's important role in the formation of the league. What specific research questions do your students form as they read about Rube's role in the formation of the league? Remind them to focus on a "what happened" question and a "why" question.

Have students work in partnerships to consider the questions that this page helps us understand and answer. Have students record their "What happened?" and "Why?" questions. When students report, they should raise questions such as, "What did Rube do to start the league and keep it going?" and "Why did he think this was important?"

Clarify Briefly restate today's teaching objective and explain the practice task(s)

Remind students that today they'll be reading to help them form more specific research questions about "what happened" and "why" around the historical events they've chosen. They will also be writing down the specific research questions that their reading sparks in them as researchers.

Practice Students work independently or in small groups to apply today's teaching objective

Students will read history-based nonfiction texts to gather information. Continue to emphasize with students that their reading today should help them clarify the research questions they are asking.

Wrap Up Check understanding as you guide students to briefly share what they have learned and produced today

Have students share their "What happened?" and "Why?" questions.

Writing Lesson 3

▼ **Teaching Objective**

Researchers take notes to better understand the time period.

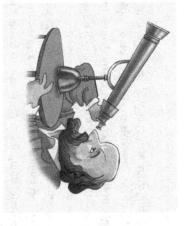

Close Reading Opportunity

▼ **Standards Alignment**

RI.4.1, RI.4.2, RI.4.6, RI.4.9, RI.4.10, W.4.4, W.4.7, W.4.10, SL.4.1a–d, L.4.6

▼ **Materials**

- Method for student note taking
- Student research folders
- Research Road Map (see Appendix 4.8)
- Selection of informational texts for students to use in their research
- Previously read text on the topic your class has chosen to study

▼ **To the Teacher**

Note taking is a skill that will help your students for years to come. Your students will feel quite grown up as they learn how to take notes and should

feel proud of this big step in their academic careers. In our lives we take notes when we have to write down information to remember it. We take notes about things that stand out to us when we're reading. Sometimes we write down full sentences, other times bullets. Sometimes we write down exact words or quotations; other times we paraphrase into our own words. Helping your students determine what type of note to write is a big step in the research process. To make the most of notes, students need to know how to take good notes.

▼ **Procedure**

Warm Up Gather the class to set the stage for today's learning

Refer to the Research Road Map to orient your students to today's important work on note taking. They will be adding to their understanding of what happened and why by reading for important details that will help them describe the event more vividly in their diary entries.

Researchers, we are off and away on our journey to understand what happened in history and why. Let's review our Research Road Map to determine where we are in today's work. So far, we've chosen topics and read with questions in mind. Now we're ready to take careful notes to be able to better understand important details that made these events from history so important to understand them and to those of us who have come after.

Teach Model what students need to learn and do

Orient your students to the importance of note taking and the procedure you would like them to follow for this work.

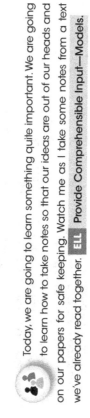

©AVAVA/Fotolia

> Today, we are going to learn something quite important. We are going to learn how to take notes so that our ideas are out of our heads and on our papers for safe keeping. Watch me as I take some notes from a text we've already read together. **ELL** Provide Comprehensible Input—Models.

Model for students how to use a heading that indicates the main idea for their notes at the top of the page. Then, use bullets to record evidence that supports the big idea. Model for students when you paraphrase in your own words, and when you want to make sure you have the exact language written down. A good rule of thumb is that when we are recording facts we need precise language. Subheadings and outlining will be part of the research process in future grades through our lesson sets. Right now you want to keep the note-taking process effective but simple for your fourth graders. Here's one way your modeling could unfold:

> Let's look back at what we underlined that helps us understand what happened to Negro League baseball players and why did the Negro league form.

Model using a single notecard for each new idea. This will help your students stay organized as they decide how they want to group information that goes together and as they make decisions about what to include in their diary entries.

- In mid-1860s most professional baseball teams had only white players
- Some African-Americans played but they were treated disgracefully
- In some states, African-Americans weren't allowed to play
- Some famous players like Welday and Moses Fleetwood Walker, Charlie Grant, and Pete Hill
- Most white ballplayers didn't want to play alongside African-Americans
- By the late 1800s, African-Americans began to disappear from pro baseball teams
- No written rule but after 1887 there weren't any more African-American players for almost 60 years
- Started own league

Continue modeling with students using page 5 of *We Are the Ship: The Story of Negro League Baseball*, which introduces Andrew "Rube" Foster:

- Rube was an old-time trick pitcher
- Knew a lot about baseball
- Demanding manager
- A well-equipped team with new uniforms, bats, and balls

Try Guide students to quickly rehearse what they need to learn and do in preparation for practice

Display or give students access to page 9 of *We Are the Ship*, which explains Andrew "Rube" Foster's important role in the formation of the league. Remind them of how you took notes earlier by focusing on the questions "what happened" and "why." Also provide your students with notecards. We suggest starting them off with 5 to 10 notecards, which will help limit how they select information worthy of notes.

Just as I took notes on the beginnings of the league, you are going to work with a partner to take notes on the page that explains more of how Rube became a key figure in starting the first Negro baseball league. Your challenge will be to stay focused on the most important information that explains what happened and why did it happen. More specifically, for this topic . . . What did Rube do and why did he do it? Decide what information is the most important to record.

Discuss and record using bullets.

Your bullets should be in mostly your own words. Remember to copy out of the book when you are trying to spell a key word correctly. When you get to the end of the section, reread your notes to make sure you've included everything you need to get the supporting details out of your head and onto your paper.

Have students work in partnerships to take notes on *why* Rube was important to the formation of the Negro Baseball League. Your students should generate notes similar to the following:

- Rube decided to organize an entire baseball league for African-Americans
- Wanted professional level of play equal to or better than the majors
- Wanted the whole league ready for the majors when integration came
- "We are the ship all else are the sea"
- Feb. 20, 1920, he called together owners of African-American baseball teams in the Midwest
- They all agreed on rules
- Named teams
- Rube kept the league going

Give students several minutes to practice note taking with a partner. Have partners share one note they took from the reading. As students share, record their notes on your larger set of class notes. This is a great opportunity to encourage the class to listen carefully to one another in order to build on each other's ideas, rather than repeat ideas that have already been shared. (SL.4.1b, SL.4.1c)

Clarify Briefly restate today's teaching objective and explain the practice task(s)

Remind students of how to take notes by putting a bullet on a single note-card to indicate an important piece of information tied to your key research question. There will be a lot of other information in their reading but the goal is to stay focused on "what happened" and "why."

Remember, friends, that researchers take careful notes to record what happened and why. Now that we've practiced with a partner I'd like you to choose one of the other readings from your research folder and practice taking notes on your own.

Goal	Low-Tech	High-Tech
Students take notes while they read to record their thinking for sharing with the larger group.	Students take handwritten pencil and paper notes. Consider using several sticky notes or index cards so that students can easily practice sorting their notes into logical categories later in these lesson sets.	There are a variety of high-tech options for student note taking. Consider the following ideas: • Students take their notes using digital Stickies (a program found on Apple computers). This application allows students to color code and visually organize their notes by category by dragging them around on the desktop. • Students use the iPad application Corkulous which allows them to create cork boards that include notes, sticky notes, photos, and To Do lists. These corkboards can be easily shared with you or their peers via email. • Students use a note-taking program such as Evernote, creating a new notebook for this project.

Practice Students work independently or in small groups to apply today's teaching objective

Students will read history-based nonfiction texts to gather information. Continue to emphasize with students that they should focus their notes on the questions "what happened" and "why."

Wrap Up · Check understanding as you guide students to briefly share what they have learned and produced today

 Have students share one notecard from their note-taking today. Remind them to choose something that they feel helps explain what happened and why. Collect this work and use it as an informal assessment to determine your students' progress with note taking. Use this Milestone Performance Assessment to determine what support your students need to be successful with this important skill. **ELL** Assess for Content and Language Understanding—Formative Assessment. This is an opportunity to assess the language supports that you will need to put into place with each student to help them in the writing process. In some cases, you may see language structures that need clarification or a model of using a particular part of speech.

Milestone Performance Assessment

Note Taking

Use this checklist to assess student note-taking skills.

Standards Alignment: RI.4.1, RI.4.2, RI.4.6, RI.4.9, W.4.4, W.4.7

	Achieved	Notes
Identify main points.		
Identify additional/ supporting points.		
Take notes independently.		
Work with a partner to take notes.		

Writing Lesson 4

▼ Teaching Objective

Researchers organize their notes and come to their own conclusions.

▼ Standards Alignment

RI.4.9, RI.4.10, W.4.4, W.4.7, W.4.10, SL.4.1a–d, L.4.1, L.4.6

▼ Materials

- Student notes
- Student research folders
- Research Road Map (see Appendix 4.8)
- Selection of informational texts for students to use in their research

▼ To the Teacher

Students may need more than one day to complete their note taking. This lesson works best when students have enough notes to start grouping them into logical categories. Once students have their notes compiled, they are ready to organize their notes to help them compose the body of their diary entry. In future grades, the categorization of notes will become more complex. For this lesson set, we are introducing the idea of categorization of notes, so it is best to stick to a simple system such as naming the category of notes, as in "The beginning of the league" and "Famous players." This grouping and naming process may be challenging for some students, but be assured that the thoughtful struggle they face will help them to develop a stronger understanding of how informational text is organized.

▼ Procedure

Warm Up   Gather the class to set the stage for today's learning

Remind students of the note-taking work they did yesterday and where they are in the Research Road Map.

Researchers, you have gathered many important notes that help you better understand the importance of these events from history, what happened, and why. I am so impressed by the thoughtful note taking you've done. Walking around the room, I've learned so much about your topics already. I can't wait to learn more! I noticed something interesting about your notes, though, and you may have noticed the same thing. I noticed that some of your notes are about the same topic and that they seem to go together. Let's consult our Research Road Map to see what we are going to do today with these important notes you've taken. Where have we been so far? Where are we going today?

Teach   Model what students need to learn and do

Use your class notes on your model topic to demonstrate how to organize notes according to topic. Introduce a categorization system to your students.

Today in writing, we are going to categorize your notes, or put them in groups based on what they are about. The big idea is your research topic, such as Why did the Negro Baseball League form. But then there are smaller ideas that seem to go together. We call these clusters of information subtopics. Informational nonfiction authors don't just list facts in any order. They group information together by subtopic. Let's take a look at our notes about the topic "Negro Baseball League." What subtopics seem to be coming up in our notes?

Students should notice some of these subtopics:

- Before 1887
- Andrew "Rube" Foster
- How teams formed
- Another league forms

Today we are going to group subtopics and give each group a name based on what the notes are about. Watch how I group notes together by naming,

Try   Guide students to quickly rehearse what they need to learn and do in preparation for practice

Have students group some of their notes that go together. Then, have students share their thinking with a partner to see if they are on the right track. Provide them with language for discussing what they notice about each other's work.

Now, open your research folder and look at your notes. Read all of your notes to yourself first. Then, turn and talk to your partner, each of you sharing some notes that seem to go together. Let your partner know if you agree with his or her ideas. Does it sound like those notes go together? **ELL** Enable Language Production—Increasing Interaction & Listening and Speaking. During this time, listen in to partner talk to see how you can scaffold or paraphrase to enhance comprehension and extend talk. By using the following sentence starters, you offer a model that ELLs can rely on to communicate their thinking. You could provide these sentence starters in a smaller version that they can hold and refer to during their partner time.

Provide your students with some sentence starters for this partner talk:

- I agree those notes about _____ do go together.
- I disagree because your notes seem to be about _____ and _____.

This gives students agreed-upon rules for discussions to effectively engage with one another in their partnerships. (SL.4.1b)

Clarify   Briefly restate today's teaching objective and explain the practice task(s)

Now that you've consulted with a partner about one of your grouping ideas, you are going to finish organizing your notes into piles or groups. When you are ready, you are going to name the groupings, just as I did with my notes.

Practice   Students work independently or in small groups to apply today's teaching objective

Students continue to group their notes into logical categories and label them according to the system you've modeled.

Milestone Performance Assessment

Coding and Sorting

 Use this checklist to assess student ability to code and sort subtopics.

Standards Alignment W.4.4, W.4.7

	Achieved	Notes
Group notes into logical categories.		
Name subtopic groups appropriately.		

At the end of class, have students return to their partners to share the rest of their grouping system and provide some feedback on whether they agree with each other's work.

Collect and analyze students' work to monitor if they are able to accurately organize their notes into logical categories. Use this as a quick assessment to determine whether your students need additional support with this skill. Based on this assessment, you may choose to continue this work as a whole group, conduct a small group, or meet with individual students. **ELL** Assess for Content and Language Understanding—Formative Assessment.

Writing Lesson 5

▶ Teaching Objective

Writers plan diary entries that spotlight a historical "headline."

▶ Standards Alignment

W.4.4, W.4.7, W.4.10, SL.4.1a-d, SL.4.2, L.4.1, L.4.6

▶ Materials

- Two sample diary entries (Appendixes 4.9 and 4.10)
- Point of View Planning Organizer (Appendix 4.11)
- Student research folders
- Research Road Map (Appendix 4.8)
- Selection of informational texts for students to use in their research

▶ To the Teacher

Today your students are making the shift from researcher to writer. Make sure your students have enough notes to be able to include important

factual information about the event from history, explain what happened, and why. Their research will now be used to guide their writing of diary entries from the point of view of someone who experienced the event. This framework was chosen because in order to be able to understand what happened and why we want our students to place themselves in the scene, to imagine how these events from history shaped the lives of those who were there. This is our way of helping students understand that history is more about human lives than it is about just memorizing dates and facts. To understand history is to understand how events impact our lives or the lives of others.

▶ Procedure

Warm Up **Gather the class to set the stage for today's learning**

Explain to your class that today they are making an important shift from researcher to writer. They are going to use their organized notes to create something new, a diary entry from the point of view of someone who lived through the important historic moment they've been reading and taking notes on.

Today is a big day! Today is the day we make a big shift from researcher to writer. Fourth graders, you have worked hard to read your independent texts closely, to understand what happened in the past and why it happened. I also know that many of you have been thinking about why these topics are important for us to think about today. Just like researchers in any field, you are now going to take the information you've found and report on your findings. Rather than just tell us what you discovered, you are going to capture every-one's attention by writing a diary entry from the point of view of someone who lived through the important historic moment you've been learning about. To really understand history we have to imagine what it would have been like to live through it.

Teach Model what students need to learn and do

Review one of our sample diary entries, based on either a child's perspective from World War II or the perspective of one of the ball-players in the Negro Baseball League. Ask students to share what makes this entry a powerful example. Draw on student thinking by asking questions like the following:

- What made you think that?
- How do you know?
- Are there words that seem to mean something special?
- Is there anything that gives you a sense of how it felt to live in this time?

As students talk, encourage them to listen thoughtfully to one another and build on each other's ideas rather than simply repeat one another. (SL.4.1b, SL.4.1c) Also, this is a good opportunity to encourage students to use the text as evidence in their conversation. (SL.4.2)

Following this conversation, it's time to orient students to how they will plan for writing their diary entries. Use the sample diary entry and work your way backwards with students to complete the Point of View Planning Orga-nizer. Ask your students to help you imagine how the writer planned for this entry by considering:

- What happened?
- Why?
- Thoughts
- Feelings

Point of View Planning Organizer

Event that happened in the story.	
Why did this event occur?	
Your thoughts on this event.	
Your feelings on this event.	

Try Guide students to quickly rehearse what they need to learn and do in preparation for practice

Have students complete the Point of View Planning Organizer with a partner.

Now that we understand the important ways the writer helped us understand the point of view of someone living in this moment in history, we can speculate how they may have planned for this. Using the Point of View Planning Organizer you'll be continuing with a partner to look for these important characteristics within this diary entry. Be ready to share your findings with the group.

Clarify Briefly restate today's teaching objective and explain the practice task(s)

Remind students that today is about planning for their writing so that they can share with everyone what they learned about this important moment from history. They will be able to plan for the facts from their notes, but the vivid details, thoughts, and feelings will need to come from their own under-standing of what it would have been like to live through this important time.

Now you're ready to use the Point of View Planning Organizer to plan for your own diary entry. Remember that you should use your notes to plan for what happened and why. But the thoughts and feelings are going to come

Goal	Low-Tech	High-Tech
Students will plan and then over the next few lessons write diary entries from the point of view of an imaginary or real historical figure to explain what happened and why.	Students write entries with pencil and paper. Students can then "antique" their diary entries using wet tea bags or crinkling the paper.	Students could write a fictional blog from the point of view of a historical figure. The blog would allow students to write collaboratively and give responses to one another's entries.

from your own ideas about what it would have been like to live through this historical event.

Practice Students work independently or in small groups to apply today's teaching objective

Students will use their notes as well as their own interpretation of what it would have been like to live in this moment in history to plan for their diary entries using the Point of View Planning Organizer. Some students will be ready to begin their writing. Remind students who are ready for this that their entries should begin with the historical date and "Dear Journal" or "Dear Diary."

Wrap Up Check understanding as you guide students to briefly share what they have learned and produced today

Have students share one element from their Point of View Planning Organizer. Ask students how they made their decisions about what to include and what to leave out. Collect student work and use it as an informal assessment of your students' understanding of cause and effect relationships in informational text. **ELL** Assess for Content and Language Understanding—Formative Assessment. At this point, you will be able to assess concepts and language that might have been confusing for your ELLs. This is also an opportunity to see, through reflecting on the graphic organizer, whether your ELLs are grasping point of view.

Milestone Performance Assessment

Planning Organizer

Use this checklist to assess student ability to plan and organize thoughts.
Standards Alignment: W.4.4, W.4.7, W.4.10

	Achieved	Notes
Include an important historical event.		
Identify why the event happened.		
Develop point of view (thoughts and feelings) regarding an event.		

> I've always believed that if you put in the work, the results will come.
>
> —Michael Jordan

Writing Lesson 6

▼ **Teaching Objective**

Writers include factual information from the time period.

Close Reading Opportunity

▼ **Standards Alignment**

RI.4.1, RI.4.6, RI.4.10, W.4.2a, W.4.2b, W.4.2d , W.4.4, W.4.6, W.4.10, SL.4.6, L.4.6

▼ **Materials**

* Key Facts Sheet (see Appendixes 4.12)
* Two sample diary entries (see Appendixes 4.9 and 4.10)
* Highlighting tools

▶ To the Teacher

Your students have a plan for how they are going to include what happened and why, as well as their own creative additions built on what they believe it would have been like to live through this historic event. This is a great start, but we also want to make sure our students are including significant factual information that they learned about in their research. This will allow for everyone else to learn from their entries, particularly if your students have been researching different moments in time.

▶ Procedure

Warm Up Gather the class to set the stage for today's learning

Remind students of the great work they did yesterday as they moved from notes to planning their writing.

Fourth graders, I am so impressed by how thoughtfully you have planned for your diary entries. As I reviewed them, I noticed that you included important points about what happened and why these events happened. You have also thought carefully about how you are going to make this feel real by including thoughts and feelings from the point of view of someone living through this historic event. But, you have a lot of other information in your notes and we want to make sure it has a place in your diary entry.

Teach Model what students need to learn and do

Ask students what kinds of information they have in their notes that could be included in their entries. Your students should have things like facts about the place, facts about people, facts about the time period. Guide students in reviewing one or both of the sample diary entries to note where these facts are present.

Wow, fourth graders, you have a lot of important information here that can help your readers learn about what really happened. What I notice about your ideas is that there are facts you want to include in your entries. These seem to be:

- Facts about the Place
- Facts about People
- Facts about the Time Period

Let's read our sample diary entries and see if we can find any of these kinds of facts included in the entries. Watch me as I highlight important facts in our first entry.

Try Guide students to quickly rehearse what they need to learn and do in preparation for practice

Have students read the second diary entry highlighting facts about the place, facts about people, and facts about the time period. Have them share what they found with a partner and record on the Key Facts Sheet the important facts they both found.

©Monkey Business/Fotolia

Clarify Briefly restate today's teaching objective and explain the practice task(s)

In your independent writing today, you are going to continue to move from research to writing. First, you are going to highlight your notes that are facts about the place, facts about people, and facts about the time period that you want to include. Not every fact you have will make its way into your diary entry. So, select your notes carefully by thinking about what are the most important facts that will help your reader understand why this event was so important.

Once they've planned the facts they want to include, all of your students should now begin their writing. Remind students that their entries should begin with the historical date and "Dear Journal" or "Dear Diary."

Practice Students work independently or in small groups to apply today's teaching objective

Students will select key facts to include in their entries and begin or continue their entries.

Wrap Up Check understanding as you guide students to briefly share what they have learned and produced today

 Have students share how they chose which facts to include and which to leave out. This is something to continue discussing in the days to come. Collect this work and use it as an informal assessment to determine your students' progress with this skill. **ELL** Assess for Content and Language Understanding—Formative Assessment

Writing Lesson 7

▶ Teaching Objective
Writers use the five senses to vividly describe the event.

▶ Standards Alignment
RI.4.10, W.4.2b, W.4.4, W.4.6, W.4.10, L.4.6

▶ Materials
- Two sample diary entries (see Appendixes 4.9 and 4.10)
- Highlighting supplies

▶ To the Teacher
Today's lesson builds on the previous lessons that are part of this important planning stage. Now your students will be moving from focusing on facts

---

Milestone Performance Assessment

Writing a Diary Entry

Use this checklist to assess student ability to assimilate facts to write a diary entry.

Standards Alignment: W.4.2a, W.4.2b, W.4.2d, W.4.4, W.4.6, W.4.10

	Achieved	Notes
Identify facts about the place.		
Identify facts about the people.		
Identify facts about the time period.		
Begin writing diary entries.		

---

to ensuring that their writing makes readers feel as though they are there in the historic moment.

▶ Procedure

Warm Up Gather the class to set the stage for today's learning

Remind your students of the important planning they did yesterday and the day before by reviewing their notes and generating a plan for elements they'll include to make their diary entries feel vivid and real.

Fourth graders, yesterday we continued to use our notes to plan for our diary entries. Our goal with these entries is to make readers feel like they are in the moment in history with you—that we learn about the event and what caused it but that we also experience what it felt like, what might have gone through someone's head, and what that person saw all around. One of the hardest things to plan for is the vivid details. Today we are going to learn a strategy writers use to make those vivid details come alive.

Teach Model what students need to learn and do

Model for students using the sample diary entries how writers use the five senses to make the entries feel real, like we are right there with them in the moment in time.

Today we are going to reread the diary entries we've read before about two different important historic moments. Yesterday we read them to consider how a writer would have planned for these entries. Today, you are going to read with a new focus in mind. You are going to read by looking for how the writer used the five senses to make the event feel real to us as readers. Listen as I read the first entry. As I'm reading I'm going to highlight places where the writer used one of the five senses to make me feel as though I'm right there, too.

Try Guide students to quickly rehearse what they need to learn and do in preparation for practice

Give students a few minutes to read and highlight the next diary entry on their own, reflecting on how the writer uses the five senses to make the event feel real for us as readers.   **ELL** Frontload the Lesson— Activate Prior Knowledge & Build Background. You could pull your newcomer ELLs aside to preview, through demonstration and visuals, the five senses. For example, a picture of a nose, while you demonstrate smelling a flower, demonstrates the sense of smell.

Clarify Briefly restate today's teaching objective and explain the practice task(s)

In your writing today, you are going to use your plans as a guide, but I also want you to think about how you are going to create vivid details using the five senses as a guide. This will make your writing come alive for your readers and listeners.

Practice Students work independently or in small groups to apply today's teaching objective

Students will be writing their diary entries with the five senses in mind.

Wrap Up Check understanding as you guide students to briefly share what they have learned and produced today

Have students share one sentence in their entries that uses one of the five senses to make the entry feel more vivid.

> " The test of a good teacher is not how many questions he can ask his pupils that they will answer readily, but how many questions he inspires them to ask him which he finds it hard to answer."
>
> —Alice Wellington Rollins

Writing Lesson 8

▼ **Teaching Objective**

Writers use signal words to help readers identify cause and effect.

▼ **Standards Alignment**

RI.4.10, W.4.2c, W.4.4, W.4.6, W.4.10, SL.4.1a–d, L.4.1, L.4.2, L.4.3, L.4.6

▼ **Materials**

- Cause and Effect Signals chart from Reading Lesson 3 and reproduced in this lesson
- Student diary entries

▶ To the Teacher

Your students have been introduced to the idea that signal words help readers identify cause and effect. Now you're going to apply that lesson to their writing. Your students' entries should be well developed by this lesson, so this is part of the beginning of revision. Help your students revise their writing by using signal words to convey to the reader moments where causes and effects become clear.

▶ Procedure

Warm Up Gather the class to set the stage for today's learning

Remind your students of the work they did in reading earlier in the lesson set around signal words as a marker for cause and effect.

Fourth graders, we all know that reading and writing go hand in hand. Let's look back at an important reading lesson when we learned about how we can use signal words to identify cause and effect text structures.

Review with students the chart you created:

Cause and Effect Signal Words

because, so, consequently, therefore, due to the fact, since, as a result, the reason for, thus, nevertheless, why, in order that, if . . . then, since, in order that

Teach Model what students need to learn and do

These words help us as readers, but guess what? They also let us as writers help our readers understand the important causes and effects of the events from history we researched. Let's read our sample diary entries to see if we can find these signal words.

Highlight for students the words in the text. Then start a conversation about why these words are important by asking:

Do they help us as readers? How so? What do these words help us identify as readers?

Identifying the signal words is an important step, but more importantly you want your students to discuss why these words help us as readers. As

fourth graders, they should be gaining comfort with transitional words and phrases. Once you have discussed with students the importance of these signal words to orient the reader to important historical events and what caused them to happen, have students look for places in a partner's text where signal words would help them identify the cause and effect they want to get across in their diary entry.

Try Guide students to quickly rehearse what they need to learn and do in preparation for practice

Before we read our own writing to see where signal words could help a reader identify cause and effect, we're going to trade our drafts with a partner. Since signal words are clues for the reader, this is best done by having someone else read your work. As a reader, when you find yourself noticing or asking what happened and why, you want to put a star letting your partner know that this would be a good place for a signal word.

Clarify Briefly restate today's teaching objective and explain the practice task(s)

Once students have had ample time to read each other's work, place markers for signal words, and discuss their findings with each other, remind them one more time of the importance of signal words to make their writing clear for the reader. The heart of their diary entries should be description of the historic event and what caused it to happen. Signal words will make that clear for the reader.

Practice Students work independently or in small groups to apply today's teaching objective

Students will be inserting signal words into their diary entry drafts.

Wrap Up Check understanding as you guide students to briefly share what they have learned and produced today

Students will share one suggestion their partner gave them and if they agree that it is an appropriate place for a signal word to orient the reader.

Writing Lesson 9 . . . .

▼ Teaching Objective

Writers revise for cause and effect and edit for conventions of standard English.

▼ Standards Alignment

W.4.5, W.4.6, W.4.10, SL.4.6, L.4, L.4.2, L.4.3, L.4.6

▼ Materials

- Copies of Research Wrap-Up Checklist (see Appendix 4.13)
- Student diary entries
- Sample diary entries (see Appendixes 4.9 and 4.10)

▼ To the Teacher

With the diary entries written, it's time to help students with the revision process. For fourth graders, this is not always the most exciting part of the research process. They often think "We're done! We did it!" Helping them realize the importance of revision is essential not only for this lesson set but for their writing lives moving forward. Today, model for your students how you revise for a journalistic voice and edit for conventions of standard English. This lesson may be best taught over two days—one day for revision and one day of editing for conventions. Because this piece of writing requires a particular focus for revision, the Research Wrap-Up Checklist will serve as an important tool for students to independently account for the big ideas of their articles as well as the conventions that will be most critical to this piece of writing, consistent with the fourth grade Common Core State Standards. **ELL** Provide Comprehensible Input—Organizers. Organizers and outlines help ELLs understand the process they need to do to edit and revise their work. Consider providing samples of before-and-after pieces that they have done to demonstrate the steps in revision.

▼ Procedure

Warm Up Gather the class to set the stage for today's learning

You have accomplished quite a lot as historians, researchers, and writers as you took on the perspective of someone living in a particular moment in time.

Now, we're ready to reread our diary entries and check to make sure we've done our job of explaining the big ideas of our topic and why it should matter to your readers. We also want to make sure we follow the rules of English so that our readers can focus on the big ideas.

Teach **Model what students need to learn and do**

Direct students to read the sample diary entry and use that as a guide for what to do well in writing.

Today we are going to reread the sample diary entry using our Research Wrap-Up Checklist. First, we are going to read our Research Wrap-Up Checklist to know what we're looking for in this piece of writing. Then, we are going to read the diary entry once through. It's important to read it completely to re-mind yourself what the whole piece is about. After that, we are going to reread the entry with a revision and editing lens. That means we are going to use our Research Wrap-Up Checklist to identify moments in the diary entry where more needs to be added or where something isn't clear enough yet. We will also note places where conventions are not used properly using our acronym COPS (Capitalization, Order and usage of words, Punctuation, and Spelling).

Research Wrap-Up Checklist

Revising	Yes or No	Notes
Does my entry describe an important event?		
Does my entry include why this event happened?		
Does my entry make my point of view clear to the reader?		
Does my entry include facts about people, places, and events from the time period?		
COPS Editing Checklist		
Capitals—I remembered to use capitals correctly.		

as an assessment. After looking closely at their work, determine if your class needs additional time for revision and editing before moving on to reflection. **ELL** Assess for Content and Language Understanding—Summative Assessment.

Milestone Performance Assessment

Research Wrap Up

Use this checklist to assess student ability to make final revisions and edits.

Standards Alignment: W.4.5, W.4.6, SL.4.6, L.4.1, L.4.2, L.4.3

	Achieved	Notes
Describe an important event.		
Include why this event happened.		
Make the point of view clear to the reader.		
COPS Editing Checklist*		
Correct **c**apitalization.		
Correct **o**rder and usage of words.		
Correct **p**unctuation.		
Correct **s**pelling.		

*We recommend that you focus your assessment lens in these areas. Select and assess a few skills you have previously taught or that have emerged as areas of need in your ongoing assessment of student writing.

Revising	Yes or No	Notes
Order and usage of words—I have reread my sentences, and they all sound right and make sense.		
Punctuation—I have used correct punctuation.		
Spelling—I have corrected my spelling errors.		

Try Guide students to quickly rehearse what they need to learn and do in preparation for practice

Have students work with a partner to reread the other sample diary entry and to read with a revision/editing lens.

With a partner, you are going to use our Research Wrap-Up Checklist to review another diary entry that you've read before. I want you to read each sentence carefully and note places you think the writer could add some more explanation or detail, using the Research Wrap-Up Checklist as a guide.

Clarify Briefly restate today's teaching objective and explain the practice task(s)

Today you are going to read through your diary entry looking to make sure the causes and resulting effects are clear to the reader and that you have followed the rules of standard English. Then, you are going to use the Research Wrap-Up Checklist to carefully go through each sentence, making sure all of the items are complete in your diary entry.

Practice Students work independently or in small groups to apply today's teaching objective

Students will reread their diary entries using the Research Wrap-Up Checklist.

Wrap Up Check understanding as you guide students to briefly share what they have learned and produced today

 Have students share one change they made to their diary entry by using the Research Wrap-Up Checklist. Collect student work to use

Writing Lesson 10 ●

▶ **Teaching Objective**

Writers present their diary entries and reflect on what they've learned about research and writing.

▶ **Standards Alignment**

W.4.10, SL.4.1a–d, SL.4.4, L.4.1, L.4.6

▶ **Materials**

- Student diary entries
- Two sample diary entries (Appendixes 4.9 and 4.10)
- Charting supplies or interactive whiteboard
- How to Perform Point of View chart (created collaboratively with students during Teach section)

▶ **To the Teacher**

When the diary entries are complete, it's time for students to share them with one another and reflect as a class on what they've learned about research and writing. Today is all about presentation and reflection—important parts of the lesson set process both for students as individuals and for the class as a collective. Helping students gain confidence as presenters is an important part of how you help students with skills they'll use far beyond this lesson set. Also, helping them pause and think about what they've learned and what they've enjoyed can have long-lasting effects. Today's lesson is meant to be celebratory and to help students build those important reflection skills. Emphasize with students that research is ongoing and that they will continue to have questions about this topic and many others and now they have some tools for finding the answers all on their own.

▶ **Procedure**

| Warm Up | Gather the class to set the stage for today's learning

Congratulate the class on a job well done as researchers and writers!

Congratulations, students, on your diary entry success. Not only have you researched topics that matter to you but you have written diary entries that have captured the perspective of someone living in a particular moment in time. It's been quite a journey. We packed our bags and hit the road of research and luckily we had a road map to help us along the way.

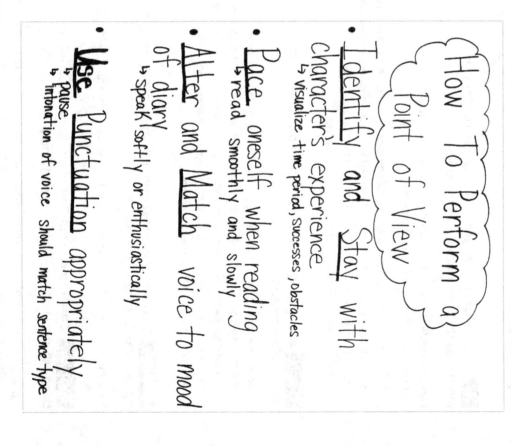

Teach Model what students need to learn and do

Today is all about sharing your entry with the class. At the end, we'll be reflecting as a group on all the things we've learned about these important moments in time, about research, and about writing in this particular way. When you are sharing your diary entry, how do you think it should sound? That's right, like you are living in that moment in time. You might read certain lines more quietly than others to indicate fear or nervousness. You might read other lines with great excitement. You might read certain lines slowly to build suspense. Watch me as I read a diary entry we know well (choose one of the sample entries) and listen for what I do with my voice and watch what I do with my body to tell us more about what I'm feeling living in this moment in time.

Try Guide students to quickly rehearse what they need to learn and do in preparation for practice

Have students share what they noticed about how you read the entry. Record these ideas on a class chart called "How to Perform a Point of View." Ask students to share their thinking about how they knew the entry reflected something scary, uncertain, or hopeful depending on the sample you choose. This discussion is critical because you will be giving students the opportunity to review the key ideas you've expressed through your performance of the diary entry. (SL.4.1d)

Clarify Briefly restate today's teaching objective and explain the practice task(s)

Review the list you created about How to Perform a Point of View and emphasize with students that this is a special kind of reading you're asking

them to do. You are asking them to take on the identity of the character they've created to write about this important historic moment. Some of these moments are perplexing, others are devastating, some are joyful. The mood of the moment from history that they've researched and written about should dictate how they perform their diary entry.

Practice Students work independently or in small groups to apply today's teaching objective

Students will perform their diary entries for one another. This will be something some students look forward to, while others will be nervous about sharing their work with their peers in this way. You may decide to have students share with partners or in small groups rather than with the whole class. Emphasize with students that these performances are an opportunity for them to present their research findings with each other in a creative format. Their entries include relevant facts and descriptive details to support the theme of their entry. As such, they need to speak at an understandable pace and demonstrate pride in their hard work. (SL.4.4)

Wrap Up Check understanding as you guide students to briefly share what they have learned and produced today

Have students share what they learned about these important historic events by viewing and listening to each other's performances. End class with:

What do you think you will remember beyond today or even this school year about one of these topics based on today's performances?

Language Companion Lesson

This lesson is best taught at nearly any point during the lesson set because it addresses a challenge that some writers face nearly every time they write.

▼ Teaching Objective

Writers have tricks to help them use frequently confused words correctly.

▼ Standards Alignment

L.4.1g

▼ Materials

- Whiteboards
- Charting supplies

▼ To the Teacher

This lesson focuses on one set of frequently confused words: To/Too/Two. For whatever reason among others, these seem to plague young writers right through high school and beyond, so much so that they earned their own Core Standard, L.4.1g: "Correctly use frequently confused words (e.g., *to, too, two; there, their*)." Use a similar lesson plan format to address other frequently confused words.

▼ Procedure

Warm Up **Gather the class to set the stage for today's learning**

Display the following sentences:

- There are two ducks in the pond.
- The ducks swam to the other side.
- The pond is too cold to swim.
- I quacked to the ducks.
- I want to swim too.

Engage students in a brief discussion about the role of each underlined word. Develop a working definition of how the word is used in each example. A sample of what this might look like follows. Students are likely to need help with defining the infinitive verb use of *to*.

Word	Example	Working Definition
Two	Two ducks	The number 2, a count of something
Too	I want to swim too.	Also, in addition
Too	Too cold	Extra, more than you want
To	To the other side To the ducks	Indicates direction, *toward* something or *at* someone
To	I want to swim.	Basic form of the verb *swim* (called an infinitive). Other examples: to walk, to run, to quack, to laugh, etc.

Teach **Model what students need to learn and do**

The following bits of information and hints are designed to help trigger students memories when using *to, too,* and *two* in writing.

Two

For most students, *two* is the easiest of the choices, and they don't use confuse it very often. We usually can easily identify when we are giving a count of something. *two trees, two books, two students,* etc.

Two **Hint:** Explain to students that TW is a clue that we refer to a number. Other TW number words: TWin, TWenty, TWice.

Too Hints

Too

Sometimes students find it easier to work with securing their understanding of *too* before *to* because the meaning of *too* is a little more concrete.

❶ (extra or excessive) *Too* has a double letter O. This can help us remember that *too* means extra or excessively—as in *too much, too many, too hot,* etc. There is an extra O in TOO, or TOO many letter Os.

❷ (also) In addition, *Too* means *also*, as in *I want to go, too*. We can remember this when we remember that an extra "O" wanted to come along, *too*.

❸ Another trick is to emphasize the extra "Os" when speaking the word *too*. Here are two examples:

▶ I want to swim **fooooooooo**. This pond is **fooooooooo** cold. You can just hear that extra "O!"

▶ Have students articulate several *too* sentences this way.

To

This form of *to* is the most abstract, but here we suggest how to make it more concrete for younger students.

To Hints

❶ (preposition *to*) Since *to* indicates direction, we can point in a direction when using *to* in this way. I am going *to* the gym. This is a letter *to* the president. The kinesthetic experience can help the proper usage stick in students' minds. Have them articulate several sentences, pointing dramatically when they say *to*.

❷ (infinitive *to*) When using *to* as part of an infinitive verb, practice saying the *to* very quickly and stressing the verb. For example, *to* GO, *to* WALK, *to* SING, *to* WRITE. The *to* is quick and short when we say it this way, and therefore we should choose the short (one-letter-O) version of the word. (It may sound like a stretch, but this hint has proven to work with students!)

Wrap Up Check understanding as you guide students to briefly share what they have learned and produced today

After practicing all of the forms, orally recite sentences that use them. Don't tell the students which form is in the sentence. Have students write the correct *two*, *too* or *to* on their whiteboards. In the beginning, to scaffold students use the obvious hints (*toooooo*, pointing, *to* WALK), but gradually take these supports away.

Encourage and guide students to apply what they learn in this lesson whenever they write.

> An author ought to write for the youth of his own generation, the critics of the next, and the school-masters of ever afterward.
>
> —*F. Scott Fitzgerald*

GLOSSARY

because: for the reason that.

cause: something that makes a thing happen.

consequently: as a result, effect, or outcome; therefore.

effect: something that happens because of something else.

history: the study of events that happened in the past.

nevertheless: in spite of that; notwithstanding; all the same.

since: between a particular past time and the present; subsequently.

so: as a result; it turned out.

therefore: in consequence of that; as a result; consequently.

thus: as a result or consequence of this; therefore.

why: for what reason or purpose.

PD TOOLKIT™

Accompanying *Core Ready for Grades 3–5*, there is an online resource site with media tools that, together with the text, provides you with the tools you need to implement the lesson sets.

The PDToolkit for Pam Allyn's *Core Ready Series* is available free for 12 months after you use the password that comes with the box set for each grade band. After that, you can purchase access for an additional 12 months. If you did not purchase the box set, you can purchase a 12-month subscription at **http://pdtoolkit.pearson.com.** Be sure to explore and download the resources available at the website. Currently the following resources are available:

- Pearson Children's and Young Adult Literature Database
- Videos
- PowerPoint Presentations
- Student Artifacts
- Handouts, Forms, and Posters to supplement your Core-aligned lesson plans
- Lessons and Homework Assignments
- Close Reading Guides and Samples
- Children's Core Literature Recommendations

In the future, we will continue to add additional resources. To learn more, please visit **http://pdtoolkit.pearson.com.**

Grade 5

Knowledge Quest: Navigating and Integrating Multiple Sources as Researchers

Introduction

Empowering upper elementary school students to ask and independently seek the answers to their own questions is essential work. In third grade, students were introduced to the research process. In fourth grade, students approached the research process again by focusing on cause and effect relationships. As fifth graders, our students are more sophisticated inquirers, ready to seek out, analyze, and integrate information from a range of sources, including those in print and those found digitally.

Helping students to analyze and integrate information from multiple sources is a hallmark of grade 5. This lesson set provides students with the opportunity to practice engaging with multiple sources in critical ways as they delve into the inquiry process again. Building from grades K–4, students in grade 5 apply their knowledge of strategies to determine the meaning of new academic or domain-specific vocabulary, which in turn increases their ability to construct meaning when reading new and unfamiliar material.

In support of the reading standards, during this lesson set students are taught to identify multiple main ideas within a single informational text as

well as their related supporting details. Beyond that, students will think critically about *how* key details work to support a main idea as well as explain the relationships between important individuals, events, ideas, or concepts within the text. Students will also have many opportunities to discuss their thinking and learning with a research partner and to offer appropriate elaboration on the ideas of classmates by building on what has been said before. By focusing on making meaning from information acquired from a number of sources on one topic, students will develop a deeper understanding of how to be critical consumers of informational texts.

Through the writing process students will practice many of the skills essential to the research process. Students will take relevant notes that include the appropriate use of summary, paraphrasing, and direct quotation. Students will also write critical reflections in response to their reading, creating evidence of their thinking as they travel through the inquiry process. As a culminating activity, students will create a multimedia presentation of their findings.

Why This Lesson Set?

In this lesson set, students will:

- Analyze and integrate information from multiple sources
- Become critical consumers of informational text
- Encounter and build understanding of content-specific vocabulary
- Think critically about the relationship between main ideas and details
- Research, take notes, paraphrase, and quote sources
- Create and deliver multimedia research presentations

Common Core State Standards Alignment

Reading Standards

RI.5.1 Quote accurately from a text when explaining what the text says explicitly and when drawing inferences from the text.

RI.5.2 Determine two or more main ideas of a text and explain how they are supported by key details; summarize the text.

RI.5.3 Explain the relationships or interactions between two or more individuals, events, ideas, or concepts in a historical, scientific, or technical text based on specific information in the text.

RI.5.4 Determine the meaning of general academic and domain-specific words and phrases in a text relevant to a grade 5 topic or subject area.

RI.5.5 Compare and contrast the overall structure (e.g., chronology, comparison, cause/effect, problem/solution, description) of events, ideas, concepts, or information in two or more texts.

RI.5.6 Analyze multiple accounts of the same event or topic, noting important similarities and differences in the point of view they represent.

RI.5.7 Draw on information from multiple print or digital sources, demonstrating the ability to locate an answer to a question quickly or to solve a problem efficiently.

RI.5.9 Integrate information from several texts on the same topic in order to write or speak about the subject knowledgeably.

RI.5.10 By the end of the year, read and comprehend informational texts, including history/social studies, science and technical texts, at the high end of the grades 4–5 text complexity band independently and proficiently.

Writing Standards

W.5.2 Write informative/explanatory texts to examine a topic and convey ideas and information clearly.

a. Introduce a topic clearly, provide a general observation and focus, and group related information logically; include formatting (e.g., headings), illustrations, and multimedia when useful to aiding comprehension.

b. Develop the topic with facts, definitions, concrete details, quotations, or other information and examples related to the topic.

c. Link ideas within and across categories of information using words, phrases, and clauses (e.g., in contrast, especially).

d. Use precise language and domain-specific vocabulary to inform about or explain the topic.

e. Provide a concluding statement or section related to the information or explanation presented.

W.5.4 Produce clear and coherent writing in which the development and organization are appropriate to task, purpose, and audience.

W.5.5 With guidance and support from peers and adults, develop and strengthen writing as needed by planning, revising, editing, rewriting, or trying a new approach.

W.5.7 Conduct short research projects that use several sources to build knowledge through investigation of different aspects of a topic.

W.5.8 Recall relevant information from experiences or gather relevant information from print and digital sources; summarize or paraphrase information in notes and finished work, and provide a list of sources.

W.5.9 Draw evidence from literary or informational texts to support analysis, reflection, and research.

b. Apply grade 5 reading standards to informational texts (e.g., "Explain how an author uses reasons and evidence to support particular points in a text, identifying which reasons and evidence support which point[s]").

W.5.10 Write routinely over extended time frames (time for research, reflection, and revision) and shorter time frames (a single sitting or a day or two) for a range of discipline-specific tasks, purposes, and audiences.

Speaking and Listening Standards

SL.5.1 Engage effectively in a range of collaborative discussions (one-on-one, in groups, and teacher-led) with diverse partners on grade 5 topics and texts, building on others' ideas and expressing their own clearly.

a. Come to discussions prepared, having read or studied required material; explicitly draw on that preparation and other information known about the topic to explore ideas under discussion.

b. Follow agreed-upon rules for discussions and carry out assigned roles.

c. Pose and respond to specific questions by making comments that contribute to the discussion and elaborate on the remarks of others.

d. Review the key ideas expressed and draw conclusions in light of information and knowledge gained from the discussions.

SL.5.2 Summarize a written text read aloud or information presented in diverse media and formats, including visually, quantitatively, and orally.

SL.5.6 Adapt speech to a variety of contexts and tasks, using formal English when appropriate to task and situation.

Language Standards

L.5.1 Demonstrate command of the conventions of standard English grammar and usage when writing or speaking.

a. Explain the function of conjunctions, prepositions, and interjections in general and their function in particular sentences.

b. Form and use the perfect (e.g., I had walked; I have walked; I will have walked) verb tenses.

c. Use verb tense to convey various times, sequences, states, and conditions.

d. Recognize and correct inappropriate shifts in verb tense.

e. Use correlative conjunctions (e.g., either/or, neither/nor).

L.5.2 Demonstrate command of the conventions of standard English capitalization, punctuation, and spelling when writing.

a. Use punctuation to separate items in a series.

b. Use a comma to separate an introductory element from the rest of the sentence.

c. Use a comma to set off the words yes and no (e.g., Yes, thank you), to set off a tag question from the rest of the sentence (e.g., It's true, isn't it?), and to indicate direct address (e.g., Is that you, Steve?).

d. Use underlining, quotation marks, or italics to indicate titles of works.

e. Spell grade-appropriate words correctly, consulting references as needed.

L.5.3 Use knowledge of language and its conventions when writing, speaking, reading, or listening.

a. Expand, combine, and reduce sentences for meaning, reader/listener interest, and style.

b. Compare and contrast the varieties of English (e.g., dialects, registers) used in stories, dramas, or poems.

L.5.6 Acquire and use accurately grade-appropriate general academic and domain-specific words and phrases, including those that signal contrast, addition, and other logical relationships (e.g., however, although, nevertheless, similarly, moreover, in addition).

Essential Skill Lenses (PARCC Framework)

As part of its proposal to the U.S. Department of Education, the multi-state Partnership for Assessment of Readiness for College and Careers (PARCC) has developed model content frameworks for English Language Arts to serve as a bridge between the Common Core State Standards and the PARCC assessments in development at the time of this publication. In the grade 3 to 5 lesson sets, we expect students to engage in reading and writing through eight PARCC specified skill lenses that are rooted in the standards. The table below details how each skill lens is addressed across the grade 5 lesson set.

	Reading	Writing
Cite Evidence	Students cite text as evidence throughout this lesson set. In particular, students are asked to cite text as evidence when examining main ideas and supporting details and integrating their learning across multiple texts.	In conducting their own research, students cite text as evidence to support their thesis statement as well as when providing adequate details to support their thinking.
Analyze Content	Students analyze multiple sources on one topic, noting important similarities and differences. In addition, students analyze content to determine the main idea(s) and related supporting details.	Students work with research/writing partners to analyze each other's writing with an eye on clarity as well as the sufficient development of ideas.
Study and Apply Grammar and Usage	Students encounter and apply grammatical structures and word usage characteristic of and appropriate for informational reading and writing.	Students work with research/writing partners to edit writing for the conventions of standard English.

	Reading	Writing
Study and Apply Vocabulary	Students utilize a variety of strategies independently to identify, define, and utilize key vocabulary found in their informational texts.	Students incorporate key vocabulary specific to their topic into their written presentation.
Conduct Discussions	By working with a reading/research partner, students will discuss their thinking and construct meaning collaboratively.	Writing/research partners will engage in discussions focused on the research process as well as the ways in which their writing can be improved by revising, editing, rewriting, and trying another approach.
Report Findings	Students will share their thinking and learning with a reading/research partner throughout this lesson set.	Students publish their findings in public formats.
Phonics and Word Recognition	We recommend that teachers plan opportunities for students to build Reading Foundational Skills by exploring grade-level-appropriate skills in the context of the Core Texts from each lesson set and applying this knowledge to their independent reading.	We recommend that teachers encourage students to apply Reading Foundational Skills in the context of their daily writing.
Fluency and Stamina	Fluency and stamina are emphasized throughout this lesson set. Content area texts can easily be scaffolded to provide students with short texts which build up to longer texts as the lesson set progresses. This will help students build greater fluency and stamina within this genre.	Students compose quick writes in response to their reading and engage in longer, more extended writing with their independent research projects. When sharing their work with their writing/research partner aloud, students should read accurately and at an appropriate pace.

Core Questions

These questions should remain at the core of your teaching. Refer back to them often, encouraging your class to share their thinking as it evolves.

- What does it mean to conduct research?
- How do we find answers to our questions as we read?
- How do readers synthesize information and develop ideas through the use of multiple nonfiction sources?
- How does the use of varied media enhance the presentation of information?
- How do people share their research in dynamic ways?

Ready to Get Started?

Let's tap into our students' enthusiasm for researching those topics that excite them the most . . .

Fifth graders are actively questioning and engaging in the world around them. Similar to adults, many fifth graders are also often turning to digital resources to search for answers, find entertainment, and make their presence known globally. This lesson set not only allows students to integrate several sources of information on one topic, it presents the opportunity to develop students' ability to use digital resources in critical and responsible ways. When tailoring this lesson set to the needs of your school and students, you will want to consider what topics you study in the content areas and perhaps use one of these topics to guide your teaching and modeling. For the purposes of this lesson set, we will focus our teaching and modeling on investigating the invention of several popular toys. By engaging in the research with this topic in mind, we aim to keep the process of inquiry invigorating and inspiring.

Lesson Set Goals

Within this lesson set there are many goals we as teachers want to help our students reach.

Reading Goals

- Gather a variety of resources on a topic of interest, including print and digital resources. (RI.5.6, RI.5.7, RI.5.9, RI.5.10)
- Identify and explain common text structures in informational texts. (RI.5.1, RI.5.5, RI.5.10, SL.5.1a–d, SL.5.2, L.5.1, L.5.6)
- Understand, define, and utilize key vocabulary from the reading. (RI.5.1, RI.5.4, RI.5.10, SL.5.1a, SL.5.6, L.5.1, L.5.4, L.5.6)
- Determine multiple main ideas from a text and identify the key details that support these main ideas. (RI.5.1, RI.5.2, RI.5.10, SL.5.2)
- Identify and explain the relationship between key ideas, people, and events in informational texts. (RI.5.1, RI.5.3, RI.5.10, SL.5.1a, SL.5.2, SL.5.4, L.5.1, L.5.6)
- Present findings in an engaging format that integrates text, visual, and audio components in relevant ways. (RI.5.7, RI.5.9, W.5.4, W.5.9b, W.5.10, SL.5.1a–d, SL.5.4, SL.5.5, SL.5.6, L.5.1, L.5.2, L.5.3, L.5.6)
- Quote accurately from a text when explaining what the text says explicitly and when drawing inferences from the text. (RI.5.1)
- By the end of the year, read and comprehend a variety of informational texts at the high end of the grades 4–5 text complexity band independently and proficiently. (RI.5.10)
- Write routinely over extended time frames (time for research, reflection, and revision) and shorter time frames (a single sitting or a day or two) for a range of discipline-specific tasks, purposes, and audiences. (W.5.10)

Writing Goals

- Take effective notes on informational texts by using summary, paraphrasing, and direct quotations purposefully. (RI.5.1, RI.5.2, RI.5.10, W.5.4, W.5.7, W.5.8, W.5.10)
- Craft clear and organized responses to the reading. (RI.5.1, RI.5.10, W.5.4, W.5.5, W.5.9b, W.5.10, SL.5.1a–d, SL.5.6, L.5.1, L.5.2, L.5.3, L.5.6)
- Craft a thesis or framing statement in informational/explanatory writing that synthesizes information on one topic from multiple sources, both print and digital. (W.5.2a, W.5.4, W.5.7, W.5.10, L.5.6)
- Develop and strengthen writing by including facts, definitions, details, and quotations. (W.5.2b, W.5.4, W.5.7, W.5.10, SL.5.6, L.5.1, L.5.2, L.5.3, L.5.6)
- Provide a reference list of sources. (W.5.4, W.5.7, W.5.8, W.5.10)
- Prepare and present the research. (W.5.4, W.5.6, W.5.7, SL.5.1a–d, SL.5.6, L.5.1, L.5.2, L.5.3, L.5.6)
- With guidance and support from peers and adults, develop and strengthen writing as needed by planning, revising, editing, rewriting or trying a new approach. (W.5.5)
- Quote accurately from a text when explaining what the text says explicitly and when drawing inferences from the text. (RI.5.1)
- By the end of the year, read and comprehend a variety of informational texts at the high end of the grades 4–5 text complexity band independently and proficiently. (RI.5.10)
- In collaborative discussions, demonstrate evidence of preparation for discussion and exhibit responsibility to the rules and roles of conversation. (SL.5.1a, SL.5.1b)
- In collaborative discussions, share and develop ideas in a manner that enhances understanding of topic. Contribute and respond to the content of the conversation in a productive and focused manner. (SL.5.1c, SL.5.1d)
- Demonstrate knowledge of standard English and its conventions. (L.5.1, L.5.2, L.5.3)
- Acquire and accurately use grade-appropriate conversational, general academic, and domain-specific vocabulary and phrases. (L.5.6)

- Write routinely over extended time frames (time for research, reflection, and revision) and shorter time frames (a single sitting or a day or two) for a range of discipline-specific tasks, purposes, and audiences. (W.5.10)
- In collaborative discussions, demonstrate evidence of preparation for discussion and exhibit responsibility to the rules and roles of conversation. (SL.5.1a, SL.5.1b)
- In collaborative discussions, share and develop ideas in a manner that enhances understanding of topic. Contribute and respond to the content of the conversation in a productive and focused manner. (SL.5.1c, SL.5.1d)
- Demonstrate knowledge of standard English and its conventions. (L.5.1, L.5.2, L.5.3)
- Acquire and accurately use grade-appropriate conversational, general academic, and domain-specific vocabulary and phrases. (L.5.6)

Choosing Core Texts

For this lesson set, you will need to gather print and digital informational texts that utilize a variety of structures (chronology, comparison, cause/effect, problem/solution, description) for your students to investigate. You can rely on everyday resources that are easy to find, as well as resources you may already have in your classroom. There is no need to find a wealth of never-seen-before texts for this investigation. Below, find some examples or ideas for each structure.

Chronology

Directions or manuals

Family trees

Historical time-lines

Recipes (consider epicurious.com or Foodnetwork.com for online sources, in addition to printed recipes)

Transportation timetables such as bus and subway routes

Comparison

Many good examples of comparison text may be found online. Try the following search terms: hurricanes vs. tornadoes comparison; frogs vs. toads comparison; planets vs. stars comparison; rugby vs. football comparison; spiders vs. insects comparison. You will find a variety of comparative formats including tables, Venn diagrams, and paragraphs of text.

Cause/Effect

Books/articles on natural disasters (tornadoes, earthquakes, hurricanes, volcanoes) usually have strong cause/effect relationships. The Core Book, *Mistakes That Worked: 40 Familiar Inventions and How They Came to Be* by Charlotte Foltz Jones includes fun, engaging scenarios with strong cause/effect relationships.

Weather reports

Problem/Solution

Texts about efforts to address environmental issues

Texts about successful community service programs

Description

Advertisements and catalogues where products, hotels, services, etc., are described

Biographies

Restaurant reviews (where atmosphere, meals, etc., are described)

Science-based texts containing descriptions of animals, inventions, habitats, geological features, etc.

Travel brochures

You will also want to gather a variety of print and digital resources around a particular topic for your own teaching and modeling. For the purposes of this lesson set, we will be focusing on the invention of toys. Below are the texts you will see mentioned in our expanded reading and writing lessons:

Books

Horses by Seymour Simon

The Kid Who Invented the Popsicle and Other Surprising Stories about Inventions by Don L. Wulffson

Mistakes That Worked: 40 Familiar Inventions and How They Came to Be by Charlotte Foltz Jones

Toys! Amazing Stories Behind Some Great Inventions by Don Wulffson

The Ultimate Lego Book: Discover the Lego Universe by DK Books

Web Resources

"#157: Who Invented the Kite?" posted on Wonderopolis.org

"50th Birthday of the Lego Brick" posted on the Lego website

Good Pet, Bad Pet by Elizabeth Schleichert

"History of Lego" posted on Wikipedia.org

"History of Lego" video on YouTube

"The History of Silly Putty" by Jennifer Rosenberg on About.com

Webpage for Ole Kirk Christiansen located on Brickipedia, Lego's wiki page

Here are suggestions for other resources appropriate to fifth grade, clustered around particular topics, that you may want to consider using as well.

Resources about the Ocean

Discover the Oceans: The World's Largest Ecosystem by Lauri Berkenkamp

National Geographic Readers series (*Great Migrations: Whales, Sharks, Dolphins*) Lower level

Ocean by Miranda MacQuitty

Ocean Life from A to Z by Cynthia Stierle

Shipwrecks: Exploring Sunken Cities Beneath the Sea by Mary M. Cerullo (Penguin)

Resources about Natural Disasters

Earthquakes by Seymour Simon or *Tornadoes* or *Hurricanes*, also by Seymour Simon

Earthquakes and Other Natural Disasters by Harriet Griffey

Hurricane and Tornado by Jack Challoner

Tornado!: The Story behind These Twisting, Turning, Spinning, and Spiraling Storms by Judy Fradin

Volcano & Earthquake by Susanna van Rose

Weather by Brian Cosgrove

Weather Forecasting by Gail Gibbons

Resources about the Solar System

"13 Planets: The Latest View of the Solar System" (National Geographic Kids) by David A. Aguilar (lower level)

Time for Kids: Planets! (very low level)

A Note about Addressing Reading Standard 10: Range of Reading and Level of Text Complexity

This lesson set provides all students with opportunities to work with texts deemed appropriate for their grade level as well as texts at their specific reading level. Through shared experiences and focused instruction, all students engage with and comprehend a wide range of texts within their grade level complexity band. We suggest a variety of high-quality complex texts to use within the whole-group lessons and recommend a variety of additional titles under Choosing Core Texts to extend and enrich instruction. During independent practice and in small-group collaborations, however, research strongly suggests that all students need to work with texts they can read with a high level of accuracy and comprehension (i.e., at their developmentally appropriate reading level), in order to significantly improve their reading (Allington, 2012; Ehri, Dreyer, Flugman, & Gross, 2007). Depending on individual needs and skills, a student's reading level may be above, within, or below his grade-level band.

Goal		
Students engage with multiple sources of informational texts around a specific topic of interest.	**Low-Tech**	**High-Tech**
	Students work with the following sources:	Students work with the following sources: online articles (including following related links) and multimedia websites
	• Books	• Bookmarked websites
	• Printed copies of online informational articles	• Books
	• Print articles	• Print articles

Teacher's Notes

Your fifth graders have a wonderful foundation in the process of conducting research. In third grade, they concentrated on the process itself. In fourth grade, students focused on the importance of text structures and how authors build their work in particular ways to convey their ideas. As fifth graders, we want to push them to synthesize information from a number of print and digital resources in order to develop a general observation (or thesis) to drive the presentation of their findings. This is complicated work! In order to support students' ability to construct and express their ideas, you will notice that throughout these lesson sets we ask students to work in reading/writing research partnerships. These partnerships do not need to conduct their research on similar topics—not at all! Rather, these partnerships are intended to serve as an additional layer of support for your students as they work their way through the wonderfully messy process of research. Periodically, students will check in with their reading/writing research partners to discuss their thinking about a specific text, and express their overall observations clearly.

The following steps are an important road map for your research with students. This process and most of these terms should be familiar to your students from both third and fourth grades.

- Choose topic and read
- Form questions
- Narrow the topic
- Create key words
- Find resources
- Identify important information
- Take notes
- Organize information
- Come to conclusions
- Present information

Additionally, the following materials will help you organize the research process for students:

- Student research folders
- Ready to Review baskets for submission
- Reminder charts

Core Message to Students

Before the first lesson, use this as a shared reading or read-aloud to set the stage and engage students in discussion about your upcoming study. See Appendix 5.1 for an enlarged version to reproduce and share with students.

We have so much information at our fingertips. These days, when I want to learn something new or answer a question, I almost immediately turn to the Internet to get started. I search for websites, books to check out, and articles to read. Researchers are such good readers and writers because they can take all this information, figure out what is the most important to them, and come up with a new way to look at it all. Over the next few days and weeks, we're going to dig into the topics that interest you the most—are you ready to research?

Questions for Close Reading

The Core Ready lessons include many rich opportunities to engage students in close reading of text that require them to ask and answer questions, draw conclusions, and use specific text evidence to support their thinking (Reading Anchor Standard 1). These opportunities are marked with a close reading icon. You may wish to extend these experiences using our recommended Core Texts or with texts of your choosing. Use the following questions as a resource to guide students through close reading experiences reading any informational text.

- What is the purpose of this text?
- What is the most important information in the text? How do you know?
- What features are built in to help the reader understand the information?
- How is this information important/useful to you?
- Does this text meet your research needs? What other information or type of text might you need?

Building Academic Language

A list of academic language to build your students' comprehension of the focus of this lesson set and facilitate their ability to talk and write about what they learn is included here. Rather than introduce all the words at once, systematically add them to a learning wall as your teaching unfolds. See the glossary at the end of this chapter for definitions of the words. Also listed are sentence frames that may be included on a sentence wall (Carrier and Tatum, 2006), a research-proven strategy for English language learners (ELLs) (Lewis, 1993; Nattinger, 1980), or as a handout to scaffold student use of the content words. Some students, especially ELL students, may need explicit practice in using the sentence frames. Encourage all students to use these words and phrases regularly in their conversations and writing.

Core Words

analyze	multimedia	summary
author's purpose	observation	supporting/key
cause and effect	paraphrase	details
chronology	point of view	therefore
comparison	problem and	thesis
consequently	solution	
definition	quote/quotation	
description	recipe	
fact	since	
focus	source	
integrate	specifically	
main idea	structure	

Core Phrases

- For instance, _____.
- For example, _____.
- In contrast, _____.
- I think this because _____ reminds me of _____ that we've read about because _____ (textual evidence to support your thinking).
- In addition, _____.
- Consequently, _____.
- More specifically, _____.
- Therefore, _____.

Recognition

At the end of this lesson set, it is important to recognize the hard work your students have put into their learning and the way they've thought about themselves and others. Reading and writing instruction is highly integrated throughout this lesson set, as students work toward creating a multimedia presentation of their findings.

Goal	Low-Tech	High-Tech
Students create an engaging presentation on a research topic that incorporates both text and multimedia components.	Students curate a museum display about their research topic by: • Writing an informative text about their research topic and using a word processing program to type up their final draft • Incorporating visual images, artifacts and drawings, with supporting captions, to enhance their presentation	Students craft a mock Wonderopolis page (samples at http://Wonderopolis.org) framed around their research question by: • Writing an informative text about their research topic • Incorporating relevant hyperlinks, images, and videos to enhance their page.

Assessment

Assessment in this lesson set is both ongoing and culminating, meaning that as teachers we are constantly kid-watching and observing how students make meaning and how they are interpreting new material. Throughout this lesson set, look for performance-based assessments, called Milestone Performance Assessments, each marked with an assessment icon. Milestone Performance Assessments are opportunities to notice and record data on standards-aligned indicators during the course of the lesson set. Use the results of these assessments to determine how well students are progressing toward the goals of the lesson set. Adjust the pace of your teaching and plan instructional support as needed.

Also, we encourage you to use the Reading and Writing Rubrics, also marked with an assessment icon, with each lesson set to evaluate overall student performance on the standards-aligned lesson set goals. In this lesson set, the finalized multimedia presentation of student findings is an important piece of the summative assessment that can be analyzed and then placed in a portfolio of student work.

In addition, we have provided a Speaking and Listening Performance Checklist (Appendix 5.9) that provides observable Core Standards–aligned indicators to assess student performance as speakers and listeners. There are multiple opportunities in every Core Ready lesson set to make such observations. Use the checklist in its entirety to gather performance data over time or choose appropriate indicators to create a customized checklist to match a specific learning experience.

Core Support for Diverse Learners

This lesson set was created with the needs of a wide variety of learners in mind. Throughout the day-by-day lessons, you'll find examples of visual supports, graphic organizers, highlighted speaking and listening opportunities, and research-driven English language learner supports aimed at scaffolding instruction for all learners. Also, we urge you to consider the following areas of challenge with which some of your students may need guided support. The following sections are written to spotlight important considerations as you move through the lesson sets.

Reading

Choosing texts that are at students' reading levels is essential for their reading success and reading identity. When finding texts, make sure you have various levels represented in your classroom reading collection. Some of your students will benefit from repeated exposure to a lesson's teaching objective over several days. This can be accomplished with the whole class when appropriate or more often in small-group settings.

Closely monitor your students who are reading below grade level to determine whether they are reading with accuracy and fluency to support comprehension. Encourage students to use context to confirm or self-correct word recognition and understanding and to reread when necessary. Refer to the Common Core Foundational Skills Standards—both at the grade 5 level as well as kindergarten and grades 1–4 standards—for direct, explicit foundational skills support that your students reading below grade level may need.

Special needs and ELL students conducting research are likely to encounter a variety of multi-syllabic words that will require teacher support to decode and understand. In addition, your student researchers will often come across content-specific terms that may be unfamiliar. Refer to our Core Words guide for vocabulary that you may want to frontload with small groups of students. Be cognizant of unfamiliar language embedded within the topics you and your students choose for both whole-class teaching as well as independent reading and preview the texts you provide to students reading below grade level.

As you continue your work with students, use observational notes and reading assessment data to create two to three specific short-term goals for your students with diverse needs. For example, as stated previously, these goals may be related to increasing word accuracy, building vocabulary, improving fluency, or enhancing comprehension. Throughout this lesson set, tailor your individualized and small-group instruction so that it addresses and evaluates student progress toward these goals.

Writing

Inspired writers are motivated writers. Allowing students to choose the topic of their writing is critical for their ultimate success and their positive development of identity as a writer. When immersing your students in a new genre, form, or purpose for writing, emphasize the meaning and function this particular type of writing may have in their own lives. Many of your students will also benefit from exposure to strong mentor texts and examples of your own writing, as well as the experience of sharing their own work—both the final product and the work in process.

Many of your special needs and ELL students will significantly benefit from the opportunity to visually organize their research before adding text. For example, some students will require extra support in writing to move from drawing to writing or to move from story mapping to sentences. You can also provide additional scaffolding by having students draw out a visual representation of their findings. This is especially helpful for visual learners and students who need to "sketch to stretch." Even your most proficient writers can benefit from this step, but many of your resistant or hesitant writers will feel more comfortable with getting their ideas on paper through drawing first.

As your students move from determining their ideas based on their research and begin organizing this information, provide your students with a variety of paper choices that are fifth grade appropriate. For students with fine motor control issues, providing students with a variety of paper choices that have handwriting lines with a dotted line in the middle can offer support, as letter formation may require significant energy for some writers. Also consider having students type and electronically publish their research if that is a medium more conducive to their writing success. Using apps when possible will inspire your most struggling writers to use new technology to bring their words to life.

We want our fifth graders to share their research with an audience, and supporting them as developing writers is essential. In addition to providing students with topic choice and the opportunity to draw or select inspiring photo images prior to writing, we can provide further scaffolding by having students orally rehearse how they plan to present their research to us or to a peer. For some students, the oral rehearsal will provide a springboard to writing. For others, they will have greater success dictating their findings to you.

As with the reading lessons, your students may benefit from several days on a single lesson's teaching objective. This can be done with the whole class or in small group settings.

English Language Learners

Although it is always our goal as teachers to get to know all of our students deeply both in and out of the classroom setting, this work is perhaps more critical when considering our English language learners. Honoring families' cultural traditions and experiences is important to getting to know, understand, and work with your students in meaningful ways.

English language learners are learning about the research process alongside native English speakers in your classroom, but they are also simultaneously learning English. For English language learners, it is essential to simultaneously develop their ability to easily hold conversations about their reading and writing and build their academic language base. Goldenberg (2010) defines "academic English" as the more abstract, complex, and challenging language that permits us to participate successfully in mainstream classroom instruction. English language learners will over time be responsible for understanding and producing academic English both orally and in writing. However, language acquisition is a process, and English language learners range in their development of English language acquisition. We urge you to consider your students along a spectrum of language acquisition, from students new to this country to those who are proficient conversationally to those who have native-like proficiency.

Refer to the English language learner icons throughout this lesson set for ways to shelter instruction for English language learners. These elements will help English language learners participate successfully in the whole-group lesson and support the development of their language skills. While these moments during instruction are designed to support English language learners, many schools are adding a separate ELD (English language development) block targeted at oral English language development to further support their students in language acquisition.

Students with growing English proficiency will benefit from a research word wall to build vocabulary (refer to the Core Words and Phrases). A sentence word wall that gives sentence starters to help with conversation will also offer students another layer of support. Some students may benefit from having their own personalized copies of these words to keep in their reading or writing notebooks for quick reference. Visual aids will further support students and guide them on what words are important to this study and what they mean.

Some students will benefit from several days on the same teaching objective. You may consider gathering small groups of readers or writers for repeated instruction or using one-on-one conferences as an opportunity to revisit teaching objectives.

Complementary Core Methods

Read-Aloud

Take this opportunity to share a wide variety of informational texts during read-aloud. Use the list of Core Texts suggested at the beginning of this lesson set to help make some of your selections. Make sure to include texts that vary in length, topic, and presentation style. Use your knowledge of students' interests to select texts that will inspire and excite your class. When appropriate, use your read-aloud as another chance for students to practice one or two of the following skills:

- Discussing the structures utilized by the author
- Making a prediction about a text's potential content by skimming the text features
- Determining multiple main ideas and key details within one text
- Asking and answering questions about a text, using the portions of the text as evidence in your responses
- Identifying and exploring the meaning of new vocabulary
- Generating a list of key words to use in a search for additional information on the same topic

Shared Reading

Shared reading provides a wonderful opportunity to link science or social studies content to the work you are doing in this lesson set. Think about selecting a range of short texts that match your current lessons in either social studies or science. Use shared reading to reinforce the idea of reading to learn (versus learning to read). Below are some prompts you may want to use in your conversations about these texts:

- What is/are the main idea(s) of this text? What are the supporting details?
- After reading this text, what questions do we still have about our topic?
- What new vocabulary did we take away from this text? How can we use this new vocabulary?

- Let's summarize what we just learned in our own words . . .
- Let's paraphrase this key section . . .
- Let's compare these two texts on the same topic . . .

Shared reading can also be a great place to specifically highlight the linking words found within a shared text and discuss how they connect ideas within a specific category of information.

Shared Writing

Shared writing also provides an opportunity to link to your work in social studies or science. Use this time to:

- Create shared lists of prior knowledge around a content area topic of study
- Generate key words to use in an Internet search
- Jot notes about a shared reading
- Organize notes into logical categories
- Compose questions about a topic for further investigation
- Craft answers to shared questions
- Compose shared written responses to a prompt about your reading
- Revise shared writing to link ideas together, creating more complex sentences words and phrases such as *also, another, and, more, but.*

Core Connections at Home

Ask students to bring a piece of informational text from home. Who reads this text? Why do they read it? For homework, have students list what other sorts of informational text they see around the house. Invite families to spend time in their local library or online at home researching a topic of shared interest. Is there a family member who shares a particular hobby or passion with their child?

Have students share their final Writing Projects with their families during a special Recognition. Ask families to write a letter to their child sharing what they learned from their presentations. Display these letters alongside students' final presentations.

Grade 5

Reading Lessons

The Core I.D.E.A. / Daily Reading Instruction at a Glance table on the next page highlights the teaching objectives and standards alignment for all ten lessons across the four stages of the lesson set (Introduce, Define, Extend, and Assess). It also indicates which lessons contain special features to support ELLs, technology, speaking and listening, and formative ("Milestone") assessments.

The Core Ready Reading Rubric that follows next is designed to help you record each student's overall understanding across four levels of achievement as it relates to the lesson set goals. We recommend that you use this rubric at the end of the lesson set as a performance-based assessment tool. Use the Milestone Performance Assessments and checklists as tools to help you gauge student progress toward these goals, reteach, and differentiate as needed. See the foundational book, *Be Core Ready: Powerful, Effective Steps to Implementing and Achieving the Common Core State Standards*, for more information about the Core Ready Reading and Writing Rubrics.

The Core I.D.E.A. / Daily Reading Instruction at a Glance

Grade 5 Knowledge Quest: Navigating and Integrating Multiple Sources as Researchers

Stages of the Lesson Set	Lesson	Teaching Objective	Core Standards	Special Features
Introduce: notice, explore, collect, note, immerse, surround, record, share	1	Readers orient themselves to informational text by comparing and contrasting the overall structures of sources.	RI.5.1 • RI.5.5 • RI.5.10 • SL.5.1a–d L.5.6	Close Reading ELL
	2	Readers answer questions by gathering multiple relevant print or digital sources.	RI.5.1 • RI.5.7 • RI.5.9 • RI.5.10 SL.5.1a–d • L.5.1 • L.5.6	Close Reading ELL Tech
Define: name, identify, outline, clarify, select, plan	3	Readers can determine if there are multiple main ideas within a text and identify each one with relevant supporting details from the text.	RI.5.1 • RI.5.2 • RI.5.10 • SL.5.2 L.5.6	Close Reading ELL Milestone Assessment S&L
	4	Readers determine the overall main idea by synthesizing the important ideas from smaller sections of the whole.	RI.5.1 • RI.5.2 • RI.5.10 • SL.5.1c SL.5.1d • SL.5.2 • L.5.1 • L.5.6	Close Reading ELL S&L
Extend: try, experiment, attempt, approximate, practice, explain, revise, refine	5	Readers can identify and explain the relationship between key ideas, people, and events in informational text.	RI.5.1 • RI.5.3 • RI.5.10 • SL.5.1a SL.5.1b • L.5.1 • L.5.6	Close Reading ELL Milestone Assessment S&L
	6	Readers can determine the meaning of new vocabulary in their reading.	RI.5.1 • RI.5.4 • RI.5.10 • SL.5.1a SL.5.1b • L.5.6	Close Reading ELL S&L
	7	Readers integrate information from multiple sources to create a more complete answer to their question.	RI.5.1 • RI.5.2 • RI.5.7 • RI.5.9 RI.5.10 • W.5.9b • W.5.10 • SL.5.1c SL.5.1d • L.5.1 • L.5.6	Close Reading ELL S&L Tech
	8	Readers consider and analyze multiple accounts or texts on the same topic in order to draw conclusions about the points of view represented.	RI.5.1 • RI.5.2 • RI.5.6 • RI.5.10 SL.5.1a • SL.5.1c • L.5.1 • L.5.6	Close Reading ELL Milestone Assessment S&L
	9	Readers focus on, read, and select visuals to support their presentation of information on a given topic.	RI.5.7 • SL.5.1a–d • SL.5.5 • L.5.1 L.5.6	ELL S&L Tech
Assess: reflect, conclude, connect, share, recognize, respond	10	Readers reflect on the Core Questions.	W.5.4 • W.5.10	ELL Milestone Assessment Tech

⊞ Core Ready Reading Rubric

Grade 5   Knowledge Quest: Navigating and Integrating Multiple Sources as Researchers

Lesson Set Goal	Emerging	Approaching	Achieving	Exceeding	Standards Alignment
Gather a variety of resources on a topic of interest, including print and digital resources.	Student has little or no success gathering appropriate resources without significant support.	Student gathers a few useful resources. Or student gathers multiple resources, but few are appropriate to the task.	Student gathers a variety of relevant resources on a topic of interest, including both print and digital resources.	Student gathers a wide variety of relevant and useful resources on a topic of interest, including print and digital resources.	RI.5.6 RI.5.7 RI.5.9 RI.5.10
Identify and explain common text structures in informational texts.	Student shows little or no evidence of being able to identify and explain common text structures in informational texts.	Student attempts, with some success, to identify and explain a few common text structures in informational texts.	Student identifies and explains many common common text structures in informational texts with great accuracy. May also address uncommon or advanced features.	Student identifies and explains multiple common text structures in informational texts.	RI.5.1 RI.5.5 RI.5.10 SL.5.1a–d SL.5.2 L.5.1 L.5.6
Understand, define, and utilize key vocabulary from the reading.	Student shows little or no evidence of understanding, defining, and utilizing key vocabulary from his or her reading.	Student shows some evidence of understanding, defining, and utilizing key vocabulary from his or her reading.	Student shows solid evidence of understanding, defining, and utilizing key vocabulary from his or her reading.	Student shows exceptional evidence of understanding, defining, and utilizing key vocabulary from his or her reading.	RI.5.1 RI.5.4 SL.5.1a SL.5.6 L.5.1 L.5.4 L.5.6
Determine multiple main ideas from a text and identify the key details that support these main ideas.	Student struggles to determine main ideas from a text and to identify the key details that support these main ideas. Some inaccuracies may be present. May miss some key elements.	Student has some success determining main ideas and key details that support the main ideas. Some inaccuracies may be present. May miss some key elements.	Student accurately determines multiple main ideas from a text and identifies several key details that support these main ideas. Few inaccuracies or missing elements.	Student consistently and accurately determines multiple main ideas from a text and identifies multiple key details that support these main ideas.	RI.5.1 RI.5.2 RI.5.10 SL.5.2
Identify and explain the relationship between key ideas, people, and events in informational texts.	Student has little or no success in identifying and explaining the relationship between key ideas, people, and events. Many inaccuracies and key elements missing.	Student has some success identifying and explaining the relationship between key ideas, people, and events. Some inaccuracies may be present. May miss some key elements.	Student accurately identifies and explains the relationship between key ideas, people, and events in informational texts. Few inaccuracies or missing elements.	Student consistently and accurately identifies and explains relationships, including complex or subtle ones, between key ideas, people, and events in informational texts.	RI.5.1 RI.5.3 RI.5.10 SL.5.1a SL.5.2 SL.5.4 L.5.1 L.5.6

Core Ready Reading Rubric, Grade 5, *continued*

Lesson Set Goal	Emerging	Approaching	Achieving	Exceeding	Standards Alignment
Present findings in an engaging format that integrates text, visual, and audio components in relevant ways.	Student struggles to present findings in a clear and engaging manner. The use of text, visual, and audio components is missing or very ineffective.	Student presentation of findings is somewhat clear and engaging. Some parts may have inaccuracies or be incomplete. The use of text, visual, and audio components may vary in development and effectiveness.	Student presentation is clear and engaging. There are few inaccuracies or missing elements. The use of text, visual, and audio components is effective and relevant.	Student presentation is exceptionally clear and engaging. Very thorough and accurate. The use of text, visual, and audio components is highly effective and may be especially innovative and skillful.	RI.5.7 RI.5.9 W.5.4 W.5.9b W.5.10 SL.5.1a–d SL.5.4 SL.5.5 SL.5.6 L.5.1 L.5.2 L.5.3 L.5.6
Quote accurately from a text when explaining what the text says explicitly and when drawing inferences from the text.	Student shows little or no evidence of active, purposeful reading or searching the text for specific quotes, information, and evidence. Student makes little or no attempt to provide accurate details and examples when explaining what the text says explicitly and is unable to draw inferences from the text.	Student shows some evidence of active purposeful reading and searching the text for specific quotes, information, and evidence. Student may provide some details and examples, with limited accuracy, when explaining what the text says explicitly and when drawing inferences from the text.	Student shows solid evidence of active, purposeful reading and searching the text for specific quotes, information, and evidence. Student usually provides appropriate and accurate details and examples when explaining what the text says explicitly and when drawing inferences from the text.	Student demonstrates exceptional evidence of active, purposeful reading and searching the text for specific quotes, information, and evidence. Student provides accurate, explicit and thoughtful details and examples when explaining what the text says explicitly and when drawing inferences from the text.	RI.5.1
By the end of the year, independently and proficiently read and comprehend a variety of informational texts at the high end of the grades 4–5 text complexity band.	Student shows little or no evidence of reading and comprehending texts appropriate for the grade 5 text complexity band.	Student shows inconsistent evidence of independently and proficiently reading and comprehending texts appropriate for the grade 5 text complexity band.	Student shows solid evidence of independently and proficiently reading and comprehending texts appropriate for the grade 5 text complexity band.	Student shows solid evidence of independently and proficiently reading and comprehending texts above the grade 5 text complexity band.	RI.5.10
Write routinely over extended time frames (time for research, reflection, and revision) and shorter time frames (a single sitting or a day or two) for a range of discipline-specific tasks, purposes, and audiences.	Student shows little or no evidence of writing routinely for short or long time frames for a range of discipline-specific tasks, purposes, and audiences.	Student shows some evidence of writing routinely for short and long time frames for a range of discipline-specific tasks, purposes, and audiences.	Student shows solid evidence of writing routinely for short and long time frames for a range of discipline-specific tasks, purposes, and audiences.	Student shows exceptional evidence of consistently and accurately writing for short and long time frames for a range of discipline-specific tasks, purposes, and audiences.	W.5.10

Lesson Set Goal	Emerging	Approaching	Achieving	Exceeding	Standards Alignment
In collaborative discussions, demonstrate evidence of preparation for discussion and exhibit responsibility to the rules and roles of conversation.	In collaborative discussions, student comes unprepared and often disregards the rules and roles of conversation.	In collaborative discussions, student's preparation may be evident but ineffective or inconsistent. May occasionally disregard the rules and roles of conversation.	In collaborative discussions, student prepares adequately for discussions and draws on the preparation and other information about the topic to explore ideas under discussion. Usually observes the rules and roles of conversation.	In collaborative discussions, student arrives extremely well prepared for discussions and draws on the preparation and other information about the topic to explore ideas under discussion. Always observes the rules and roles of conversation.	SL.5.1a SL.5.1b
In collaborative discussions, share and develop ideas in a manner that enhances understanding of topic. Contribute and respond to the content of the conversation in a productive and focused manner.	Student shows little or no evidence of engaging in collaborative discussions and makes little or no attempt to ask and answer questions, stay on topic, link comments to the remarks of others, or to explain his or her own ideas and understanding in light of the discussion.	Student shows some evidence of engaging in collaborative discussions and, with marginal success, attempts to ask questions to check understanding of information presented, stay on topic, link comments to the remarks of others, and explain his or her own ideas and understanding in light of the discussion.	Student engages in a range of collaborative discussions and asks questions to check understanding of information presented. Stays on topic most of the time and frequently links his or her own ideas and understanding in light of the discussion.	Student effectively and consistently engages in a range of collaborative discussions and asks high-level questions to check understanding of information presented. Always stays on topic and, with great insight and attention to the comments of others, links his or her own ideas and understanding in light of the discussion.	SL.5.1c SL.5.1d
Demonstrate knowledge of standard English and its conventions.	Student demonstrates little or no knowledge of standard English and its conventions.	Student demonstrates some evidence of knowledge of standard English and its conventions.	Student consistently demonstrates knowledge of standard English and its conventions.	Student demonstrates an exceptional understanding of standard English and its conventions. Use of conventions is sophisticated for grade level and accurate.	L.5.1 L.5.2 L.5.3
Acquire and accurately use grade-appropriate conversational, general academic, and domain-specific vocabulary and phrases.	Student shows little or no evidence of the acquisition or use of grade-appropriate conversational and academic language.	Student shows some evidence of the acquisition and use of grade-appropriate conversational and academic language.	Student shows solid evidence of the acquisition and use of grade-appropriate conversational and academic language.	Student shows a high level of sophistication and precision with the acquisition and use of grade-appropriate conversational and academic language.	L.5.6

Note: See the Core Ready Rubrics chart in the Walk Through for descriptions of category headers.

Reading Lesson 1

▶ Teaching Objective

Readers orient themselves to informational text by comparing and contrasting the overall structure of sources.

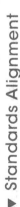

Close Reading Opportunity

▶ Standards Alignment

RI.5.1, RI.5.5, RI.5.10, SL.5.1a–d, L.5.1, L.5.6

▶ Materials

- Various informational texts that represent differing text structures (chronology, comparison, cause/effect, description, problem/solution)
- Chart paper or interactive whiteboard
- *Good Pet, Bad Pet* by Elizabeth Schleichert
- *Horses* by Seymour Simon

▶ To the Teacher

This lesson focuses on identifying the text structures most commonly used in informational texts (chronology, comparison, cause/effect, problem/solution, description) and then using this knowledge to inform *how* to read the text. For example, once readers recognize that an informational text utilizes a cause and effect format, they can begin to look for and highlight those relationships in their note taking. In fourth grade, students may have studied text structure during the lesson set What Happened and Why, exploring both timelines (chronological texts) and cause and effect relationships. If not, this lesson may be best taught if it is implemented across more than one day of instruction.

Prior to teaching this lesson, create a chart that outlines each text structure you will discuss. **ELL** Provide Comprehensible Input—Organizers. Graphic organizers provide visual support to organize thoughts for ELLs to aid in comprehension. Title the chart, "Structures in Informational Texts." You will

use this chart throughout this lesson to record (1) examples of each text structure, (2) the features of each text structure, and (3) ideas for *how* students can effectively engage in reading this sort of text. (Note: This chart is intentionally similar to the one used in grade 4.)

Text Structure	Examples . . .	Definition . . .	Features . . .	*How* to read it . . .
Chronology				
Comparison				
Cause/Effect				
Problem/Solution				
Description				

▶ Procedure

Warm Up   Gather the class to set the stage for today's learning

Gather your students. Display your chart on text structures. Ask the students, "What do you know about the different features of cause and effect writing? What is an example of a cause and effect relationship? How would you approach this kind of reading?" Spend a moment collecting student responses and charting their answers on the "Structures of Informational Text" chart. **ELL** Frontload the Lesson—Activate Prior Knowledge. Prior knowledge can help ELLs brainstorm the words in English that they may need to explain what they already understand about the topic.

Teach   Model what students need to learn and do

Remind students that writers use structures so that readers can build a better understanding of the text. Likewise, readers who recognize structures will be stronger readers of informational text. Return to your chart to focus your conversation and teaching.

Today we are going to look through a variety of informational texts. These texts use the different structures you see listed on our chart here.

- **Cause/Effect:** the result (or effect) of something is explained
- **Comparison:** two or more things are described; their similarities and differences are discussed
- **Chronology:** information is organized step by step or in order of time

Building background knowledge can offer a time when the student is learning the vocabulary in English and an opportunity to clarify for understanding.

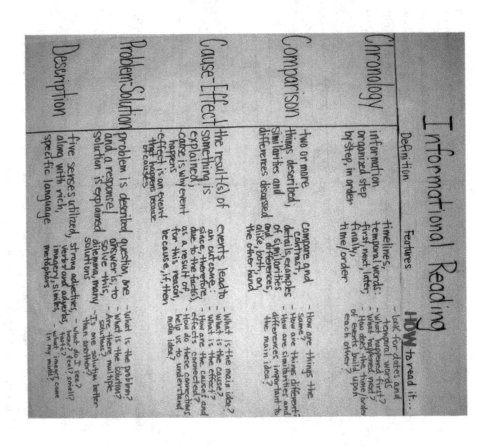

Read through the text structures on the chart. Give a brief definition of each kind of text. **ELL** Frontload the Lesson—Build Background.

- **Problem/Solution:** a problem is described and a response or solution is explained
- **Description:** a person, place, or thing is described in detail

Model reading a piece of informational text. As you read from the text, think aloud about how you are identifying its structure. **ELL** Provide Comprehensible Input—Models. Here's one way your modeling could unfold using the article "Good Pet, Bad Pet" by Elizabeth Schleichert. First read aloud the article to the class. Then, turn to explicit parts of the text as you think aloud.

I want to figure out which structure the author used to create this article. I'm thinking this article uses a problem and solution structure. Here's why. The article begins by asking, "Are you thinking about getting a pet?" which doesn't really sound like a bad problem, just a big decision for someone to make. In the second paragraph under the heading "Where to Start" the author describes all the things you need to consider before running out to get a pet. For example, she writes, "Some take a lot of time and attention and need a lot of space." This backs up my thinking that this article uses a problem and solution structure because more and more the article is focusing on the difficulty, or problem, of making this decision. Later, the author outlines some suggestions for making the decision with your family.

Indicate the section of the article that begins, "Here are some things to do before making a decision:"

These sound like a list of potential solutions to the challenge of deciding what type of pet to get. Here's an example. One of the bullet points reads, "Read some pet books or go online to learn more." **ELL** Provide Comprehensible Input—Models. Modeling your thinking, especially when you were reading, offers diverse learners a step-by-step structure of how they can solve problems independently.

Reiterate to the class how you arrived at your decision. First you read through the article. As you were reading, you kept the question about text structure in the back of your mind. Then, using the text as evidence to support your thinking, you determined which structure the author used to build the article.

Try Guide students to quickly rehearse what they need to learn and do in preparation for practice

Give your students the opportunity to engage in this type of thinking with a partner. Read aloud a brief section of *Horses* by Seymour Simon. Then, ask your students to turn and talk about the structure (description) they believe the author is using in this section of the text. **ELL** Enable Language Production—Increasing Interaction. Increasing interaction and offering opportunities to talk give ELLs time to practice their learning in English or native language. Triad partnerships (one English speaker, one ELL, and one bilingual student) are often powerful in sharing and modeling language. Remind them to use explicit examples from the text in their conversations. Listen in to several partnerships as you allow your students adequate time to discuss. Share important or interesting moments from the conversations you overheard. Be on the lookout for examples of how students wove explicit examples from the text into their conversation.

Clarify Briefly restate today's teaching objective and explain the practice task(s)

Today we are focused on identifying the specific text structure used to build various informational texts. I want you to work in groups to identify which structure is used in this packet of informational texts. You can sort the examples I give to you into different piles—one pile for each type of text structure. After you've sorted all the texts, I want you to choose two different text structures to discuss. Compare and contrast the two text structures. What features are the

same? What features are different? You can record your ideas on a Venn diagram if you find that helpful to your thinking.

Practice Students work independently or in small groups to apply today's teaching objective

Students work in collaborative groups to sort a packet of informational texts by the overall structures used. Then, each group will select two different text structures to compare and contrast.

Wrap Up Check understanding as you guide students to briefly share what they have learned and produced today

Gather your students to share their findings. Which structures did each group compare and contrast? What did they notice or discover about each text structure? Ask students to share their conversations, recording their ideas on the Structures of Informational Text chart. Once you've discussed each feature as a class, ask, "How does knowing the text structure affect the way you read a piece of informational text? Does it help? How?" Guide the class to recognize that being able to identify the structure of an informational text can help them:

- Know what to expect as they read
- Determine the main idea
- Locate supporting details
- Summarize
- Take notes

> "The cure for boredom is curiosity. There is no cure for curiosity.
> —Dorothy Parker

Reading Lesson 2

▼ **Teaching Objective**

Readers answer questions by gathering multiple relevant print or digital sources.

▼ **Standards Alignment**

RI.5.1, RI.5.7, RI.5.9, RI.5.10, SL.5.1a–d, L.5.1, L.5.6

▼ **Materials**

- Students should have their Interests and Wonderings sheet from Writing Lesson 1 handy.
- Prepared chart listing the Research Road Map (see Appendix 5.2).
- Charting supplies or interactive whiteboard

▼ **To the Teacher**

This lesson may be best addressed across multiple days. For example, you may choose to gather print resources and online resources on different days to allow students adequate time for judging the usefulness and relevance of each potential source. Another option is to spend one day narrowing the topic, revising questions and creating key words, and reserve an additional day(s) for actually locating and selecting print and online resources. Choosing to divide the gathering of materials across more than one day affords you the opportunity to teach into any misunderstandings or issues that may arise on the first day of collection. You will notice both low- and high-tech suggestions for gathering and consuming informational text. Although both options involve utilizing the Internet to gather information, the high-tech suggestion incorporates a broader range of online resources (blogs, podcasts, videos, etc.) as well as the experience of reading text online.

▼ **Procedure**

Close Reading
Opportunity

Warm Up | **Gather the class to set the stage for today's learning**

Yesterday during writing, you thought about what you are most interested in and jotted down a list of wonderings. Today it's time to dig in and see if we can find some answers to your most pressing wonderings by beginning to collect some resources. Let's take a look at our Research Road Map to get a sense of where we are in the research process.

Teach | **Model what students need to learn and do**

Display your Research Road Map. **ELL** Provide Comprehensible Input—Organizers. Organizers with descriptions, examples, or visuals can help ELLs to be independent learners. Making sure this chart is displayed in an accessible area or having a small copy for each ELL's folder will further support their learning.

We've spent time *immersing* ourselves in informational texts—just yesterday we spent our reading time looking at a variety of sources that utilize different structures to help convey the information they have to offer more clearly. We also used our writing time to think about our interests and ask questions about our wonderings. Now it's time to narrow our topic, create some key words, and begin to locate some useful sources.

Explain to the group that researchers look for sources in a number of places and formats. They conduct observations and interviews, read books related to their topic, and look for additional information online. Indicate that you will focus your energy on looking for helpful resources in print (in your classroom, school, or public library) and online.

Let's get started! Begin by reviewing the Interests and Wonderings sheet you created during Writing Lesson 1. Model narrowing your focus by choosing an interesting question that you believe will yield enough information as your focus. As you think aloud about which question to choose, consider several factors:

- Which topic or wondering are *you* most interested in knowing more about?

- Which question do you think other people will be interested in reading more about?

- Which topic do you think you will be able to find enough information about?

- Is your question "thick" enough or do you need to revise it a bit?

Now, take a moment to discuss the difference between "thick" and "thin" questions. Students who craft "thicker" questions are best equipped to find a greater number of resources and create a more dynamic presentation.

Researchers ask different types of questions—some are "thick" questions and some are "thin" questions. They ask different types of questions for different reasons. Sometimes they will ask a quick question or a thin question. There isn't much meat to a thin question. Think of them as a boring hamburger with nothing on it—there's not much to it! The answers to thin question are usually only one- or two-word answers. Here are a few examples of thin questions about inventions: When were Legos invented? Who invented Ping Pong? What year was the lightbulb invented? These questions are important to clarify confusion, but they don't make for the most interesting research projects. Then there are thick questions. These would be like the double cheeseburger packed with tons of good fixings! Researchers ask these types of questions as well. Thick questions often begin with why, how come, or I wonder. The answers are longer and usually leading to further research or discussion. For example, a thick question about inventions is, "Where does Silly Putty come from?" or "How were Legos invented?"

Begin a T-chart, using one side to list examples of thick questions and the other side to list examples of thin questions. ELL Provide Comprehensible Input—Organizers. Organizers like this T-chart offer learners concrete samples of examples and non-examples of the types of research questions they need to deepen their work. Add the questions you used as examples to the chart now. Choose one of your thick questions for the focus of your research modeling. For the purposes of this lesson set, we will focus on the question, "How were Legos invented?" but you may choose to substitute another question for modeling the research process.

Next, use your focus question or wondering to demonstrate generating a list of related search terms that will guide your resource gathering. Here is how your modeling could unfold with the question: "How were Legos invented?"

I want to list a few terms that I can type into my search bar online or use when looking up books in the library. On this list, I want to make sure to write the terms exactly as I'm going to use them in my search. You might notice that a lot of them sound very similar. I am doing this on purpose to make sure I get information that matches as closely as possible what I'm looking for—it's not always a good thing to get a ton of books or a ton of hits. We want to be more specific than that and search for materials that will really help answer our questions or wonderings. When I'm searching for books at the library, I'm going to type in "toy inventions" and "toy inventors." I might try searching for "Lego" too, but I'm afraid I'll end up with a lot of books about how to build things with Legos, which is fun, but doesn't really help me to answer my question. When I'm searching for information on the Internet, I'm going to use the terms "history of Lego" and "Lego inventor." I might also just type in my question, "How were Legos invented?" and see what happens. I'm afraid that if I just type in "toy inventions" into an Internet search bar, I'll end up with way too much information to sort through.

Explain to the class that conducting a library search for books is different from searching the Internet for information, even though the keywords and search terms you may use sound similar. In general, researchers want to cast a wider net when searching for print resources in a library, while on the Internet, it is beneficial to be as specific as possible.

Goal	Low-Tech	High-Tech
Students gather relevant resources to help them answer their question or investigate their wondering further.	Students gather materials by: • Conducting a library search for print materials	Students gather materials by: • Searching for and bookmarking useful Internet sites • Perusing relevant and topical blogs, podcasts, and videos.

As you model searching for resources for your students, think aloud about how to determine which resources will be the most useful in answering your questions. As you think aloud, highlight the idea of scanning the headings, table of contents, and index to accomplish this goal. This is a skill students practiced in both grades 3 and 4, but while familiar, it may present a challenge for some students.

Try Guide students to quickly rehearse what they need to learn and do in preparation for practice

Ask students to look at the Interests and Wonderings sheet they completed during Writing Lesson 1. Direct them to select a question on which to focus their research. Remind them that they may need to revise their question to make sure it is thick enough. After giving students a moment, have them turn and share their question with a partner. **ELL** Enable Language Production—Increasing Interaction. Increasing interaction through time to practice listening and speaking to peers helps language learners revise their thinking about which question is the strongest. As you listen in to partner conversations, select a few examples of thick questions to add to your T-chart.

Clarify Briefly restate today's teaching objective and explain the practice task(s)

Today we took many steps on our Research Road Map. We narrowed our topic by choosing a question and revising that question to make sure it is thick

enough to support our work. Then we created a list of key words that will help us locate both print and online resources. Last, we practiced skimming the resources we found to determine which resources will be the most useful and are therefore worth a closer read.

Practice Students work independently or in small groups to apply today's teaching objective

Students will select a question for further research from their Interests and Wonderings sheet. If necessary, students will revise their question to make it as thick as possible. Students will use these questions to generate a list of search terms to use when locating resources in print and online. Finally, students will evaluate the sources they gather in order to determine which resources will be the most useful in their research.

Wrap Up Check understanding as you guide students to briefly share what they have learned and produced today

Gather the class to review the process of gathering resources. Hold a class discussion. "What felt easy about finding resources to use in your research? What felt difficult?" Use the information you gain in this conversation to direct your future instruction. Do students need additional support with these skills? Are there any misunderstandings or challenges that merit an additional day of instruction and practice?

Close Reading
Opportunity

Reading Lesson 3

▼ Teaching Objective

Readers can begin to determine if there are multiple main ideas within a text and identify each one with relevant supporting details from the text.

▼ Standards Alignment

RI.5.1, RI.5.2, RI.5.10, SL.5.2, L.5.6

▼ Materials

- "Lego" in *Toys! Amazing Stories Behind Some Great Inventions* by Don Wulffson
- "History of Lego" Wikipedia page
- Main Idea and Supporting Details Graphic Organizer (see Appendix 5.3)

with each of these resources. Begin by reviewing how students can hone in on the main idea of an informational text by relying on various text features.

Teach Model what students need to learn and do

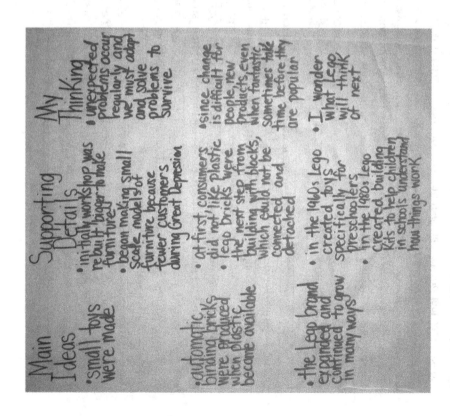

In previous grades, students practiced using headings, bolded vocabulary, graphs, and pictures to guide them toward the main idea. Quickly review this learning by modeling this process for students using a resource that includes a variety of text features. As you model your thinking, add your ideas to the Main Ideas, Supporting Details, and My Thinking graphic organizer. **ELL** Provide Comprehensible Input—Organizers and Models. Organizers and models aid in showcasing ideas in a way that will help students organize their thinking as they see you add your thinking to the chart. You can also add visuals to the headers to offer a different form of representing the category (e.g., table top as the main idea, table legs as the supporting details). Students should be familiar with the "My Thinking" column from their work in Writing Lesson 2. Briefly, this column represents a place for students to record any thoughts or additional questions they may have about the corresponding main idea and supporting details.

For this lesson, we will be using the "History of Lego" Wikipedia page. The first heading I see is "Beginnings," which is a clue. Right away, I know the first main idea of this page is going to be about how Legos began. Let me keep that in my mind as I read this section and try to come up with one sentence that captures the entire main idea about Lego's beginnings. I also need to be on the lookout for evidence from the text to support my thinking about the main idea.

Read the section aloud.

Now that I've read this section, let me come up with a sentence to capture the main idea about Lego's beginnings. "Legos began when Ole Kirk Christiansen's carpentry shop burned down and he began to make toys to make ends meet during the Great Depression." That's a good main idea statement. When I go back into the section, I can find several details that support this thinking too. First, the article tells us that Christiansen initially rebuilt a larger shop after the fire in order to expand his business, but when the Great Depression hit, Christiansen had fewer customers. The article also says that Christiansen's shop made many small scale models of furniture before building the real thing. These small models are what inspired Christiansen to make toys.

▼ To the Teacher

In previous grades, students should have had practice with determining the main idea of informational text. The work in grade 5 builds on this foundation in two ways. First, it acknowledges and encourages students to search for *multiple* main ideas within one piece of informational text. Second, this lesson set highlights how students can determine the main idea of informational texts when there are not text features upon which to rely.

▼ Procedure

Warm Up Gather the class to set the stage for today's learning

At this point in the lesson set, students have successfully gathered relevant materials to use in their research. It is now time to dig in and spend some time

In order to emphasize the idea that rich informational text may contain more than one main idea, continue using this webpage to model determining the main idea and supporting details be previewing the heading of each section. Here is what your graphic organizer might look like for this webpage.

Main Ideas	Supporting Details	My Thinking

Now it's time to highlight some strategies students can use to begin to determine the main idea and key supporting details when there are no headings or other text features to use as a guide. When there are no text features, readers can determine the main idea of an informational text by stopping and thinking, "What is this mostly about?" They can initially answer this question by 1) reading the first and last sentence of each paragraph and 2) looking for repetitive words or phrases in the body of the text.

Turn to the chapter on "Lego" in *Toys! Amazing Stories Behind Some Great Inventions* to model this work for students. Demonstrate reading to determine the main idea of a text without headings by focusing on the first and last sentences of each paragraph. Use a fresh Main Ideas and Supporting Details graphic organizer to record your thinking.

As I start reading, I notice right away that the first sentence in this paragraph is about people losing their jobs because of the Great Depression. The last sentence talks about how he would travel the countryside with his family selling his products to local farmers. So let me stop and think, what is this first paragraph mostly about? I think one of the main ideas of this chapter might be that Ole Kirk Christiansen, like many people, was forced to find a new career during the Great Depression.

Continue reading the next few paragraphs in this chapter, focusing on the first and last sentences as your guide to begin determining the main idea(s).

Try **Guide students to quickly rehearse what they need to learn and do in preparation for practice**

Select and read aloud a paragraph from the "Lego" chapter. Then, ask students to focus on the first sentence and the last sentence in the paragraph—do these help guide them toward determining a

main idea? Once students have had a moment to think, instruct them to turn and share their thinking with a partner. **ELL** Enable Language Production— Speaking and Listening. Giving extra time for ELLs to think about their speaking, as well as whispering in and helping ELLs practice their thoughts, can help them to rehearse before their partner share. As you listen in on various partnerships, prepare to share the main idea of the paragraph you've chosen to share, highlighting the conversations you overheard. Add this idea to the Main Ideas and Supporting Details graphic organizer you've started for this particular chapter. This work provides a great opportunity to pause and assess students' ability to summarize and discuss information presented orally. (SL.5.2) Quick formative assessments of this kind provide important insight into the direction of future work and support.

Once you've determined the main idea, turn to the class to solicit several key details from the text to support this main idea. Emphasize the importance of returning to the text to uncover the more relevant supporting details.

Clarify **Briefly restate today's teaching objective and explain the practice task(s)**

Today we took some important steps in our research and in our learning about informational text. First, we learned that rich pieces of informational text may have more than one main idea! Then, we reviewed how we can home in on the main idea of a chapter or article by using text features as a guide. We also talked about how we can use the first and last sentence of a paragraph as clues to the main idea when there aren't any text features to help us. And, as always, we practiced finding key details to support our main idea.

Practice **Students work independently or in small groups to apply today's teaching objective**

Students independently dig into the resources they gathered during Reading Lesson 2. Students work to determine the main ideas and key supporting details in their reading. Students should record their thinking on a Main Idea and Supporting Details graphic organizer. Students should use a different graphic organizer for each resource they engage with during their independent practice for this lesson.

Milestone Performance Assessment

Main Ideas and Supporting Details

Use this checklist to assess student understanding using the Main Idea and Supporting Detail graphic organizer.

Standards Alignment: RI.5.2, RI.5.1

	Achieved	Notes
Identify and list main ideas from text.		
Identify and list supporting details from text.		
Record thinking about the ideas in the text.		

Wrap Up Check understanding as you guide students to briefly share what they have learned and produced today

Collect students' Main Idea and Supporting Details graphic organizers. Analyze student work to determine whether there is a need for additional instruction or practice with this skill. **ELL** Assess for Content and Language Understanding—Formative Assessment. Take this time to think about language that might have been confusing or need further clarification when looking at the formative assessment. This can help drive further scaffolds in future lessons. In particular, look to see if students can successfully identify multiple main ideas (when appropriate) and pull relevant key supporting details out of the text.

Reading Lesson 4

▶ Teaching Objective

Readers determine the overall main idea by synthesizing the important ideas from smaller sections of the whole.

▶ Standards Alignment

RI.5.1, RI.5.2, RI.5.10, SL.5.1c, SL.5.1d, SL.5.2, L.5.1, L.5.6

▶ Materials

- Students should have their Main Idea and Supporting Details graphic organizers handy.
- Main Idea and Supporting Details graphic organizer from Reading Lesson 3

Close Reading Opportunity

▶ To the Teacher

The goal of this lesson is to support students in their ability to synthesize multiple main ideas from a given piece of informational text into one broad main idea that encompasses the entire piece or a large section.

▶ Procedure

Warm Up Gather the class to set the stage for today's learning

Yesterday we discovered that informational text often has more than one main idea. We practiced how to determine the main idea when there are text features and when there aren't text features to rely on.

Teach Model what students need to learn and do

Today we're going to start by reflecting on the Main Ideas and Supporting Details graphic organizers we created yesterday. I want to come up with a broad main idea for the entire piece we read by synthesizing the smaller main ideas we discovered in our reading. First, I'm going to read through the main ideas we determined yesterday. Then I'm going to ask myself, "How do these main ideas go together?"

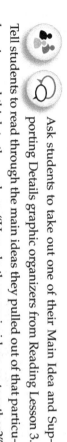

Take out the Main Idea and Supporting Details graphic organizer you created with the class during Reading Lesson 3. Reread the main ideas you highlighted on this graphic organizer. Model thinking about how these main ideas go together. **ELL** Provide Comprehensible Input—Models. Thinking aloud will offer language support as ELLs hear key vocabulary and have an opportunity to clarify questions about main ideas. Focusing on *how* these ideas go together is key, because the answer is most likely going to be reflected in your larger main idea statement. Be explicit about this fact when you are thinking aloud for your students.

Try Guide students to quickly rehearse what they need to learn and do in preparation for practice

Ask students to take out one of their Main Idea and Supporting Details graphic organizers from Reading Lesson 3. Tell students to read through the main ideas they pulled out of that particular piece and think to themselves, "How do these main ideas go together?" Once you've given students a moment to think, ask them to turn and share their ideas with a partner. **ELL** Enable Language Production—Listening and Speaking. Increasing Interaction. The time to speak with peers with their graphic organizers offers ELLs time to clarify their thinking and vocabulary about ideas that they wrote as well as expand their thinking through the peer conversation. Can they come up with a clear broad main idea that encompasses the entire article or a large section of an article or chapter? As you circulate and listen in to these conversations, take the opportunity to reinforce good listening

and speaking etiquette including explicitly drawing on materials to explore the idea under discussion and making comments that contribute to the discussion (SL.5.1a, SL.5.1c).

Clarify Briefly restate today's teaching objective and explain the practice task(s)

Rich informational text often has more than one main idea. However, it is also helpful to be able to come up with one broad main idea statement that encompasses an entire article or chapter. Today we practiced doing just this by reflecting on the various main ideas we pulled from a piece of informational text and asking ourselves, "How do these main ideas go together?" As you continue your research today, I want you to reflect on a large main idea for an entire chapter or article and add it to the bottom of your Main Ideas and Supporting Details graphic organizer.

Practice Students work independently or in small groups to apply today's teaching objective

Students read in their selected informational texts, continuing to use graphic organizers to record the main ideas and supporting detail they pull from the text. At the end of an article or chapter, students should stop to determine the main idea of the larger section encompassing the smaller sections, using the graphic organizer.

Wrap Up Check understanding as you guide students to briefly share what they have learned and produced today

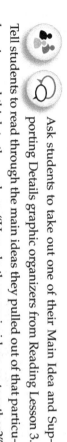

Ask one or two students to share their Main Idea and Supporting Details graphic organizers with the class. As students share their thinking, they should emphasize how they synthesized the various main ideas from one piece to come up with one broader, yet clear, main idea statement. Prompt other students to ask specific questions, focused on the speaker's thought process or aimed at clarifying their conclusions. (SL.5.1c)

Reading Lesson 5

▼ Teaching Objective

Readers can identify and explain the relationship between key ideas, people, and events in informational text.

Close Reading Opportunity

▼ Standards Alignment

RI.5.1, RI.5.3, RI.5.10, SL.5.1a, SL.5.1b, L.5.1, L.5.6

▼ Materials

- Research Road Map (Appendix 5.2)
- Key Ideas, People, and Events Graphic Organizer (Appendix 5.4)

▼ Procedure

Warm Up | Gather the class to set the stage for today's learning

Remind students of where you are on the Research Road Map, indicating and recapping briefly each step you've already completed. Relate to students that so far, it might appear as if the process of conducting research is linear—you just follow one step after another in order and voila, You've researched! However, today's lesson intends to highlight the messy nature of true research.

Today we're going to start to organize our information a bit by thinking about the key ideas, events, and people that go along with the topic we're researching. Once we do that, we'll be able to clearly see a few places where we can gather more sources, locate new information, and incorporate it into our note taking and findings.

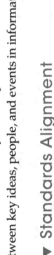

Teach | Model what students need to learn and do

Introduce the Key Ideas, People, and Events graphic organizer. The introduction to the organizer gives ELLs time to clarify their understanding about what key ideas, people, and events are. If needed, showcase these three categories by providing

ELL Provide Comprehensible Input—Organizers. The introduction to the organizer gives ELLs time to clarify their understanding about what key ideas, people, and events are. If needed, showcase these three categories by providing

a visual from a familiar text in the header. Low-tech ways to do this could be just showing the book; copying visuals from the book; or having the students draw these visuals in their organizers. Explain to students that this is one way to begin to organize the information you've collected so far. It is also a method for highlighting additional areas for further research that could prove to be very interesting. Model adding your topic to the top of the graphic organizer and listing these various components. Rely on the recurring main ideas you've pulled out of various texts. If you've chosen to use "How were Legos invented?" as your focus question, here is what your graphic organizer might look like.

Topic: How Were Legos Invented?

Key Ideas	Key Events	Key People
Christiansen built miniature furniture models to help his designs	Ole Kirk Christiansen's woodshop burning down	Ole Kirk Christiansen Godtfred (his son)
Legos lock together, unlike regular blocks making Legos out of plastic, instead of wood	The Great Depression Another fire in the warehouse	

Point out to the class that while each of the ideas, events, and people you have listed may make interesting topics for additional research, it is the *relationships* between these ideas, events, and people that are perhaps the most interesting. Think aloud about some of the relationships on the chart you've created so students can get an idea of what this thinking sounds like and should encompass.

Let's think for a moment about how some of these key events and ideas go together. When Ole Kirk Christiansen's original warehouse burned down, he rebuilt it thinking he would continue his business. But then the Great Depression hit and people he had to find other ways to make money because he had fewer and fewer customers. That's when he tried turning his furniture models into toys. The reality of life during the Great Depression is what pushed

Christiansen to change his business and try something new. I wonder, if the Great Depression had never happened, would Legos have been invented?

Recap your thinking process for the class. **ELL** Identify and Communicate Content and Language Objectives—Repeat. Repetition is a powerful strategy for ELLs, giving them multiple times, ways, and opportunities to hear the same information. This helps ELLs increase their vocabulary and understanding around the information.

Did you notice how I first listed the key events, ideas, and people that go along with my topic? Then I took a look at two entries from different columns and thought about how they go together. I focused on the *relationship* between them. As a result, I think I might do a little more digging for information about the Great Depression to add to my findings.

Try Guide students to quickly rehearse what they need to learn and do in preparation for practice

Tell students to take a moment and begin to fill out their Key Ideas, Events, and People graphic organizer. As students work, circulate and support their efforts. **ELL** Enable Language Production—Reading and Writing. This is an informal time for you to support ELL language acquisition in real time. You

may find it helpful to carry sticky notes for quick support and modeling. This is also an opportunity for ELLs to ask for support or clarification in a smaller-scale setting.

Clarify Briefly restate today's teaching objective and explain the practice task(s)

Today we began to organize the information we've gathered on our topics so far by listing the key ideas, events, and people on a graphic organizer. Creating this list helps us to focus on the relationships between some of these factors. This work is important because a) you'll need to mention these key aspects when you report your findings and b) explaining the relationships is often the most interesting part of your research.

Explain to the class that you'd like them to complete their graphic organizers independently. Then, each student should think about how various items on their graphic organizer are related. Ask students to jot down their thinking about this relationship on the back of their graphic organizer.

Practice Students work independently or in small groups to apply today's teaching objective

Students complete the Key Ideas, People, and Events graphic organizer, highlighting and explaining their thinking about one relationship they discover. If time allows, students should continue spending time engaged with their resources and taking appropriate notes.

Wrap Up Check understanding as you guide students to briefly share what they have learned and produced today

Ask students to have their Key Ideas, People, and Events graphic organizers handy. Have students turn and talk to a partner, sharing the relationship they discovered as a result of this exercise. Be sure that students also name the additional areas they would like to research further. Choose one or two students to share their work and thinking with the class. Use this Wrap Up as an opportunity to highlight the importance of coming to discussions prepared in order to specifically draw on that preparation while talking with a partner. (SL.5.1a) Collect and analyze student's graphic organizers to determine if students 1) can accurately name the key ideas, events, and people related to their topic; and 2) if they can clearly describe the relationship between two or more of these elements,

demonstrating a deeper understanding of both their topic and informational reading. **ELL** Assess for Content and Language Understanding—Formative Assessments. When looking at the formative assessment, take time to think about language that might have been confusing or need further clarification. This can help drive further scaffolds in future lessons.

	Achieved	Notes
Identify key people from text.		
Identify key ideas from text.		
Identify key events from text.		
Explain the relationship between one or more people, ideas, and events.		

Milestone Performance Assessment

Identifying Key Ideas, People, and Events

 Use this checklist to assess student work on the Key Ideas, People, and Events graphic organizer.

Standards Alignment RI.5.1, RI.5.3

Reading Lesson 6

▶ Teaching Objective

Readers can determine the meaning of new vocabulary in their reading.

▶ Standards Alignment

RI.5.1, RI.5.4, RI.5.10, SL.5.1, SL.5.1a, SL.5.1b, L.5.1, L.5.6

▶ Materials

- Prepared chart titled, Strategies for Finding the Meaning of New Words

▶ Procedure

Warm Up Gather the class to set the stage for today's learning

We've spent the last few days immersed in our topics. I have been observing you do your research, implementing our learning. I have noticed that many of you are coming across new and interesting words that you may have never seen before or may not understand. That happens no matter how old you are or how much research you do. Today we're going to think about some ways to discover the meanings of these words and use this as an opportunity to expand our vocabularies.

Close Reading Opportunity

Teach Model what students need to learn and do

 Display the Strategies for Finding the Meaning of New Words chart. **ELL** Provide Comprehensible Input—Organizers. This organizer is an especially powerful support because these strategies are used constantly in navigating a new language. You may find it helpful to sketch examples of each strategy to provide a visual of the strategy. This chart lists a variety of strategies for students to use. In previous years, students have practiced the following strategies (which are purposefully included on the chart) to determine the meaning of new or unknown words:

- Using context clues
- Looking for words within words
- Looking at the graphic aids on the page
- Looking to a glossary, dictionary, or other online tool

Today you will focus on using context clues by modeling reading the sentences before and after the tricky word(s) (but also encourage students to name and utilize any and all strategies). In particular, be sure to emphasize the need to rely on and be comfortable with a variety of strategies as the same strategy may not work for all words. Model encountering a new word and using context clues by reading the sentence before and after to determine the word's meaning. **ELL** Provide Comprehensible Input—Models. For the purposes of this lesson, we are using the chapter on Silly Putty from *Toys! Amazing Stories Behind Some Great Inventions.*

I was flipping through my book on toys, when I stopped to check out this chapter on Silly Putty. I loved Silly Putty when I was a kid! I was reading along when I came to these two tricky words: boric acid and silicone oil. Yikes! I want you to watch me as I use context clues to help me find the meaning of these two tricky words. Notice how I read the sentence before and after the tricky words to get a better idea of what they might mean.

Model reading the sentences before and after the words *boric acid* and *silicone oil* at the beginning of the chapter on Silly Putty. Notice that the sentence before these terms contains the words *chemical combination.* This tells you that boric acid and silicone oil are probably both chemicals. The sentence after these tricky words discusses how when mixed together, boric acid and silicone oil become a soft substance.

These clues, found in the sentences before and after the tricky words, tell us that boric acid and silicone oil must be chemical substances that get mixed together to form Silly Putty!

Try Guide students to quickly rehearse what they need to learn and do in preparation for practice

Find another potentially tricky word or phrase later in the same article or chapter you used to model. For example, later in this same chapter on Silly Putty, students come upon the word *query.* Read aloud the sentences that come before and after this word. Then, ask students to turn and talk—what do they think this word might mean based on the clues given in these sentences? **ELL** Enable Language Production—Increasing

interaction. This partnership time would be a good opportunity to pair ELLs at different language proficiencies together so that they model how they use strategies as learners in a second language.

Note: It is important to highlight instances where this strategy may not be helpful in determining the meaning of new words. If this occurs during your turn-and-talk, walk students through the process of trying alternative strategies from the Strategies To Find the Meaning of New Words chart.

Clarify Briefly restate today's teaching objective and explain the practice task(s)

Today we reviewed some of the strategies you've already learned to try when you come across a tricky word. We took some time to practice using context clues by reading the sentences that come directly before and after these new words. Many times, this strategy will help you to find the meaning of these unknown words.

Tell students to continue working with the resources they have gathered on their topic. In particular, they should pay attention to new vocabulary, trying to use context clues (or any strategy) to solve for word meaning. All students should be prepared to share one new word with the class and be able to explain the strategy they used to find the meaning of this new word. (SL.5.1a)

Practice Students work independently or in small groups to apply today's teaching objective

Students continue to work with the resources they've gathered on their topic, taking appropriate notes. However, today, each student should highlight at least one unknown word he had to problem solve.

Wrap Up Check understanding as you guide students to briefly share what they have learned and produced today

Ask each student to bring at least one new word she encountered in her research. Have students share with a partner the word, its meaning, and the strategy they used to understand it. Choose one or two students to share their work and thinking with the entire class.

Reading Lesson 7

Close Reading Opportunity

▶ Teaching Objective

Readers integrate information from multiple sources to create a more complete answer to their question.

▶ Standards Alignment

RI.5.1, RI.5.2, RI.5.7, RI.5.9, RI.5.10, W.9b, W.5.10, SL.5.1c, SL.5.1d, L.5.1, L.5.6

▶ Materials

- "5 Ws, 1H" Graphic Organizer (see Appendix 5.5)
- Notes gathered from various resources

▶ Procedure

Warm Up Gather the class to set the stage for today's learning

We are beginning to create our final products in writing, so it's time to put together everything that we've learned about our topics in an organized way that is easy for the reader to understand. All of you have a lot of notes to sort from—you've gathered quite a bit of information. Sometimes it can be overwhelming to think across all your notes, especially when you have looked at multiple sources. Today we're going to practice strategies for integrating the information from different sources into one organized presentation.

Teach Model what students need to learn and do

Model skimming through the notes you've taken from multiple sources related to your topic, thinking aloud about how to organize like information into logical categories. Keep the categories you create simple and general, using sub-questions as your guide. In front of the class, demonstrate generating sub-questions on the graphic organizer, placing one question in each box. For example, the sub-questions that would guide the categories created in this project include:

Goal	Low-Tech	High-Tech
Students read through their notes on a topic and organize their information into a logical sequence.	Students read through their handwritten notes. Students organize their notes by utilizing different colored pens to code for logical categories. Students can then decide on a logical sequence for presenting their information by filling out a graphic organizer.	Students read through the notes they have taken using a digital note-taking resource. Students organize their notes by cutting and pasting to create logical categories. Students can then decide on a logical sequence for presenting their information by filling out a digital graphic organizer.

- *Who* invented Legos?
- *What* are Legos?
- *When* were Legos invented?
- *Where* were Legos invented?
- *Why* were Legos invented?
- *How* were Legos invented?

Keep your coding system simple as well. For example, code *who* information in red, *what* information in yellow, *where* information in green, *when* information in blue, *why* information in purple, and *how* information in orange. Be sure to explicitly demonstrate the method you'd like your class to use, whether you choose to do this work on paper or on the computer. Clear modeling will help to alleviate any problems with the actual process itself and free students to focus on the critical thinking needed for this type of work. **ELL Provide Comprehensible Input—Models.** Also, be sure to emphasize that students may not have information or notes related to each of these categories. Emphasize that these categories are a way of organizing the information they already have, not a method for finding additional information at this point in the process. Here is one way your modeling could unfold:

The question I'm trying to answer with my research is "*how* were Legos invented?" but I'm really interested in a lot more than just the how. I'm also interested and found great information about the who, what, when, where, and why Legos were invented. Using these question words, who, what, where, when, why, and how, is a great way to help organize our research notes into logical categories. I'm going to pick a color to represent each of these question words, or categories. Then, as I'm reading through the notes that I've taken, I'm going to pay attention to notes related to each of the question words. Watch me as I read a bullet point, ask myself, "Does this piece of information tell me about who, what, where, when, why, or how Legos were invented?" and then code the information appropriately. When I'm done, I'll have an easy way to categorize or think across the information I've collected across a variety of sources.

Here is what your graphic organizer might look like:

Main Ideas	Supporting Details	My Thinking

Once your notes have been organized into logical categories (such as who, what, where, when, why and how), return to your original research question. For this lesson set, we have focused on the question, "How were Legos invented?" Consider the most logical sequence to present your information. Which category will you discuss first? How will you connect each category in a logical fashion? For example, in answering the question, "How were Legos invented?" it would make the most sense to begin with the information related to the how box on the graphic organizer.

Try Guide students to quickly rehearse what they need to learn and do in preparation for practice

Distribute graphic organizers to your students. Ask them to jot their research question at the top of the page. Then, direct students to generate who, what, where, when, why, and how questions based on their research topic to help categorize and synthesize the information they gathered across

multiple categories. As students work, check in with various individuals, looking for examples of categories to share with the class before sending them off to work independently.

Clarify Briefly restate today's teaching objective and explain the practice task(s)

It's time to read through our notes and organize our thinking to help us craft clear presentations on our topics. Today, I'd like you to read through your notes and organize them into logical categories, using who, what, where, when, why, and how questions as a guide. Then, considering your original research question, put your categories into a logical sequence that will be easy for the reader to follow and understand. Fill out this graphic organizer to record your ideas.

Practice Students work independently or in small groups to apply today's teaching objective

Students read through their notes, organizing the information they've collected into logical categories. Then, students fill out a graphic organizer that arranges these categories into a logical sequence.

Wrap Up Check understanding as you guide students to briefly share what they have learned and produced today

Gather the class, asking students to have their graphic organizers ready. Have them share their graphic organizers with a partner. Partners should respond with suggestions for clarifying categories or the sequence of information being presented. This lesson presents a wonderful opportunity to highlight the importance of posing and responding to specific questions by making comments that contribute to the discussion. Partners are expected to be active listeners who assist in revising and clarifying their classmate's original ideas. (SL.5.1c)

Reading *Lesson 8*

▼ Teaching Objective

Readers consider and analyze multiple accounts or texts on the same topic in order to draw conclusions about the points of view represented.

▼ Standards Alignment

RI.5.1, RI.5.2, RI.5.6, SL.5.1a, SL.5.1c, L.5.1, L.5.6

▼ Materials

- "50th Birthday of the Lego Brick" posted on www.wikipedia.org
- "History of Lego" posted on www.lego.com
- Venn diagram

▼ To the Teacher

This lesson asks students to compare and contrast information found in multiple accounts on the same topic. However, beyond using this information to confirm the importance of some details or put together a more complete image of a particular event, students will analyze these sources to assess the impact of purpose or point of view on the content of the text. With this focus in mind, it is often key for students to be able to notice and think about what details are *not* included in certain accounts as well as *how* key events, ideas, and people are presented.

▼ Procedure

Warm Up Gather the class to set the stage for today's learning

You've gathered a tremendous amount of information on your topics already. I know I've read quite a bit about Legos and how they were invented. Each time I work with a new resource, I find a few more details or another piece of important information that helps to shape my thinking about this event.

Close Reading Opportunity

Teach Model what students need to learn and do

I know many of you have read more than one source about your topic. You've read articles online, chapters from books, and various articles. Just as I have, you've put all of this information together to help answer your question. You've become very good at reading across informational texts in order to find a wealth of information about a specific topic. Well, today we're going to look across our resources in a different way. We're going to analyze the different resources you have and focus on the different points of view or purposes they represent.

Take a moment to define "point of view" and "author's purpose" for the class. **ELL** Identify and Communicate Content and Language Objectives—Academic Vocabulary. Academic vocabulary can pose a different challenge to your ELLs. If your ELLs need further clarification, you could form small groups and use familiar text at their level that will help them see examples of point of view and author's purpose. These examples can be your graphics for the Venn.

▶ **Author's purpose**: the author's reason for something existing, or occurring. *What was the author's purpose for writing this?*

▶ **Point of view**: a way of thinking about or looking at something. *The coach did not agree with the referee's point of view.*

Using two or more sources from your model study, demonstrate relying heavily on the text itself for this type of analysis. Students should be on the lookout for:

- What is said in every source?
- What is *not* said in every source? Why do you think a source may have left something out?
- Were there differences between sources in how they conveyed the same basic information?
- How do you think the author's purpose or point of view affected the message?

The purpose of this lesson is for students to consider how author's purpose and point of view impact the content of informational text. We will be utilizing two online sources: "50th Birthday of the Lego Brick" and "History of Lego." Both accounts focus on the beginnings of the Lego company, yet contain different information as a result of the intended audience and purpose of the website.

When I took another look at these two accounts of the beginning of the Lego company, I was struck right away by a big difference. This piece in Wikipedia goes into a lot of detail about the fires in Ole Christiansen's workshop, as well as how the Great Depression forced him to diversify his original furniture business to include toys. I also found out that Christiansen didn't start his toy company by making Legos. At first, he made a variety of wooden pull toys and piggy banks. But this article, posted on the Lego website, doesn't say anything about the fires, the other toys Christiansen made, or the Great Depression. If I read this article and nothing else, I would have a very different idea about how Legos were invented.

Use the Venn diagram to record your thinking about the similarities and differences between these two resources thus far. Here's an example of what your Venn diagram might look like. Discuss with students how this is an example of how intended audience impacts the author's purpose and, therefore, the content of any given source they may encounter on a particular topic. Critical readers of informational text should analyze their resources with this in mind.

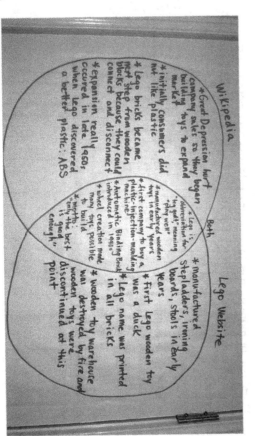

Try Guide students to quickly rehearse what they need to learn and do in preparation for practice

Why would the Lego webpage choose to leave out the information about Christiansen's true beginnings?

Think aloud about the purpose and intended audience of each online source. (Wikipedia is an online encyclopedia that attempts to have complete and unbiased information. The article on the Lego website was posted in the section for parents.) Lead the class in a discussion that investigates this question, guiding students to realize that perhaps the Lego website chose not to include this information for a variety of reasons, including:

• The Lego company didn't want the invention of Legos, a very successful toy, to seem like an accident.

• The purpose of this article is to celebrate the birth and success of Legos rather than to explain it in detail.

• The intended audience of the Lego webpage is more specific than the audience for Wikipedia pages. Specifically, it was written for the parents of children who play with Legos, who may not be interested in historical details.

As your class discussion unfolds, craft a shared response that begins to answer this question at the bottom of your Venn diagram. Be sure to emphasize the need to incorporate specific examples from the text as you explain your thinking.

Clarify Briefly restate today's teaching objective and explain the practice task(s)

We want to be critical readers of informational text. That means we need to think across our resources and consider how they are the same and how they are different. It is important to do this work keeping in mind how the intended audience and author's purpose can impact the content of any given resource. Today I want you to put two or three of your resources side by side. What is the same and what is different across these texts? Consider the intended audiences and author's purpose for these sources. How do they interact to impact the content? Be prepared to share your thinking about this at the end of our reading time today. Jot down any notes that will make it easy for you to share your ideas with a classmate.

Practice   Students work independently or in small groups to apply today's teaching objective

Students analyze multiple resources on their topic, considering the interaction and impact of intended audience and author's purpose on the content of each account. Students use a Venn diagram to record the similarities and differences they notice. At the bottom of the Venn diagram, students should jot down their thinking in a way that supports their ability to report their findings to a classmate. Thinking about the relationship between content, purpose, and point of view will be a challenging task for many fifth graders, but we see it as an early and important step to becoming critical readers. Some students may be able to try a triple Venn diagram to compare three sources.

Wrap Up   Check understanding as you guide students to briefly share what they have learned and produced today

Gather the class, asking them to bring along any notes or examples they may need to discuss their thinking with a partner. Then, instruct the class to turn and share their ideas with a partner. Circulate, listening for key exemplar conversations to share with the larger group. This Wrap Up serves as another great opportunity to emphasize the importance of coming to discussions prepared to speak intelligently and listen actively. These skills are hallmarks of the Common Core and essential in grade 5. (SL.5.1a, SL.5.1c)

Collect and analyze students' Venn diagrams to determine if there is a need for additional support or practice with understanding or expressing these ideas. Are students able to identify key similarities and differences that

are reflective of the author's point of view? Are students able to explain these observations in a clear way that is grounded in examples from the text itself?

Milestone Performance Assessment

Compare and Contrast

Use this checklist to assess student ability to compare and contrast information found in multiple accounts on the same topic.

Standards Alignment: RI.5.1, RI.5.2, RI.5.6, SL.5.1a, SL.5.1c

	Achieved	Notes
Record similarities between sources.		
Record differences between sources.		
Provide reasonably logical reasons why sources differ from each other.		
Form connections with author's purpose and point of view.		

"The foundation of every state is the education of its youth.

—Diogenes

Reading Lesson 9

▼ Teaching Objective

Readers focus on, read, and select visuals to support their presentation of information on a given topic.

▼ Standards Alignment

RI.5.7, SL.5.1a–d, SL.5.5, L.5.1, L.5.6

▼ Materials

- Charting supplies or interactive whiteboard
- Computer with Internet access

▼ To the Teacher

In third grade, students worked to "read" the visuals included in informational text as a way to support their understanding of the topic and to encourage the idea of lingering in a text. In this lesson, we ask students to again focus on visuals; however, with the incorporation of Internet-based resources, students must consider a wider range of visual support including, but not limited to, illustrations, photographs, related hyperlinks, and videos. The end goal for this lesson is for students to consider a wide range of visuals, think about how those visuals enhance the information presented, and integrate those that will best support their final presentations.

This lesson may be best if divided across more than one day of instruction. If you choose to divide the work in this lesson, have students notice, chart, and discuss the various types of visual media available to them by looking through the resources they have gathered on their topic on one day. On another day, ask students to search for or create the visual media they will use in their final presentations.

▼ Procedure

Warm Up ☐ Gather the class to set the stage for today's learning

You have all worked very hard to mine your resources for as much information as you possibly can! However, there may be an additional resource

in your research that you have yet to consider—the visuals! Illustrations, photographs, videos, and links to additional sources enhance the information presented in any given resource. Today, we're going to focus on the visuals we've encountered and choose visuals to use in our own final presentations.

Teach ☐ Model what students need to learn and do

Begin a simple T-chart titled, "Visuals That Support Our Work." You will use the left side of the chart to describe that type of visual and the right side of the chart to record the type of visual might support student work. **ELL** Provide Comprehensible Input—Organizers, Visuals. Visuals are a universal, nonverbal way for ELLs to communicate their work.

Now, return to the sources you have used for your model research. Model looking through these resources again, focusing on the types of visual resources presented. As you encounter a new type of resource, think aloud about what it is and how it supports the information presented. Then, add your thinking to the T-chart. Here are a few types of visuals you will want to list and provide examples of:

- Photographs: *The Ultimate Lego Book* by DK Publishers
- Illustrations: *Toys! Amazing Stories Behind Some Great Inventions* by Don Wulffson, illustrated by Laurie Keller
- Videos: "Who Invented the Kite?" posted on Wonderopolis.org
- Hyperlinks: "History of Lego" posted on www.wikipedia.org

Now that you have a list of possible visual resources to include in your final presentation, think aloud about the types of visual support you will include in your final presentation. Model conducting a search for possibilities. **ELL** Provide Comprehensible Input—Models. This is an opportunity to aid ELLs in the exact key words they need for a search. Return to the graphic organizer you used to originally plan your presentation during Reading Lesson 7. Read through your first supporting detail about the original fire in Christiansen's factory. Think aloud about the type of image that would best illustrate this detail as well as what types of images are readily available to you.

When I think about the kind of image I want to use to illustrate this key detail, right away I know I won't include a video. There can't be any video from a fire that happened this long ago—there weren't any video cameras in the 1920s. Plus, I don't think a video of any old fire, which I could find, would really do the trick. Instead, I'm thinking I might be able to find a historical photograph to include. I know I saw some in the reading I did. I could copy one of those or do a Google search using some key words.

Goal	Low-Tech	High-Tech
Students choose and locate visuals to support their presentation of information on a specific topic.	Students locate and utilize visuals in the following ways: • Looking through print resources, photocopying relevant visuals • Creating drawings or diagrams as appropriate	Students locate and utilize visuals in the following ways: • Conducting a Google Image search for related photographs, drawings or illustrations • Conducting a search for photographs on Flickr • Searching YouTube or TeacherTube for videos • Finding additional web resources to use as hyperlinks (web pages, images, videos, etc.)

Try Guide students to quickly rehearse what they need to learn and do in preparation for practice

Actively involve your students in deciding which visuals will best support your final presentation on the invention of Legos through a class discussion. **ELL** **Enable Language Production—Listening and Speaking** Use your graphic organizer as a jumping off point, pushing them to think of explicit examples of visual support for the two remaining supporting details included on your graphic organizer, as well as how they might go about finding these examples. Be sure to

emphasize the importance of considering what types of visuals are readily available.

Clarify Briefly restate today's teaching objective and explain the practice task(s)

Reiterate the importance of visuals in enhancing the presentation of information. Call students' attention back to the chart "Visuals That Support Our Work," asking them to consider their options and choose visuals that will best support their final presentations.

Practice Students work independently or in small groups to apply today's teaching objective

Students look through the visuals available to them, considering how each visual works to enhance the information presented. Then, students choose visuals to integrate into their final presentations. Tell students they should be prepared to share their process with the class. As you support students during their independent practice, emphasize the importance of returning to their research question and intended message as a basis for making decisions about the integration of various multimedia components. The goal is to select multimedia elements that enhance, rather than distract from, the student's intended focus. (SL.5.5)

Wrap Up Check understanding as you guide students to briefly share what they have learned and produced today

Gather the class to discuss this process. Use the following questions to focus your conversation:

Which visuals do you feel are the most useful in enhancing informational text? How did choosing visuals for your final presentation go? What felt easy? What felt difficult?

Reading Lesson 10

▼ **Teaching Objective**

Readers reflect on the Core Questions (on page 179).

▼ **Standards Alignment**

W.5.4, W.5.10

▼ **Materials**

- Chart that lists the Core Questions (on page 179) for this lesson set

▼ **To the Teacher**

Reflection is an essential part of this work. It provides students with the necessary time to think about and articulate their own learning as well as develop and express their identity as readers and writers. Helping students pause and think about what they've learned and what they've enjoyed will have long-lasting effects. This is something you may also want to discuss with families when they visit your classroom or through newsletters

© Monkey Business/Fotolia

or other communication you send home. Emphasize with students that searching for the answers to their questions will be a skill that will serve them throughout their lives, no matter what path they choose to take.

▼ **Procedure**

Warm Up | **Gather the class to set the stage for today's learning**

"I am so impressed with the work you have created over the last few weeks! In this classroom, we now have a wealth of experts on all sorts of topics and dynamic presentations to put out into the world.

Teach | **Model what students need to learn and do**

Today I want us to take some time and reflect on everything we've learned about asking and answering our own questions. One thing we learned was that conducting our own research can be a complex process. Now that we've finished going through this process ourselves, I want us to reflect. 'What does it mean to conduct research?'"

Try | **Guide students to quickly rehearse what they need to learn and do in preparation for practice**

Lead the class in a discussion around this question. As the discussion unfolds, begin to craft a shared response to the question. **ELL** Provide Comprehensible Input—Models. This is an opportunity for students to hear sentence frames and structures that they will need in preparing for independent practice. Ideally, your class response should describe the complex process of research using terminology from the Research Road Map as well as concrete examples from resources they explored and from their own experience.

Clarify | **Briefly restate today's teaching objective and explain the practice task(s)**

"It's important to take some time to reflect on your learning after completing a project. This helps make what you learn stay in your brain so you can use it later! I want to know what you have learned about yourself as a reader through this process. Today, you are going to write a response to one of our remaining Core Questions.

178

Post the questions in a central location for students to refer back as they work.

- What does it mean to conduct research?
- How do we find answers to our questions as we read?
- How do readers synthesize information and develop ideas through the use of multiple nonfiction sources?
- How does the use of other media enhance the presentation of information?
- How do readers share their research in dynamic ways?

Practice Students work independently or in small groups to apply today's teaching objective

Students individually craft responses to the Core Questions posed. Check in with ELLs to provide sentence support; remind them of and refer them to the group constructed response.

ELL Enable Language Production—Reading and Writing. Check in with ELLs to provide sentence support; remind them of and refer them to the group constructed response.

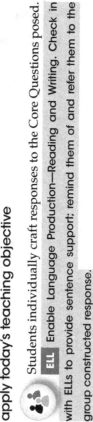

Goal	Low-Tech	High-Tech
Students craft a written response to one or two reflection questions.	Students answer the questions using pencil and paper. Students share their responses orally. You could choose key snippets of conversation to write up and create a reflection bulletin board.	Students draft a response on a Word document, practicing their keyboarding skills. They can share this document with you by dragging it into a shared folder on Dropbox or via email. In addition, students can • Post their reflections to a class blog to share with their peers. As homework, students could comment thoughtfully on the reflections of two (or more) of their classmates. • Create a VoiceThread to post and preserve audio and visual representations of class reflections on the Core Questions.

Wrap Up Check understanding as you guide students to briefly share what they have learned and produced today

After students have had sufficient time to complete their responses, call the class together to share their ideas.

Collect student work to assess their understanding of reading and conducting research using multiple informational resources. Let this information help you determine where students need additional guidance or support. **ELL** (Assess for Content and Language Understanding—Summative Assessment)

Milestone Performance Assessment

How to Use Multiple Sources in Research

Use this checklist to assess student written reflection on the Core Questions.

Standards Alignment: W.5.4, W.5.10

	Achieved	Notes
Define research.		
Explain methods for answering reading questions.		
Explain how to synthesize and develop ideas using multiple sources.		
Explain how other media enhances the presentation of information with specific examples.		
Share examples of how researchers share their research in dynamic ways.		

Writing Lessons

The Core I.D.E.A. / Daily Writing Instruction at a Glance table on the next page highlights the teaching objectives and standards alignment for all ten lessons across the four stages of the lesson set (Introduce, Define, Extend, and Assess). It also indicates which lessons contain special features to support ELL students, technology, speaking and listening, and formative ("Milestone") assessments.

The Core Ready Writing Rubric that follows next is designed to help you record each student's overall understanding across four levels of achievement as it relates to the lesson set goals. We recommend that you use this rubric at the end of the lesson set as a performance-based assessment tool. Use the Milestone Performance Assessments and checklists as tools to help you gauge student progress toward these goals, reteach, and differentiate as needed. See the foundational book, *Be Core Ready: Powerful, Effective Steps to Implementing and Achieving the Common Core State Standards,* for more information about the Core Ready Reading and Writing Rubrics.

Grade 5

The Core I.D.E.A. / Daily Writing Instruction at a Glance

Grade 5 Knowledge Quest: Navigating and Integrating Multiple Sources as Researchers

Instructional Stages	Lesson	Teaching Objectives	Core Standards	Special Features
Introduce: notice, explore, collect, note, immerse, surround, record, share	1	Writers find inspiration for their research.	RI.5.10 • W.5.7 • SL.5.1a–d • L.5.1 • L.5.6	ELL S&L Tech
	2	Writers take organized notes to record their thinking and learning.	RI.5.10 • W.5.7 • W.5.8 W.5.10 • SL.5.1 a–d L.5.1 • L.5.6	ELL Tech
Define: name, identify, outline, clarify, select, plan	3	Writers understand when and how to summarize, paraphrase, and quote accurately when taking notes on a text.	RI.5.1 • RI.5.2 • RI.5.10 • W.5.7 • W.5.8 W.5.10 • SL.5.1a–d • L.5.1 • L.5.6	Close Reading ELL Milestone Assessment
	4	Writers articulate their thoughts about their reading in writing.	RI.5.10 • W.5.4 • W.5.5 • W.5.9b W.5.10 • SL.5.1a–d • L.5.1 L.5.6	ELL S&L
Extend: try, experiment, attempt, approximate, practice, explain, revise, refine	5	Writers craft clear and organized responses to their reading.	RI.5.10 • W.5.4 • W.5.5 • W.5.9b W.5.10 • SL.5.1a–d • L.5.1 • L.5.6	ELL Milestone Assessment S&L
	6	Writers introduce their topic clearly by providing a thesis or focus statement.	W.5.2a • W.5.4 • W.5.7 • W.5.10 SL.5.1a–d • L.5.1 • L.5.2 L.5.3 • L.5.6	ELL
	7	Writers develop their topic by providing facts, definitions, details, and quotations.	W.5.2b • W.5.4 • W.5.5 • W.5.7 W.5.10 • SL.5.1a–d • L.5.1 L.5.6	ELL S&L
	8	Writers revise, edit, and consider a new approach when appropriate.	W.5.5 • W.5.7 • W.5.10 • L.5.1 L.5.2 • L.5.3 L.5.6	ELL Milestone Assessment
	9	Writers provide a list of sources.	W.5.7 • W.5.8 • W.5.10 • SL.5.1a–d L.5.6	ELL
Assess: reflect, conclude, connect, share, recognize, respond	10	Writers publish and share their research with others.	W.5.6 • W.5.7 • SL.5.1a–d • SL.5.6 L.5.1 • L.5.6	ELL Milestone Assessment S&L

Core Ready Writing Rubric

Grade 5   Knowledge Quest: Navigating and Integrating Multiple Sources as Researchers

Lesson Set Goal	Emerging	Approaching	Achieving	Exceeding	Standards Alignment
Take effective notes on informational texts by using summary, paraphrases, and direct quotations purposefully.	Student shows little evidence of success taking effective notes using any of the three methods. Lacks understanding of how method works. Information is missing or unclear.	Student shows some evidence of taking effective notes using all three methods. May not grasp all three methods equally. Some information may be missing or unclear.	Student takes clear and complete notes by using all methods purposefully and appropriately.	Student takes clear and complete notes by using all methods purposefully and appropriately. Demonstrates thorough and advanced understanding of topic and note taking methods.	RI.5.1 RI.5.2 RI.5.10 W.5.4 W.5.7 W.5.8 W.5.10
Craft clear and organized responses to the reading.	Student shows little or no evidence of success crafting clear and organized responses to his or her reading.	Student crafts basic responses to his or her reading. May lack some clarity or organization.	Student crafts clear and organized responses to his or her reading.	Student crafts highly effective, clear, and well-organized responses to his or her reading. May demonstrate advanced understanding or insight.	RI.5.1 RI.5.10 W.5.4 W.5.5 W.5.9b W.5.10 SL.5.1a-d SL.5.6 L.5.1 L.5.2 L.5.3 L.5.6
Craft a thesis or framing statement in the informational or explanatory writing that synthesizes information on one topic from multiple sources, both print and digital.	Student struggles to craft a thesis or framing statement that synthesizes information from multiple sources. Statement may be very unclear or neglect to use multiple sources.	Student attempts to craft a thesis or framing statement. May need support in improving clarity or addressing multiple sources.	Student crafts a clear thesis or framing statement that synthesizes information from multiple sources.	Student crafts an exceptionally clear or powerful thesis or framing statement that effectively synthesizes information from multiple sources.	W.5.2a W.5.4 W.5.7 W.5.10 L.5.6
Develop and strengthen writing by including facts, definitions, details and quotations.	Student demonstrates little or no evidence of developing and strengthening writing with facts, definitions, details, or quotations. Writing is underdeveloped and lacks required elements.	Student demonstrates some evidence of developing and strengthening writing with facts, definitions, details, or quotations. Some elements may be more developed than others.	Student develops and strengthens writing by including facts, definitions, and quotations. All required elements present.	Student demonstrates exceptional understanding of how to develop and strengthen writing by including all required elements in a highly effective manner.	W.5.2b W.5.4 W.5.7 W.5.10 SL.5.6 L.5.1 L.5.2 L.5.3 L.5.6

Core Ready Writing Rubric, Grade 5, *continued*

Lesson Set Goal	Emerging	Approaching	Achieving	Exceeding	Standards Alignment
Provide a reference list of sources.	Student neglects to provide a reference list of sources, or list is very incomplete, inaccurate, or in an inappropriate format.	Student provides a reference list. May be somewhat incomplete or have minor errors in accuracy or format.	Student provides a reference list of sources that is accurate, complete, and formatted correctly.	Student provides a comprehensive reference list of sources that is accurate, complete, and formatted correctly.	W.5.4 W.5.7 W.5.8 W.5.10
Prepare and present research using appropriate technology and resources.	Student presents research with little or no evidence of preparation. Struggles to use technology and resources appropriately for presentation.	Student presents research to an audience with insufficient rehearsal or preparation. Student incorporates some appropriate technology or resources at a very basic level.	Student successfully prepares and presents research to an audience using appropriate technology or resources to enhance presentation.	Student delivers a well-rehearsed, confident, and polished presentation of his or her research. Uses appropriate technology thoughtfully and effectively to enhance presentation.	W.5.4 W.5.6 W.5.7 SL.5.1a–d SL.5.6 L.5.1 L.5.2 L.5.3 L.5.6
With guidance and support from peers and adults, develop and strengthen writing as needed by planning, revising, editing, rewriting, or trying a new approach.	Student shows little to no evidence of attempting to develop and strengthen writing as needed by planning, revising, editing, rewriting, or trying a new approach.	Student makes a marginal or limited attempt to develop and strengthen writing as needed by planning, revising, editing, rewriting, or trying a new approach. Writing may still contain significant errors or lack clarity.	Student develops and strengthens writing as needed by planning, revising, editing, rewriting, or trying a new approach. Some areas of the planning, revision, and editing may be more developed than others.	Student extensively develops and strengthens writing as needed by planning, revising, editing, rewriting, or trying a new approach. Few or no errors or lapses of clarity evident.	W.5.5
By the end of the year, independently and proficiently read and comprehend a variety of informational texts at the high end of the grades 4–5 text complexity band.	Student shows little or no evidence of reading and comprehending texts appropriate for the grade 5 text complexity band.	Student shows inconsistent evidence of independently and proficiently reading and comprehending texts appropriate for the grade 5 text complexity band.	Student shows solid evidence of independently and proficiently reading and comprehending texts appropriate for the grade 5 text complexity band.	Student shows solid evidence of independently and proficiently reading and comprehending texts above the grade 5 text complexity band.	RI.5.10
Write routinely over extended time frames (time for research, reflection, and revision) and shorter time frames (a single sitting or a day or two) for a range of discipline-specific tasks, purposes, and audiences.	Student shows little or no evidence of writing routinely for short or long time frames for a range of discipline-specific tasks, purposes, and audiences.	Student shows some evidence of writing routinely for short and long time frames for a range of discipline-specific tasks, purposes, and audiences.	Student shows solid evidence of writing routinely for short and long time frames for a range of discipline-specific tasks, purposes, and audiences.	Student shows exceptional evidence of consistently and accurately writing for short and long time frames for a range of discipline-specific tasks, purposes, and audiences.	W.5.10

Core Ready Writing Rubric, Grade 5, *continued*

Lesson Set Goal	Emerging	Approaching	Achieving	Exceeding	Standards Alignment
In collaborative discussions, demonstrate evidence of preparation for discussion and exhibit responsibility to the rules and roles of conversation.	In collaborative discussions, student comes unprepared and often disregards the rules and roles of conversation.	In collaborative discussions, student's preparation may be evident but ineffective or inconsistent. May occasionally disregard the rules and roles of conversation.	In collaborative discussions, student prepares adequately and draws on the preparation and other information about the topic to explore ideas under discussion. Usually observes the rules and roles of conversation.	In collaborative discussions, student arrives extremely well prepared for discussions and draws on the preparation and other information about the topic to explore ideas under discussion. Always observes the rules and roles of conversation.	SL.5.1a SL.5.1b
In collaborative discussions, share and develop ideas in a manner that enhances understanding of topic. Contribute and respond to the content of the conversation in a productive and focused manner.	Student shows little or no evidence of engaging in collaborative discussions and makes little or no attempt to ask and answer questions, stay on topic, link comments to the remarks of others, or to explain his or her own ideas and understanding in light of the discussion.	Student shows some evidence of engaging in collaborative discussions and, with marginal success, attempts to ask questions to check understanding of information presented, stay on topic, link comments to the remarks of others, and explain his or her own ideas and understanding in light of the discussion.	Student engages in a range of collaborative discussions and asks questions to check understanding of information presented. Stays on topic most of the time and frequently links his or her own ideas and understanding in light of the discussion.	Student effectively and consistently engages in a range of collaborative discussions and asks high-level questions to check understanding of information presented. Always stays on topic and, with great insight and attention to the comments of others, links his or her own ideas and understanding in light of the discussion.	SL.5.1c SL.5.1d
Demonstrate knowledge of standard English and its conventions.	Student demonstrates little or no knowledge of standard English and its conventions.	Student demonstrates some evidence of knowledge of standard English and its conventions.	Student consistently demonstrates knowledge of standard English and its conventions.	Student demonstrates an exceptional understanding of standard English and its conventions. Use of conventions is sophisticated for grade level and accurate.	L.5.1 L.5.2 L.5.3
Acquire and accurately use grade-appropriate conversational, general academic, and domain-specific vocabulary and phrases.	Student shows little or no evidence of the acquisition or use of grade-appropriate conversational and academic language.	Student shows some evidence of the acquisition and use of grade-appropriate conversational and academic language.	Student shows solid evidence of the acquisition and use of grade-appropriate conversational and academic language.	Student shows a high level of sophistication and precision with the acquisition and use of grade-appropriate conversational and academic language.	L.5.6

Note: See the Core Ready Rubrics chart in the Walk Through for descriptions of category headers.

Writing Lesson 1

▶ Teaching Objective

Writers find inspiration for their research.

▶ Standards Alignment

RI.5.10, W.5.7, SL.5.1a–d, L.5.1, L.5.6

▶ Materials

- Research Road Map (Appendix 5.2)
- Inspire and Wonder graphic organizer
- Computers with Internet access (optional)

▶ To the Teacher

Your choice of final product will influence your modeling throughout this lesson set. Please make a choice that best suits the needs of your students and the resources available to you. These choices were originally discussed in the Recognition section of this lesson set and are summarized in this table.

Goal	Low-Tech	High-Tech
Students create an engaging presentation on a research topic that incorporates both text and multimedia components.	Students curate a museum display about their research topic by: • Writing an informative text about their research topic and using a word processing program to type up their final draft • Incorporating visual images, artifacts and drawings, with supporting captions, to enhance their presentation	Students craft a mock Wonderopolis page framed around their research question by: • Writing an informative text about their research topic • Incorporating relevant hyperlinks, images, and videos to enhance their page

Make your vision for the final product clear to the students from the beginning of this lesson set so that they may gather materials and craft their writing to be appropriate for the intended purpose and audience.

▶ Procedure

Warm Up Gather the class to set the stage for today's learning

Gather the class and share your vision for their upcoming research project. Excite them about the freedom to choose a topic of their interest, academic or nonacademic, and the creativity inherent in both versions of the final presentation. This will be an exciting and engaging journey for the entire class!

Teach Model what students need to learn and do

Display the Research Road Map for your class to see. **ELL** Provide Comprehensible Input Organizers. Displaying the road map demonstrates steps in this process and aids ELLs in understanding the process they will be following. The first step in your research journey is to find inspiration for your work and immerse yourself in the topic. Highlight the messiness of true research. It is essential that researchers simply investigate a topic for some time before choosing a direction for future work. Today will be all about exploring in the topics that interest your students the most.

Goal	Low-Tech	High-Tech
Students find inspiration for and immerse themselves in a topic to pursue further through a research project.	Students find inspiration for and immerse themselves in a topic for further research by: • Browsing through the classroom, school, or local library • Talking with a partner • Reflecting on their interests and passions outside of school	Students find inspiration for and immerse themselves in a topic for further research by: • Browsing other related "wonders" on Wonderopolis.org • Taking virtual field trips to various related museum exhibits • Browsing through popular children's websites (such as *National Geographic Kids, Time for Kids,* and *Weekly Reader Kids*) • Reflecting on their interests and passions outside of school • Talking with a partner

Relying on the chart at the bottom of the previous page, model your chosen methods for finding inspiration for a topic to study. Whether you opt for the low-tech or high-tech option, emphasize your own thought process when it comes to finding inspiration for a topic to pursue. Reflect on your interests outside of school, making sure to choose a topic that does not feel too ponderous or heavy; rather, choose something that feels intriguing and interesting for yourself and your students. As you model the above strategies, keep track of your inspiration and wonderings on the Inspire and Wonder graphic organizer. Use the Inspiration bubble to record your interest, passion, or source of inspiration. Use the corresponding Wondering bubbles to note any questions you might have about this particular topic. Here's an example of what your graphic organizer might look like:

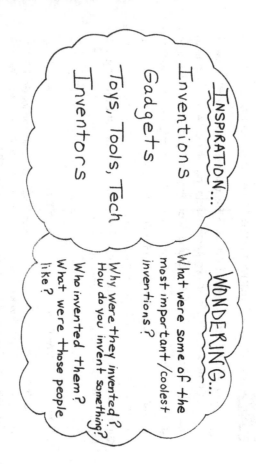

INSPIRATION...

Inventions

Gadgets

Toys, Tools, Tech

Inventors

WONDERING...

What were some of the most important/coolest inventions?

Why were they invented? How do you invent something?

Who invented them? What were those people like?

For the purposes of this lesson set, we have chosen to pursue the idea of inventions, specifically the invention of Legos. You will notice that the remainder of the lessons in this set rely on informational texts about this topic, but you may choose to select another topic for study that more closely reflects your own passions and interest outside of the school day.

Try Guide students to quickly rehearse what they need to learn and do in preparation for practice

Give students a moment to reflect upon their interests and passions outside of school. **ELL** Frontload the Lesson—Activate prior knowledge. This is a good time to encourage ELLs to share a picture or visual of their interest to help promote their own language production. Do they have any hobbies, collections, or fascination with a particular topic? After giving students a moment to collect their thoughts, ask them to turn and share their ideas with a partner. **ELL** Enable Language Production—Listening and Speaking. This time is an authentic opportunity for ELLs to learn and expand their vocabulary with their peers. Using a visual of their passion/interest is another opportunity for the students to increase their language skills through dialogue. The goal of these conversations should be to narrow students' search as they begin to immerse themselves in a topic for further pursuit. Having students share something as personal as their interests and passions provides the perfect opportunity to highlight and reinforce conversational etiquette such as following agreed-upon rules for discussions as well as posing and responding to specific questions by making comments that contribute to the discussion (SL.5.1b, SL.5.1c)

Clarify Briefly restate today's teaching objective and explain the practice task(s)

Today we are beginning our investigations of topics that are near and dear to our hearts! Your job now is to spend time finding inspiration for and immersing yourself in the topic of your choice. Record your inspirations and wondering on this graphic organizer.

Practice Students work independently or in small groups to apply today's teaching objective

Based on your choice of the low-tech or high-tech option outlined above, students spend time finding inspiration for and immersing themselves

> *"The educated don't get that way by memorizing facts; they get that way by respecting them.*
>
> —Tom Heehler

in a topic that reflects their personal passion or interest. Students record their sources of inspiration and corresponding wonderings and potential questions for future research on the Inspire and Wonder graphic organizer.

Wrap Up Check understanding as you guide students to briefly share what they have learned and produced today

Gather the class, asking them to have their Inspire and Wonder graphic organizers handy. Organize students into groups of three or four and instruct them to share their inspiration and potential questions ("wonders") with the group.

Writing Lesson 2

▶ Teaching Objective

Writers take organized notes to record their thinking and learning.

▶ Standards Alignment

RI.5.10, W.5.7, W.5.8, W.5.10, SL.5.1a–d, L.5.1, L.5.6

▶ Materials

- Method for student note taking
- Research Road Map (Appendix 5.2)
- Method to record two-column chart: Main Ideas and My Thinking (note-taking sheet—either paper or digital)
- Webpage for Ole Kirk Christiansen located on Brickipedia, Lego's wiki page

▶ To the Teacher

Note taking is a skill that will help your students for years to come. Your students will feel quite grown up as they learn how to take notes and should feel proud of this big step in their academic careers. In our lives we take

notes when we have to write down information to remember it. We take notes about things that stand out to us when we're reading. Sometimes we write down full sentences, other times bullets. Sometimes we write down exact words or quotations; other times we paraphrase into our own words. Helping your students negotiate what type of note to write is a big step in the research process. To make the most of notes, students need to know how to take good notes. In this lesson set, we begin by asking students to simply jot down the main idea(s) of a piece of informational text along with their related thinking about this main idea. As fifth graders, students should become comfortable not only noting critical information to be remembered from their reading, but also snippets of their own thinking as they read. This lesson will focus on emphasizing the process of recording their own thinking as well as on organizing notes by resource. In Writing Lesson 3, students expand their note-taking skills by recording key supporting details in addition to the main idea and their thinking.

▶ Procedure

Warm Up Gather the class to set the stage for today's learning

Call students' attention to the Research Road Map, highlighting the journey they have already taken. Today, students begin to take notes as they engage deeply with their research topics of choice.

Researchers, we are deep into our journey to understand more about the topics that interest us the most. Let's review our Research Road Map to determine where we are in today's work. So far, we've chosen topics, crafted thick research questions, and gathered the most relevant sources we could find. Now we're ready to take careful notes in order to highlight important details that will help us to answer our questions.

Teach Model what students need to learn and do

Orient your students to the importance of note-taking and the procedure you would like them to follow for this work.

Goal	Low-Tech	High-Tech
Students take organized notes to record their thinking and learning.	Students take handwritten pencil and paper notes on a graphic organizer. Notes should be organized so that the original source is easy to identify.	Students take notes on a digital copy of the graphic organizer(s) designed for this lesson set.

Today, we are going to practice something quite important. We are going to practice taking notes so that our ideas are out of our heads and on our papers for safe keeping. Watch me as I take some notes from a text we've already read together.

Model for students how to begin their note taking by recording the title and author of the resource chosen at the top of their graphic organizer. **ELL** Provide Comprehensible Input—Models. This model is powerful in demonstrating the thought process in note taking, as well as the act of taking notes. Then, model reading from the source, thinking aloud about the main idea of each section. Record the main idea and your related thinking on the Main Idea(s) and My Thinking two-column chart. Here's one way your modeling could unfold using the webpage for Ole Kirk Christiansen located on Brickipedia, Lego's wiki page. Read the section, "The First Fire."

Wow! Let me stop and think for a moment. One of the main ideas here is that Ole Kirk Christiansen didn't start his business by making toys. He was a

furniture maker who had to develop new products to make money during the Great Depression. I'm thinking it sounds like Legos were invented by chance. If all these things didn't happen to Christensen, would Legos have ever been invented?

Jot the main idea and your related thinking in the appropriate columns on the graphic organizer. Model good note-taking strategies, such as using initials for important people (rather than writing out their full name each time).

Try Guide students to quickly rehearse what they need to learn and do in preparation for practice

Read the second section titled "The Second Fire" aloud to the class. Guide the class in determining the main idea of this section. Modeling effective note taking, add this main idea to the graphic organizer. Then, ask partners to turn and talk about their thinking related to this main idea.

Remember, keeping track of our own thinking as we read informational text is an important skill that will help us to shape our final presentations.

Give students a moment to talk with a partner. **ELL** Enable Language Production—Increasing Interaction. Listen in to various partnerships and collect snippets of interesting responses to add to the graphic organizer.

Clarify Briefly restate today's teaching objective and explain the practice task(s)

Today, we are working on not only keeping track of the important information in our reading, we are also jotting down our own thinking about this learning. Researchers keep careful track of their thinking as well as the new information they encounter in their reading. Begin to look through the sources you've gathered for your project and begin taking notes using this graphic organizer, focusing on identifying the most important information and recording your own thinking as you go.

Practice Students work independently or in small groups to apply today's teaching objective

Students begin to read the resources they gathered on their topic during Reading Lesson 2. As students read, they use the Main Ideas and

Supporting Details graphic organizer and My Thinking graphic organizer from Reading Lesson 4 to take notes.

Wrap Up Check understanding as you guide students to briefly share what they have learned and produced today

Gather the class together for a discussion. Ask them to reflect on their work today.

Today was your first real chance to dig into the resources you gathered around your topic. You've begun to take notes and now it's time to take a moment and think—will you be able to answer your question with the resources you have available to you? As you discuss this question with a small group, decide if you are all set, need to revise your question, or should begin with a new topic entirely.

 Have students discuss this question in small groups. **ELL** Enable **Language Production—Increasing Interaction. This is an important time for students to get feedback from their peers as they discuss whether they feel they want to pursue the topic. This is a helpful time to listen in and see how you can further support language development around their chosen topic.**

Writing Lesson 3

▶ Teaching Objective

Writers understand when and how to summarize, paraphrase, and quote accurately when taking notes on a text.

▶ Standards Alignment

RI.5.1, RI.5.2, RI.5.10, W.5.7, W.5.8, W.5.10, SL.5.1a–d, L.5.1, L.5.6

▶ Materials

- Charting supplies or interactive whiteboard
- "Lego" in *Toys! Amazing Stories Behind Some Great Inventions* by Don Wulffson

▶ To the Teacher

The difference between summarizing, paraphrasing, and using a direct quotation is one that confuses many writers. It is this slight, but important, difference that will be highlighted in this lesson. As students develop their skills as researchers and note takers, it is essential to discuss the notion of plagiarism and to provide them with the resources to utilize the work of other people effectively and respectfully.

Close Reading Opportunity

When we *summarize*, we write down the main ideas of someone else's work in our own words. A summary is always shorter than the original since the purpose is to include only the main ideas and related key details of the original work and to leave out any irrelevant information. Typically, a summary is approximately one-third the size of the original. When we *paraphrase*, we rewrite another writer's words or ideas in our own words without changing the meaning. Paraphrasing should result in a writing that is about the same length as the original since the purpose is to rephrase without leaving out anything, rather than to shorten.

When we use a *direct quotation*, we copy another writer's words exactly.

▶ Procedure

Warm Up Gather the class to set the stage for today's learning

Yesterday we began taking notes. At the top of each note-taking sheet, I asked you to record the title and author of the source you were working with. It's important that researchers are able to give credit to the resources they used by listing them at the end of their presentation. This is often called your reference list. We'll talk more about how to write a reference list later on. But for today, we need to discuss the difference between summarizing, paraphrasing, and the danger of plagiarizing.

Teach   Model what students need to learn and do

Begin by explaining the difference between summarizing, paraphrasing, and using direct quotations. **ELL** Identify and Communicate Content and Language Objectives—Academic vocabulary. Create a three-column chart titled "Summarizing, Paraphrasing, or Direct Quote?" and add these definitions to your chart as you discuss them with your class. **ELL** Provide Comprehensible Input—Organizers

Explain the decision between summarizing, paraphrasing, and using direct quotations while taking notes. Here are some good rules of thumb for deciding when to summarize, when to paraphrase, and when to use a direct quote. Opt for using a summary when:

- You want to identify only the main ideas of the writer.
- You want to give an overview of the topic (from several sources).
- You want to simplify a complex argument or topic.

Opt for paraphrasing when:

- The ideas of the other writer are more important than his or her style.
- You want to include all of the ideas in a section, not just the most important ones.
- You think that the words of the other writer are too difficult for your readers.

Opt for using a direct quotation when:

- You want to use another writer's words without plagiarizing.
- The author's style or exact words are so unique or important that you can't effectively paraphrase or summarize them.
- You find an interesting fact or statistic you'd like to use.

Try   Guide students to quickly rehearse what they need to learn and do in preparation for practice

Return to the chapter titled "Lego" in *Toys! Amazing Stories Behind Some Great Inventions*. Resume reading and note taking where you left off during

Reading Lesson 3. As you read the remainder of the chapter to the class, stop at the end of each paragraph and discuss the notes you're taking aloud. Involve students in making decisions about what to jot down after reading a full paragraph. Use these shared notes to model examples of each type of note-taking strategy.

Clarify   Briefly restate today's teaching objective and explain the practice task(s)

Recap the differences between summarizing, paraphrasing, and using a direct quotation, calling students' attention to the chart and examples you have created together. Instruct students to take advantage of these three note-taking strategies as they continue to work with the resources they've gathered on their topic. Ask students to be prepared to share an example of one note-taking strategy they used and explain why they chose to use that particular strategy.

Practice   Students work independently or in small groups to apply today's teaching objective

Students continue to work with the resources they've gathered on their topic, taking notes on key information as they go. Students consider the three note-taking strategies discussed today, making effective choices in their own work.

Wrap Up   Check understanding as you guide students to briefly share what they have learned and produced today

Gather the class, asking them to have their examples handy. Students turn and share their example with a partner. Remind the class to include their decision-making process: *Why did they summarize, paraphrase, or use a direct quotation?* As you listen in to partnerships, select two or three students to share their examples and thinking with the class. Collect student notes and analyze them to determine if students need additional support to understand the difference between these note-taking strategies, if students need additional practice using these strategies effectively, or if students need additional support with choosing relevant information to record. **ELL** **Assess** for Content and Language Understanding—Formative Assessment.

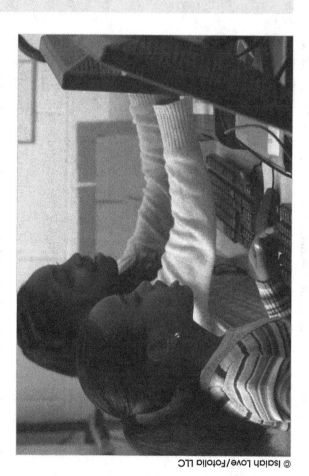

© Isaiah Love/Fotolia LLC

Milestone Performance Assessment

Researcher Skills

 Use this checklist to assess student ability to summarize, paraphrase, and use a direct quotation.

Standards Alignment: RI.5.1, RI.5.2, W.5.7, W.5.8

	Achieved	Notes
Take notes that effectively capture the content of a larger piece.		
Attempt all three note-taking strategies.		
Explain decision to summarize, paraphrase, or quote with logical reasoning.		

Writing Lesson 4

▶ Teaching Objective

Writers articulate their thoughts about their reading in writing.

▶ Standards Alignment

RI.5.10, W.5.4, W.5.5, W.5.9b, W.5.10, SL5.1a–d, L.5.1, L.5.6

▶ Materials

- *The Ultimate Lego Book* by DK DK Publishers (should this book not be available to you, an alternate text, *The History of LEGO*, may be found on the Core Ready PDToolkit)
- Charting supplies or interactive whiteboard

▶ Procedure

Warm Up **Gather the class to set the stage for today's learning**

Throughout this lesson set, you have been sharing your thinking with partners. We do so much sharing about our reading and writing so that we can be really good at explaining our thinking out loud to our friends. But, sometimes you will be asked to express your thinking in writing. It is always important to be able to clearly express your thinking about a new topic or piece of information in writing.

Teach **Model what students need to learn and do**

Instead of asking you to turn and share your thinking about your reading with a partner, I'm going to ask you to write about it. Today, I'd like each of you to pick an important text from your pile of resources and respond to the following task in writing: "Determine two or more main ideas of your text and explain how they are supported by key details."

Model writing this type of response using a salient text from your group of resources. **ELL** Provide Comprehensible Input—Models. This helps ELLs practice in a group how to craft their responses on their own. For this lesson, we will rely on the chapter titled, "A System of Play" in *The Ultimate Lego Book*. First, read the section aloud to the class. Then, craft a written response that clearly identifies the main idea(s) and supporting details, explaining *how* the details support the main idea. Here is what your work might look like.

The Ultimate Lego Book by DK Publishers

"A System of Play" The main idea of this section is that making Legos out of plastic opened up new possibilities for the company. For example, Lego began making bricks that automatically stuck together. Another example is that the company also created systems for playing with the blocks. One of the first systems included various sets that helped children build a town. These key details support the main idea because they are examples of the innovations Lego was able to make after switching to plastic.

Draw your students' attention to the types of sentences you crafted in your written response.

Did you notice how I took the question apart and wrote different sentences to address each part? My first sentence clearly summarizes the main idea. Then, I added three more sentences that paraphrased the examples given in the text. My last sentence explains the relationship between the main idea and the key details.

Writing Lesson 5

▼ Teaching Objective

Writers craft clear and organized responses to their reading.

▼ Standards Alignment

RI.5.10, W.5.4, W.5.5, W.5.9b, W.5.10, SL.5.1a–d, L.5.1, L.5.6

▼ Materials

- Key Ideas, People, and Events graphic organizer (from Reading Lesson 5)

Try Guide students to quickly rehearse what they need to learn and do in preparation for practice

Choose another section or relevant text from your gathered resources. Read the text aloud to the class. Then, lead the class in a shared writing exercise in which you craft a written response to this question.

Clarify Briefly restate today's teaching objective and explain the practice task(s)

It's important to be able to clearly communicate your thinking about your reading in writing. Today, each of you is going to choose a text from the resources you've gathered on your topic. After you've taken the time to read or reread that text, respond to the following task in writing: "Determine two or more main ideas of your text and explain how they are supported by key details."

Practice Students work independently or in small groups to apply today's teaching objective

Students work independently to choose a text and respond to the posted task in writing.

Wrap Up Check understanding as you guide students to briefly share what they have learned and produced today

Ask students to share their written responses with a partner. Partners should actively participate in helping their classmates develop and strengthen their writing through revising, editing, or rewriting. Not only does this Wrap Up provide a wonderful opportunity to highlight the roles and responsibilities involved in peer editing, it also is a natural place to reinforce the importance of coming to discussions prepared, following conversational etiquette, and posing and responding to specific questions. (SL.5.1a–d)

▸ Procedure

Warm Up Gather the class to set the stage for today's learning

Today, during our reading lesson, we began to organize the information we've gathered on our topics by listing the key ideas, events, and people on a graphic organizer. Creating this list helped us to focus on the relationships between some of these factors. I think we found that these relationships are often the most interesting parts of our studies. They help us see areas for future research and help us think about interesting and new information to present to our readers.

Teach Model what students need to learn and do

Display the chart of Key Ideas, People, and Events that you created during Reading Lesson 5. Remind students that you realized how the realities of life during the Great Depression pushed Christiansen to expand his business to include toys. Without the Great Depression, Legos might have never been invented.

I think this discovery is so interesting that I want to make sure I include it in my final presentation, which means I'll have to be able to explain my thinking clearly through writing. Let me show what this kind of writing might look like.

Model crafting a strong written response to the following prompt: "Explain the relationships or interactions between two or more key individuals, events, or ideas in your topic." **ELL** Provide Comprehensible Input—Models. ELLs will benefit from this modeling by showing strong examples so that they can understand non-examples of strong responses. As you model, remind students of the importance of referencing the text as evidence of your thinking. Here's an example of what your modeled response might look like.

▲ The Great Depression had a significant impact on Ole Kirk Christiansen. Christiansen was originally a furniture maker. During the Great Depression, Christiansen's business was suffering and he was forced to create new and interesting products to attract new customers. Christiansen had always made miniature models of the furniture he built. These miniature models gave Christiansen the idea to try creating toys. His first wooden toys, which included toys like the pull toy, were popular and he had some success. It was only a matter of time before Legos were born. If Christiansen's fam-

ily had not suffered during the Great Depression, Christiansen might never have been forced to create new products and Legos might never have been invented.

Try Guide students to quickly rehearse what they need to learn and do in preparation for practice

A crucial, but basic, element in crafting a strong written response to reading is understanding the question being asked. Take this opportunity to allow students to process the information they must provide in order to answer this question completely. Ask students to turn and talk to a partner about the prompt ("Explain the relationship between two or more key individuals, events, or ideas in your topic and why this relationship is important.") Ask the students, "What information do you need to include to answer this question completely?" As you listen in to partnerships and share exemplar responses, guiding your students toward realizing they must include the following components in order to answer the prompt fully:

- Clear statement of the relationship being discussed (_____ had an impact on _____).
- Explanation of what that relationship was mainly about.
- Statement about the importance of the relationship—what makes it significant enough to write about?

Clarify Briefly restate today's teaching objective and explain the practice task(s)

Today we're continuing to practice how we can best express our thinking about reading in our writing. You just spent time analyzing with a partner the question being asked to decide what information you need to include in your response in order to provide a complete answer. Every time you are asked to write about your thinking in reading, take a moment to pause and consider the question being asked. Think to yourself, "What information do I need to include in my response to make sure I'm answering this question completely."

Tell the class that you'd like each of them to select one of their resources and answer the following prompt in writing: "Explain the relationship between two or more key individuals, events, or ideas in your topic and why this relationship is important."

Milestone Performance Assessment

Written Responses

Use this checklist to assess student ability to craft a strong written response.

Standards Alignment: W.5.5, W.5.9b, SL.5.1a–d

	Achieved	Notes
Identify and describe the relationship between two or more key individuals, events, or ideas.		
Explain what about this relationship is important.		
Provide details/ evidence from the text to support thinking.		
Provide improvements to strengthen a partner's work.		

Practice — Students work independently or in small groups to apply today's teaching objective

Students work independently to craft a strong written response to their reading.

Wrap Up Check understanding as you guide students to briefly share what they have learned and produced today

Ask students to share their written responses with a partner. Partners should actively participate in helping their classmate develop and strengthen their writing through revising, editing, or rewriting. Not only does this Wrap Up provide a wonderful opportunity to highlight the roles and responsibilities involved in peer editing, it also is a natural place to reinforce the importance of coming to discussions prepared, following conversational etiquette, and posing and responding to specific questions. (SL.5.1a–d) Collect students' written responses and analyze them to determine if students need additional support in responding completely to the question being asked, including providing relevant information or conveying their ideas clearly. **ELL** Assess for Content and Language Understanding—Formative Assessments. This is a perfect time to see what kinds of language structures are needed for your ELLs, based on their responses. You could also offer structures and supports to help them expand the ways they can explain their thinking.

Writing Lesson 6 •

▼ Teaching Objective

Writers introduce their topic clearly by providing a thesis or focus statement.

▼ Standards Alignment

W.5.2a, W.5.4, W.5.7, W.5.10, SL.5.1a–d, L.5.1, L.5.2, L.5.3, L.5.6

▼ Materials

- Research Road Map (Appendix 5.2)
- Charting supplies or interactive whiteboard

▼ To the Teacher

In third grade, students wrote informational articles that utilized a variety of exciting leads to capture the readers' attention. In fifth grade, we want to continue crafting engaging beginnings; however, we also want to push our students to include a general observation or focus for their topic. Additionally, this general observation or focus for their topic should reflect the students' point of view.

▼ Procedure

Warm Up **Gather the class to set the stage for today's learning**

Call students' attention to the Research Road Map. Briefly recap the steps you've worked through thus far and locate where you are in the process. "We're wrapping up our work on coming to conclusions and getting ready to start presenting our information!"

Teach **Model what students need to learn and do**

It's important to get our presentations off to a strong start with an engaging introduction that sets the reader up with what they can expect in the rest of your presentation. This is the place to share your point of view, so think about who is going to be reading your work and the message you'd like to send to them about your topic.

ELL **Provide Comprehensible Input—Organizers.** Have a chart prepared that includes some common ways informational articles begin. Note that these types of leads were shared with students in grade 3 as well.

• Generalization (Legos are _____.)
• Question (Did you know . . . ?)
• What if or if (What if we all _____? / If you are like many kids, then _____.)
• Quotation (One expert said, "_____.")

One way to decide the type of introduction that will work best for your topic is to try them all on first. Watch me as I create four different introductions to my topic. I want you to notice that my point of view stays the same in each one—it's the style that I'm considering.

Model writing four introductions to your topic, illustrating each of the suggestions listed. **ELL** **Provide Comprehensible Input—Models.** This chart helps ELLs organize language structures in relation to the different types of introductions. Be sure that your point of view on the topic is clear and consistent in all four examples. Here is what your model introductions might sound like if you've chosen to study the invention of Legos alongside us:

• (Generalization) Almost everyone loves playing with Legos, so everyone is really going to love hearing the story of how they were invented!
• (Question) Did you know that there are 1,700 different shapes of Lego blocks?
• (What if, or If) What if Legos had never been invented? When you hear this story, you'll realize it's not too hard to imagine!
• (Quotation) The motto of Ole Kirk Christiansen, the inventor of Legos, was, "Only the best is good enough."

Try **Guide students to quickly rehearse what they need to learn and do in preparation for practice**

Ask students to discuss these four possible introductions with a partner. *What do you notice about these introductions? Which introduction is the strongest? Which one should we choose and why?* Emphasize that while any technique can be effective, the strongest lead both engages the reader and informs him about the content of the piece.

Clarify **Briefly restate today's teaching objective and explain the practice task(s)**

Today we are beginning to think about how we present all the information we've learned. No matter if you're writing for a newspaper, the Internet, a museum display, or a book—capturing the attention of your audience is a must! So, clear, engaging introductions are essential. We've reviewed four types of introductions you can try today. Remember, try writing each kind of introduction for your topic first, and decide which one best suits your purpose and audience after.

Practice Students work independently or in small groups to apply today's teaching objective

Students work to craft four different introductions to their topic independently.

Writing Lesson 7 ● ● ● ● ● ● ● ● ● ● ● ● ● ●

▼ **Teaching Objective**

Writers develop their topic by providing facts, definitions, details, and quotations.

▼ **Standards Alignment**

W.5.2b, W.5.4, W.5.5, W.5.7, W.5.10, SL.5.1a–d, L.5.1, L.5.6

▼ **Materials**

- Graphic organizer from Reading Lesson 7
- Variety of pre-prepared facts, definitions, and quotations related to your topic

▼ **To the Teacher**

Your students created a solid outline of the body of their final presentation of information during Reading Lesson 7. During Writing Lesson 6, they crafted strong introductions for these final presentations that consisted of a general observation or focus to guide the remainder of their work. Now it's time to guide students as they round out and complete their presentations by adding relevant and interesting facts, definitions, details, and quotations. Making smart choices about where to put this information may prove to be difficult—you may find that some students over use these details, rendering their work difficult to follow. Other students may have

trouble finding any places to add this type of information. The goal for this lesson is to teach students how to choose those details that are most relevant to their writing and to select the most logical place to add them.

This lesson may be best taught across a number of days. You will need one day to teach and for students to begin their planning. You will also need additional days for students to write and develop the body and conclusion of their final presentations. Be sure that students have completed their final presentation and are ready for the revising and editing phase before moving on to Writing Lesson 8.

▼ **Procedure**

Warm Up Gather the class to set the stage for today's learning

During our reading work today, you came to some important conclusions about the information you've gathered on your topic. You also spent time organizing that information into logical categories that unfold in a clear sequence for your audience. We have one last layer to add to the body of our presentations—the details! Today we will be talking about how facts, definitions, details, and quotes can improve your work, as well as where to put them.

Teach Model what students need to learn and do

Take a moment to define and explain the differences between facts, definitions, details, and quotes. **ELL** Identify and Communicate Content and Language Objectives—Academic Vocabulary. This could also be an

Wrap Up Check understanding as you guide students to briefly share what they have learned and produced today

Gather the class, asking them to have their potential introductions handy. Have students share their work with a partner. Classmates should be prepared to help their classmate to strengthen their writing through revising, editing, and rewriting as necessary. **ELL** Enable Language Production—Increasing Interaction.

opportunity to show these examples through a graphic organizer that could be added into their folder for future reference.

TOPIC: How were Legos invented?

KEY DETAILS	KEY EVENTS	KEY PEOPLE
·Christiansen built miniature furniture to help his designs	·Ole Kirk Christiansen's workshop burning down	·Ole Kirk Christiansen
·Legos lock together, unlike regular blocks	·The Great Depression	·Godfred (his son)
·Making Legos out of plastic, instead of wood	·Another fire in the warehouse	*Ole Kirk Christiansen's motto was "Only the best is good enough."
	*Between 1949 + 1998, there were more than 203 billion Legos made	

Draw your students' attention back to the graphic organizer you created during Reading Lesson 7. Explain that you are going to use this graphic organizer to help you decide where you might be able to add relevant facts, definitions, details, or quotations.

I've collected quite a few facts, definitions, details, and quotations in my notes. We've already used the graphic organizer to decide which categories of information we're going to include in our presentations as well as the sequence that seems the most logical. Now it's time to add relevant facts, definitions, details, and quotations into the graphic organizer so I can get writing.

Display and read through the facts, details, definitions, and quotes you have prepared in advance. Here are some examples of what you might include if you have chosen to study the invention of Legos along with us:

- Facts
  - For every million Legos made, only 26 are thrown away or rejected as defective.
  - There are Legoland parks in Denmark, California, and England.
  - Between 1949 and 1998, there were more than 203 billion Legos made.

- Definitions
  - *Lego* is a Latin word that means "I put together."
- Details
  - At first, Legos were made out of wood.
  - The first plastic Legos only came in red and white.
  - Ole Kirk Christiansen started his toy business by making dolls, blocks, hobbyhorses, and marionettes.
- Quotations
  - Ole Kirk Christiansen's motto was "Only the best is good enough."

Model how to take two or three of these items and decide on the most relevant place to include them on your graphic organizer. **ELL** **Provide Comprehensible Input—Models** Think aloud about where these details may be best used to enhance the category you are writing about. In addition, be sure to include some non-examples in your modeling—that is, moments where a fact, definition, detail, or quotation does *not* fit into your graphic organizer and must be discarded.

Try Guide students to quickly rehearse what they need to learn and do in preparation for practice

Ask students to help you make decisions about the placement of the remaining facts, details, definitions, and quotations.

Clarify Briefly restate today's teaching objective and explain the practice task(s)

Today we are pulling some of the facts, definitions, details, and quotations out of our notes and deciding where they best belong in our writing. We want to make sure that these additions make our writing stronger and don't end up distracting our audience.

Explain to the class that they will look through their notes to find these items and then make decisions about where they fit into their writing plan. Each student should add relevant facts, definitions, details, or quotes to his graphic organizer.

Practice Students work independently or in small groups to apply today's teaching objective

Students pull relevant facts, definitions, details, and quotes out of their notes and make logical decisions about where to add these items to their writing plan by jotting them on their graphic organizers. Once students have incorporated these details into their plan for writing, they should start to draft the body and conclusion of their final presentations.

Wrap Up Check understanding as you guide students to briefly share what they have learned and produced today

Gather the class, asking students to have their graphic organizers handy. Have students share the changes to their graphic organizers with a partner.

Writing Lesson 8

▼ **Teaching Objective**

Writers revise, edit, and consider a new approach when appropriate.

▼ **Standards Alignment**

W.5.5, W.5.7, W.5.10, L.5.1, L.5.2, L.5.3, L.5.6

▼ **Materials**

- Student copies of Research Wrap-Up Checklist (see Appendix 5.6)
- Linking Words and Transitions Resource Sheet (see Appendix 5.7)

▼ **To the Teacher**

Now that students are done drafting their final presentations, it's time to help them with the revision process. As fifth graders, this is not always the most exciting part of the research or writing process. They often think "We're done! We did it!" Helping them realize the importance of

Partners should be prepared to assist their classmate with this thinking by asking questions such as: *Why did you put this particular fact/definition/detail/quotation here? How do you think this fact/definition/detail/quotation helps this section of your work?* Students should revise their graphic organizers as needed.

These types of focused conversations provide the perfect opportunity to reinforce the importance of several key speaking and listening goals. Specifically, this lesson lends itself to supporting students as they follow agreed-upon rules for discussions, posing and responding to specific questions, make comments that contribute to the discussion, and reviewing the key ideas expressed. (SL.5.1b–d)

revision is essential not only for this lesson set but for their writing lives moving forward. Today, model for your students how you revise for clarity of content, look for places to clarify your work with linking words, phrases and clauses, and edit for conventions of standard English. This lesson may be best taught over two days—one day for revision and one day for the editing of conventions. Since this piece of writing requires a particular focus for revision (linking words, phrases, and clauses), the Research Wrap-Up Checklist will serve as an important tool for students to independently account for the big ideas of their articles as well as the conventions that will be most critical to this piece of writing consistent with the fifth grade Common Core State Standards. **ELL** Provide Comprehensible Input—Graphic Organizers/Outlines. This graphic organizer helps ELLs to monitor their progress. If needed, offer visuals or examples for the points.

▼ **Procedure**

Warm Up Gather the class to set the stage for today's learning

You have accomplished a lot as writers over the course of this lesson set. Now we're ready to reread our work and check to make sure we've done our job of explaining the big ideas of our topic while still considering our purpose and audience. To present our thinking as clearly as possible, we need to make sure we've connected all our ideas by using linking words, phrases, and clauses. We also want to make sure we follow the rules of English so that our readers can focus on the big ideas.

Teach Model what students need to learn and do

Call students' attention the model piece on Legos that you created during this lesson set.

Today we are going to reread my work on the invention of Legos using our Research Wrap-Up Checklist. First, we are going to read the checklist to know what we're looking for in this piece of writing. Then, we are going to read my writing once through. It's important to read it completely to remind yourself what the whole piece is about. After that, we are going to reread the work with a revision and editing lens. We will use our Research Wrap-Up Checklist to identify moments where more needs to be added or where something isn't clear enough yet. In particular, we are looking for places to add linking words and phrases to connect our ideas. Last, when working with your own writing, you will also note places where conventions are not used properly by using our acronym COPS (Capitalization, Order and usage of words, Punctuation, and Spelling).

Research Wrap-Up Checklist

Revising	Yes or No	Notes
Did I include an informative and engaging introduction?		
Did I answer my research question(s) with enough details?		
Did I include information from more than one source?		
Did I include key people, places, and things related to my research questions and explain how they are related to each other?		

Revising	Yes or No	Notes
Did I include visuals that enhance my presentation?		
Are all my ideas clustered together logically?		

COPS Editing Checklist

Capitals—I remembered to use capitals correctly.		
Order and usage of words—I have reread my sentences, and they all sound right and make sense.		
Punctuation—I have used correct punctuation.		
Spelling—I have corrected my spelling errors.		

 Share with your class the Linking Words and Transitions Resource Sheet that they may want to use in their writing (Appendix 5.7). **ELL** Provide Comprehensible Input—Organizers. This list can be formalized and put into their folder for future reference. Be careful not to overwhelm them with too many choices. The focus of this work should be on identifying the places where these linking words are necessary, not on using an overly broad range of phrases.

Try Guide students to quickly rehearse what they need to learn and do in preparation for practice

Guide the class in reading your work with a revision lens. (By grade 5, we ask students to read and edit their own work independently.)

> *We cannot hold a torch to light another's path without brightening our own.*
>
> —Ben Sweetland

Again, as you work through the Research Wrap-Up Checklist, focus on revising for clarity by the use of linking words and phrases.

Clarify Briefly restate today's teaching objective and explain the practice task(s)

Today you are going to read through your writing, looking to make sure that your ideas are presented clearly to the reader and that you have followed the rules of English. Remember, in particular we are looking for moments where we can add linking words and phrases to clarify the connection we are making between ideas. Then, you are going to use the Research Wrap-Up Checklist to carefully go through each sentence, making sure all of the items are complete in your final presentation.

Practice Students work independently or in small groups to apply today's teaching objective

Students will reread, revise, and edit their writing using the Research Wrap-Up Checklist.

Wrap Up Check understanding as you guide students to briefly share what they have learned and produced today

Have students share one change they made to their writing by using the Research Wrap-Up Checklist. Collect student work to use as an assessment. After looking closely at their work, determine if your class needs additional time for revision and editing before moving on to reflection. **ELL** Assess for Content and Language Understanding—Summative Assessment

Milestone Performance Assessment

Revising

Use this checklist to assess student ability to revise for voice, look for places to clarify and edit.

Standards Alignment: W.5.5, W.5.7

	Achieved	Notes
Include an informative and engaging introduction.		
Answer research question(s) with enough details.		
Include information from more than one source.		
Include key people, places, and things related to research questions and explain how they are related to each other.		
Include visuals that enhance presentation.		
Cluster ideas together logically.		
COPS Editing Checklist*		
Correct **c**apitalization.		
Correct **o**rder and usage of words.		
Correct **p**unctuation.		
Correct **s**pelling.		

*We recommend that you focus your assessment lens in these areas. Select and assess a few skills you have previously taught or that have emerged as areas of need in your ongoing assessment of student writing.

Writing Lesson 9

▶ Teaching Objective

Writers provide a list of sources.

▶ Standards Alignment

W.5.7, W.5.8, W.5.10, SL.5.1a–d, L.5.6

▶ Materials

- Prepared chart of reference list formats

▶ To the Teacher

Many students incorrectly assume that they only need to list a resource as a reference if they have taken a direct quotation from that resource. Others assume that there is no need to cite Internet pages as references. This is not true. Researchers must give credit to any and all resources they utilized during their research process. Take this time to review the concept of plagiarism. Plagiarism is using others' ideas or words without clearly acknowledging the source of that information. Remind students of the basic rules to avoid plagiarism. In general, writers need to give credit to the authors of their sources when they

- Use another person's idea, opinion, or theory
- Use any facts, statistics, graphs, or illustrations that aren't considered common knowledge
- Use direct quotations from the text
- Paraphrase from the text

▶ Procedure

Warm Up Gather the class to set the stage for today's learning

Giving other authors credit for their work is extremely important. Let's begin today by talking a bit more about plagiarism.

Review the concept and dangers of plagiarism. Then, take a moment to list and discuss the instances when writers need to give credit to other authors.

Teach Model what students need to learn and do

Look back through the resources you've collected and used during this lesson set. Begin a list titled "References" ELL Provide Comprehensible Input—Models on the formatting chart ELL Provide Comprehensible Input—Organizers to create your list. Emphasize that reference lists are organized alphabetically by the author's last name.

How to Cite a Reference

Books with one author	Author's last name, Author's first name. *Title.* Place of publication: Publisher, publication date.
	Example: Wulffson, Don. *Toys! Amazing Stories Behind Some Great Inventions.* New York, NY: Henry Holt and Company, 2000.
Books with two authors	First author's last name, first author's first name, and second author's last name, second author's first name. *Title.* Place of publication: Publisher, publication date.
	Example: Baichtal, John, and Meno, Joe. *The Cult of Lego.* San Francisco, CA: No Starch Press, 2011.
Books with no author listed	*Title.* Place of publication: Publisher, publication date.
	Example: *The Ultimate Lego Book.* New York, NY: DK Publishing, Inc.. 1999.
Magazine or newspaper articles	Author's last name, Author's first name. "Title of article," *Name of Newspaper,* date of newspaper, page number(s).
	Example: Michaels, Daniel. "For Some Grown-Ups, Playing With Legos Is a Serious Business." *The Wall Street Journal,* November 17, 2011, page A1.
Internet	Author's last name, Author's first name. "Title of Document." (Online) Document date. URL (visited: date of visit).
	Example: Pisani, Joseph. "The Making of . . . a LEGO." (Online) November 29, 2006. *Bloomberg Businessweek.* http://www.businessweek.com/stories/2006-11-29/the-making-of-a-legobusinessweek-business-news-stock-market-and-financial-advice (visited September 19, 2012).

Try Guide students to quickly rehearse what they need to learn and do in preparation for practice

Ask students to help you identify the type of resource you need to cite and to find the correct example for formatting. Then, ask students to help you locate the information necessary as you continue to create your reference list.

Clarify Briefly restate today's teaching objective and explain the practice task(s)

Today we discussed the dangers of plagiarism and the importance of giving other authors credit for their work. I want each of you to create a reference list in which you give credit to each of the sources you used to create your final product. Use this chart to help you enter each item correctly.

Writing Lesson 10 · · · · · · · · · · · · · · · · ·

▼ Teaching Objective

Writers publish and share their research with others.

▼ Standards Alignment

W.5.6, W.5.7, SL.5.1a–d, SL.5.6, L.5.1, L.5.6

▼ Materials

• Students' final products

▼ To the Teacher

The details of this lesson will be influenced by the type of final product your students have created. If your students have curated museum displays, consider setting up a museum walk during which members of the class, as well as children from other classes, or parents, can circulate through the various displays and speak to the curators. If your students have created a mock Wonderopolis page, consider uploading their pages to a school website or on a classroom blog for students to share with their families. In addition, students

can browse through and comment on their classmates' pages. Today's lesson is meant to be celebratory and help students build important reflection skills. Emphasize with students that research is ongoing and that they will continue to have questions about many topics and now they have some tools for finding the answers all on their own!

▼ Procedure

Warm Up Gather the class to set the stage for today's learning

I am proud of all your hard work and so excited for you to share your projects with the world. What an exciting journey it has been to watch you be inspired, and create and build such wonderful presentations.

Teach Model what students need to learn and do

Today we are gathering to learn from and enjoy the work of our classmates. Lay out some ground rules for engaging with classmates' work. Be sure to emphasize the idea of respecting the efforts of others, listening with care, and responding thoughtfully to one another. Take a moment and share your final product with the class, discussing your choices as a researcher along the way.

Practice Students work independently or in small groups to apply today's teaching objective

Students work independently to create a reference list.

Wrap Up Check understanding as you guide students to briefly share what they have learned and produced today

Gather your class together to wrap up your discussion on plagiarism by sharing acceptable and unacceptable paraphrases (a resource that can be found easily and for free by searching the terms "acceptable and unacceptable paraphrases").

Try Guide students to quickly rehearse what they need to learn and do in preparation for practice

Ask students to discuss your presentation. What did they notice? What type of language did you use—was your speech casual or more formal in tone? (SL.5.6)

Clarify Briefly restate today's teaching objective and explain the practice task(s)

Today we are sharing and celebrating the work of our classmates. It is important to be proud of your work and show what you know. One way you can do that is by taking your own work seriously and speaking about it using proper, more formal English.

Practice Students work independently or in small groups to apply today's teaching objective

Students share and interact with the work of their classmates. This is also a good opportunity for students to share their work with the wider world. There are many websites for children that encourage cross-world sharing of children's writing via Skype calls and postings online. Visit the PDToolkit for links to global student sharing sites.

Wrap Up Check understanding as you guide students to briefly share what they have learned and produced today

Have students share what they learned about the research process.

Describe at least two things you learned that you can carry into your next research endeavor. What felt hard, and why? What did you enjoy most, and why?

Collect students' final presentations and use the Lesson Set Rubrics to analyze their work. **ELL** Assess for Content and Language Understanding—Summative Assessment. As you look at the summative assessment, take this time to think about your ELLs' language needs. This will help to guide their needs in upcoming units.

Milestone Performance Assessment

Research Process Reflection

Use this checklist to assess student research process reflections.

Standards Alignment: W.5.6, W.5.7, SL.5.6

	Achieved	Notes
List two lessons to carry into future research.		
Identify what felt hard and why.		
Identify favorite part and why.		

Language Companion Lesson

This lesson is best taught toward the beginning of the drafting process so that students may apply what they learn about separating items in a series to their work.

▼ Teaching Objective

Writers use commas to separate items in a series. We can list many types of items in a series such as nouns, verbs, participles, and infinitives.

▼ Standards Alignment

L.5.2a

▼ Materials

- Charting supplies/tools
- Students, writing materials

▼ To the Teacher

This lesson focuses on several types of items in a series (nouns, verbs, participles, and infinitives). The feature teaching method is sentence modeling, in which the teacher provides a model sentence and the students compose new sentences that mimic the structure of the model sentence and insert their own unique content.

▼ Procedure

Warm Up Gather the class to set the stage for today's learning

Engage students in some funny fill-in-the-blank exercises. Laugh heartily at the silly combinations your students are likely to create.

❶ Say: *I need a student's name. I need three common nouns.* Fill in students' responses.

▼ Example: _____ (student name) has a/an _____ (common noun), a/an _____, and a/an _____ (common noun), in his/her backpack.
(common noun)

▼ Example: Maria has an alligator, a nostril, and an airplane in her backpack.

❷ Say: *I need three present tense verbs.* Fill in student's responses.

Each day, our class _____ (present tense verb) in our notebooks, _____ (present tense verb) new books, and _____ (present tense verb) at recess.

▼ Example: Each day, our class sneezes in our notebooks, paints new books, and flies at recess.

❸ Say: *I need a teacher's name. I need three participles (-ing verbs).* Fill in student's responses.

After school, _____ (teacher name) will be _____ (participle), _____ (participle), and _____ (participle) at the mall.

▼ Example: After school, Mrs. Collins will be dancing, screaming, and wandering at the mall.

❹ Say: *I need three infinitive verbs (verbs that follow "to").* Ex: "to swim."

We must remind the principal not to forget _____ (infinitive verb) the doors, _____ (infinitive verb) the parents, or _____ (infinitive verb) the students.

▼ Example: We must remind the principal not to forget to scratch the doors, to poke the parents, or to fire the students.

Teach Model what students need to learn and do

All of the silly examples have something in common. Did anyone notice what it was? Every sentence presented a list of things, or items in a series separated by commas. You may not have noticed that there were four types of series that writers use all the time—nouns, verbs, participles, and infinitives. Most of you are familiar with type 1, a series of nouns.

1—Series of Nouns:

▲ *Maria has an alligator, a nostril, and an airplane in her backpack.*

Use the Nouns example to point out the structure and punctuation of this type of series sentence. Emphasize the position and importance of the commas. Note that while some sources say that a final comma before the "and" (a coordinating conjunction) is not necessary; it is usually standard in professional editing to include it.

Have the students compose one or more other sentences using the same structure and punctuation with their own content.

_____ has a/an _____, a/an _____, and
(student name)   (common noun)   (common noun)

a/an _____, in his/her backpack.
       (common noun)

2, 3, 4—Verb, Participles, and Infinitives

Repeat this process with the other three varieties of series. Students should use the examples as models for their own original sentences, trying each type of series.

Advanced Concept: Explain to students that it is important that the items in a series match each other in type (i.e., all nouns, all present tense verbs, all participles, all infinitives). This is called parallel structure.

Wrap Up Check understanding as you guide students to briefly share what they have learned and produced today

Have students share their original examples. Guide students to create a class poster that showcases their favorite examples of each type of series to post as a reference in the room.

GLOSSARY

analyze: to separate into parts for close study; examine and explain.

author's purpose: the author's reason for something existing or occurring.

cause and effect: a connection between two events in which one causes the other to happen.

chronology: the order of events in time.

comparison: the act of comparing or the result of being compared.

consequently: as a result; therefore.

definition: the statement of the meaning of a word or phrase.

description: a statement or account describing something.

fact: something said or known to be true.

focus: the area of greatest attention or activity.

integrate: to bring together and mix into a whole.

main idea: most important or chief or primary theme in the piece.

multimedia: the combination of sound, still pictures, and video.

observation: the act or an instance of perceiving the environment through one of the senses.

paraphrase: a restatement of a passage or text in somewhat different words so as to simplify or clarify.

point of view: a way of thinking about or looking at something.

problem and solution: a question or condition that is difficult to understand or to deal with, and the act or process of solving a problem or question.

quotation: a quoted passage from a text or speech.

recipe: a list of ingredients and instructions for making something, usually a food dish, but can be used metaphorically.

since: because.

source: the start or cause of something.

specifically: certain and exact; particular.

structure: a thing that is made up of different parts that are connected in a particular way.

summary: a short and usually comprehensive statement of what has been previously stated.

supporting/key details: details that assist or support the main points of a piece of writing.

therefore: for that reason.

thesis: a statement or proposition put forward and supported by proof or argument.

PD TOOLKIT™

Accompanying *Core Ready for Grades 3–5*, there is an online resource site with media tools that, together with the text, provides you with the tools you need to implement the lesson sets.

The PDToolkit for Pam Allyn's *Core Ready Series* is available free for 12 months after you use the password that comes with the box set for each grade band. After that, you can purchase access for an additional 12 months. If you did not purchase the box set, you can purchase a 12-month subscription at **http://pdtoolkit.pearson.com**. Be sure to explore and download the resources available at the website. Currently the following resources are available:

- Pearson Children's and Young Adult Literature Database
- Videos
- PowerPoint Presentations
- Student Artifacts
- Photos and Visual Media
- Handouts, Forms, and Posters to supplement your Core-aligned lesson plans
- Lessons and Homework Assignments
- Close Reading Guides and Samples
- Children's Core Literature Recommendations

In the future, we will continue to add additional resources. To learn more, please visit **http://pdtoolkit.pearson.com**.

APPENDIX 3.1   Core Message to Students

Who has ever had a burning question and desperately needed an answer? What did you do? Did you talk to someone who you thought was an expert on the topic? Did you go the library or log on to the Internet to find what you were looking for? In this lesson set we're all going to be journalists— first by asking questions and then by seeking the answers. Journalists research, write, and report on the information they've learned on a topic. As journalists we're going to read and write about a topic of great importance in our world today. In this lesson set, your questions are going to be as important as the answers we find. So, let's think about,

"What do we want to know?"

Name: _____   Date: _____

K—Know	W—Want to Know	L—Learned

Polar Bears Protected by Law

Did you know that polar bears are in danger? In May of 2008, the U.S. government put polar bears on the list of **threatened** species under the Endangered Species Act (ESA). The Department of the Interior will work to protect polar bears in Alaska, the only state in the United States where they live. Polar bears are endangered because of changes in their **habitat**.

Polar bears live and hunt on **perennial sea ice**, which usually stays frozen during the summertime but in recent years has begun to melt. The rate of melting seems to be increasing. The government will outlaw some activities that harm the bears, but will not take any steps against global warming, which many scientists believe is responsible for melting the polar ice caps. If the melting does not stop, polar bears will be in serious danger: a recent U.S. Geological Survey report predicted that two-thirds of the world's polar bears could be gone by 2050.

Physical Traits of Polar Bears

Polar bears are the largest of all land predators. A fully grown male weighs between 770 and 1,500 pounds. The bears live in the Arctic north, and their bodies are designed for their cold, icy home. They have a heavy coat of fur and a thick layer of **blubber** under their skin that keeps them warm even in icy water. Their feet are large with long claws, allowing them to grip the slippery ice and move quickly. They can swim very far—over 100 miles at a time—but they spend most of their time on the ice, mating and sometimes even giving birth there.

Hunting and Eating

Polar bears like to be at the edge of ice and the ocean: that's where it's easiest for them to hunt seals and other sea mammals. In the winter, thinner seasonal ice forms over large areas of the Arctic Ocean and polar bears **expand** their hunting range. When the thin ice melts in the summer, the bears will often **fast** for months because they cannot get to good hunting **grounds**. They're able to wait until winter to eat again, but if the sea ice melts **permanently**, they will starve.

Polar Bears Now

Polar bears now have to travel farther and farther to find food. In 2007, the water surface covered by sea ice in the Arctic was 39% less than the average from 1979 to 2000. U.S. Interior Secretary Dirk Kempthorne said, "While the legal standards under the ESA **compel** me to list the polar bear as threatened, I want to make clear that this listing will not stop global climate change or prevent any sea ice from melting. Any real solution requires action by all major economies for it to be effective." But, at least the government's action will make it more difficult for people to hunt polar bears as trophies. Scientists will continue to watch polar bear populations carefully.

Glossary

blubber—special fat for warmth and energy

compel—force

expand—grow, increase

fast—(verb) eat nothing

habitat—home

list, listed—(verb) put on a list; with a species, it usually means the species is "threatened" or "endangered"

perennial sea ice—very thick ice that usually does not melt in the Arctic summer, growing thicker year by year

permanently—forever

threatened—in danger

Source: Adapted from John Roach, "Polar Bears Listed as Threatened Species in U.S." *National Geographic News.* Retrieved from http://news.nationalgeographic.com/news/2008/05/080514-polar-bears.html

©outdoorsman/Fotolia

The Amazing Humpback Whales

Humpbacks in Danger

Have you ever seen a humpback whale? Probably not. They are pretty rare. Not too long ago, humpback whales used to be common in all of the world's oceans. Now, after almost two centuries of **whaling**, the population has been reduced to just a fraction of its original size. There are reasons why the humpback has been **overhunted**. The humpback's friendliness to humans, slow cruising speed (about 3 to 6 miles per hour), and habit of staying close to shore all made it an easy target for whaling ships. The humpback whale is now listed as a protected species, but illegal whaling continues in some parts of the world.

Other dangers to the humpback are getting tangled in fishing nets, collisions with boats and ships, pollution, and loss of habitat. The humpback breeds in the warm, shallow waters off the coast of tropical islands, which are becoming increasingly popular as vacation spots for humans.

Whale Games

Despite all of the dangers from humans, the humpback whale is not shy toward us. The are often seen at play near boats and people. Herman Melville, the author of *Moby Dick*, called humpbacks "the most **gamesome** and lighthearted" of the whales. Humpbacks are famous for **breaching** and slapping the water with their tails or long fins. Humpbacks are famous for breaching and slapping playful behavior may be how they communicate with each other. But anyone who has seen humpbacks at play will tell you that it looks as if they're just doing it for fun.

Physical Traits and Life Span

Do you know why humpback whales have that name? It's because they bend their backs when they dive. A humpback whale **calf** measures around 12 to 14 feet in length at birth. Adults may reach a length of up to 50 feet and live for between 60 and 90 years. It is easy to tell humpback whales apart by the distinctive patterns of their **flukes**. No two whales are exactly the same.

Humpback Groups

Humpback whales are social mammals. They like to travel in groups, which we humans call "pods." They swim from the cold-water feeding grounds off the coasts of Greenland or Alaska to the warm-water breeding grounds near the equator.

Feeding

Humpback whales are toothless, so their diet consists of little fish, crustaceans, krill, and plankton. Sometimes groups of whales will work together at feeding time. They form a circle around a school of fish and blow bubbles together to round up their prey, like cowboys rounding up a herd of cattle.

(continued)

Whale versus Whale

Sometimes, however, the whales aren't so friendly to one another. During mating season, the male whales fight for the females' attention. A whale duel is an amazing sight to see, and often leaves the two competitors bloodied and bruised.

Save the Whales

Humans must take care of the humpback whales if they are to survive in the future. Kids can help, too! There are many groups dedicated to saving the humpback whales. Join one today!

Glossary

breaching—leaping out of the water

calf—baby whale

duel—battle

grounds—place (on land or in the water) where a species likes to gather for a specific purpose

fluke—whale tail

gamesome—playful

overhunted—hunted too much, so the species may not survive

school—group of similar fish that stay close together

whaling—hunting whales for their oil, meat, skin, and bones

APPENDIX 3.5   Features of Informational Text

Print Features

bold print

bullets

captions

colored print

font

headings

italics

labels

subheadings

titles

Visual Aids

charts

cross-sections

diagrams

drawings

figures

graphs

maps

photographs

sketches

tables

timelines

Organizational Aids

appendix

glossary

index

preface

pronunciation guide

summary

table of contents

Name: _____ Date: _____

Title of Article: _____

MAIN IDEA

This article is mostly about:

SUPPORTING DETAILS

Supporting Idea 1:

Supporting Idea 2:

Supporting Idea 3:

Supporting Idea 4:

Name: _____ Date: _____

Title of source _____

I think this source is mostly about _____

I think that because _____

Are you going to use this source for your research? _____

Why or why not? _____

Name: _____   Date: _____

We Learn from Each Other

1. The main idea of my partner's article is _____
   _____
   _____

2. One detail I learned is _____
   _____
   _____

3. My partner used various text features including _____
   _____
   _____

4. My favorite illustration/photograph is _____ because I learned _____
   _____

5. The point of view of the piece is _____
   _____
   _____

6. I agree/disagree with the point of view because _____
   _____
   _____

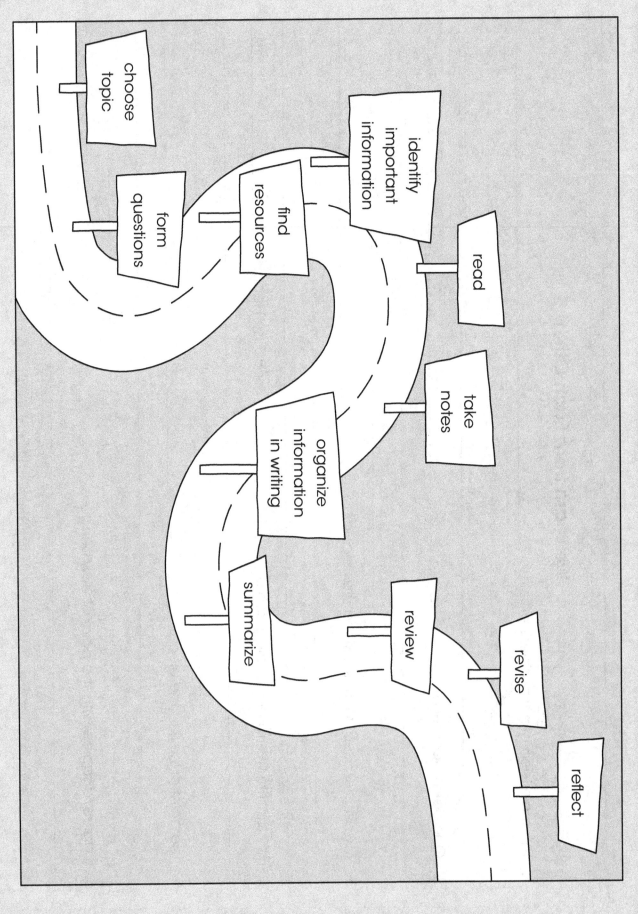

choose topic

form questions

find resources

identify important information

read

take notes

organize information in writing

summarize

review

revise

reflect

PD**d** TOOLKIT™

Name: _____ Date: _____

EXTRA! EXTRA!

My Ideas for Headlines and Leads

Headlines:

_____

_____

_____

_____

_____

Possible Leads:

_____

_____

_____

APPENDIX 3.11 Layout Plan Graphic Organizer 1

HEADLINE:

Author: Date:

Heading: Picture:

Heading: Caption:

Heading:

Picture:

Heading:

Caption:

APPENDIX 3.12 Layout Plan Graphic Organizer 2

HEADLINE:

Author: _____ Date: _____

Heading:

Picture:

Caption:

Heading:

Picture:

Caption:

Heading:

Picture:

Caption:

Heading:

Picture:

Caption:

	Achieved	Notes
Revision: Ideas Check		
I included a lead that hooks the reader.		
All information in each paragraph is connected to the main idea of the paragraph.		
The headings match the content of paragraph.		
The ideas in each paragraph are in an order that makes sense.		
I used linking words and phrases (*also, another, and, more, but*) to connect ideas.		
I included a clincher ending (quotation, shocking fact, summary, appeal).		
COPS Editing Checklist		
Capitals—I remembered to use capitals correctly.		
Order and usage of words—I have reread my sentences, and they all sound right and make sense.		
Punctuation—I have used correct punctuation.		
Spelling—I have corrected my spelling errors.		

APPENDIX 3.14 Revising and Editing Segments from "The Amazing Humpback Whales"

#1 (opening paragraphs)

Humpbacks in Danger

Humpback whales use to be common in all of the worlds oceans. Now, after almost too centuries of whaling, the populshun has been reduced to just a fraction of its original size. There are reasons why the humpback was hunted so often.

The humpback whale are now listed as a protected species, but theres still illegal whaling in some parts of the world. Other dangers to the humpback are fishing nets ships pollushun and loss of habitat. The humpback breeds in the warm shallow waters off the coast of tropical islands.

#2

Physical Traits and Life Span

Do you know how the humpback whale gets its name? It is easy to tell humpback whales apart by the distinctive patterns of there flukes. The humpback whate gets it's name from the way it bends it's back

whent dives. A humpback whale calf measures around 12 to 14 feet in length at birth Adults may reach a length of up to 50 feet. No tow whales are exactly the same.

#3

Blowing Bubbles

Humpback whales are toothless, so there diet consists of little fish crustaceans krill and plankton. Sometimes groups of whales will work together at feeding time. They form a circle and blow bubbles together to round up their prey, like cowboys rounding up a herd of cattle. Humpback whales have very smooth skin.

#4 (closing paragraph)

Save the Whales

Humans must take care of the humpback whale if they are to survive in the future I hoped you liked reading about whales.

APPENDIX 3.15 Humpback Article Revision and Editing Key

Segment	Editing Needed	Revision Needed
1	use to/used to	Lead is not very engaging.
	worlds/world's	Reasons why humpbacks were hunted not listed.
	th/the	
	too/two	Breeding sentence does not explain why swimming in shallow water is dangerous.
	populshun/population	
	theres/there's	Sentence about diving style as the source of the name is misplaced.
	pollushun/pollution	
	worlds/world's	
	humpback whale are/humpback whales	
	are/humpback whale is	
	serial commas missing (fishing nets, pollution, and loss of habitat)	
2	there/their	Life span is in heading but not in details
	whale/whale	Sequencing of ideas is incorrect
	it's/its	
	whent/when it	
	tow/two	
	period missing after birth	
3	there/their	The heading Blowing Bubbles does not summarize the content of the paragraph.
	serial commas missing (fish, crustaceans, krill, and plankton)	Sentence about skin does not belong.
	there/their	
4	capitalization in heading	Not a "clincher" ending.
	thEy/they	More details needed about how humans can help.
	period missing after future	

☐ Teaches about a topic

☐ Includes headings to show main ideas

☐ Includes facts

☐ Includes glossary of important or difficult words

☐ Asks question

☐ Includes quotes from experts

☐ Written in paragraphs

☐ Directly addresses the reader ("you")

☐ Includes picture and caption

Ending Techniques	Give It a Try
Quote	
Shocking fact	
Summary	
Appeal to the reader	

Singular Antecedents

boy	dog
girl	house
Joe	flower
Annie	

each	everything
either	nobody
neither	no one
anybody	nothing
anyone	somebody
anything	someone
everybody	something
everyone	

. . . should always be followed by . . .

Singular Pronouns

he	The **flower** opened **its** petals.
him	**Joe** is my brother. **He** is 15.
his	
himself	
she	**Everyone** needs **his or her** lunchbox.
her	or
hers	
herself	**Everybody** should speak for **himself**.
it	
its	
itself	

Plural Antecedents

boys	
girls	
Joe and Annie	
dogs	
houses	
flowers	

both
several
few

. . . should always be followed by . . .

Plural Pronouns

they	The **boys** ran with **their** dogs.
them	
their	
theirs	
themselves	**Few** wanted **their** dinners.

Reading Lesson 1

Milestone Performance Assessment: K-W-L

Standards Alignment: RI.3.1, W.3.7, W.3.8, W.3.10

Use this checklist to assess student performance on their K-W-L chart.

Name: _____   Date: _____

	Achieved	Notes
List facts they know about the topic.		
Generate questions about their topic.		
Record what they learned.		

Reading Lesson 3

Milestone Performance Assessment: Finding Main Idea and Support Details

Standards Alignment: RI.3.1, RI.3.2, RI.3.5

Use this checklist to assess student performance on the Main Idea and Supporting Details graphic organizer.

Name: _____   Date: _____

	Achieved	Notes
Identify main ideas.		
Identify supporting details.		
Connect main ideas to supporting details.		

Standards Alignment: RI.3.1, RI.3.2, RI.3.8

Reading Lesson 6

Milestone Performance Assessment: Finding the Cause and Effect

Use this checklist to assess student ability to identify and understand the relationship between cause and effect.

Name: _____

Date: _____

	Achieved	Notes
Identify causes.		
Identify effects.		
Understand relationship between cause and effect.		

Standards Alignment: RI.3.1, RI.3.2, RI.3.6

Reading Lesson 10

Milestone Performance Assessment: Peer Assessment

Use this checklist to assess student ability to read and respond to peer's work.

Name: _____

Date: _____

Peer assessment:	Achieved	Notes
Identify the main idea in a classmate's work.		
Identify the supporting key details in a classmate's work.		
Identify various text features in a classmate's work.		
Explain significance of illustration/photo in a classmate's work.		

Standards Alignment: W.3.4, W.3.5, W.3.7 W.3.8, W.3.10, SL.3.1a–d, SL.3.2, SL.3.6, L.3.1, L.3.6

Writing Lesson 4

Milestone Performance Assessment: Categorizing Notes

Use this checklist to assess student understanding of basic categorization of notes.

Name: _____   Date: _____

	Achieved	Notes
Organize notes logically in clusters of related information.		
Create appropriate labels for groups.		
Discuss notes with a partner and make revisions based on discussion, as needed.		

Standards Alignment: W.3.2a–c, W.3.4, W.3.5, W.3.10, SL.3.6, L.3.1, L.3.6

Writing Lesson 6

Milestone Performance Assessment: Creating a Paragraph

Use this checklist to assess student ability to create a paragraph.

Name: _____   Date: _____

	Achieved	Notes
Use notes to create paragraph content.		
Use punctuation correctly.		
Use transitional phrases.		
Use complete sentences.		
Create a focused, complete paragraph.		

Standards Alignment: W.3.2d, W.3.4, W.3.5, W.3.10

Writing Lesson 7

Milestone Performance Assessment: Creating an Ending

Use this checklist to assess student ability to organize thoughts into a final conclusion.

Name: _____ **Date:** _____

	Achieved	Notes
Draft a variety of endings.		
Choose an ending that logically concludes content of writing.		

Standards Alignment: W.3.2a–d, W.3.4, W.3.5, W.3.10, SL.3.6, L.3.1, L.3.6

Writing Lesson 9

Milestone Performance Assessment: Research Wrap Up

Use this checklist to assess student ability to complete the research.

Name: _____   Date: _____

	Achieved	Notes
Include a lead that hooks the reader.		
Connect all information in each paragraph to the main idea of the paragraph.		
Use headings that match the content of paragraph.		
Put the ideas in each paragraph in an order that makes sense.		
Use linking words and phrases (e.g., *also, another, and, more, but*) to connect ideas.		
Include a clincher ending (quote, shocking fact, summary, appeal).		
COPS Editing Checklist		
Correct **c**apitalization.		
Correct **o**rder and usage of words.		
Correct **p**unctuation.		
Correct **s**pelling.		

The following checklist provides observable Core Standards–aligned indicators to assess student performance as speakers and listeners. Use it in its entirety to gather performance data over time or choose appropriate indicators to create a customized checklist to match a specific learning experience.

Name: _____   Topic of Study: _____   Time Frame: _____

Performance Indicator	Achieved	Notes
Actively engages in collaborative discussions in a variety of settings (student partnerships, student groups, teacher-led). [SL.3.1]		
Prepares for discussions in advance and uses this preparation to enhance discussion. [SL.3.1a]		
Follows agreed-upon rules for discussions (active listening, taking turns to speak, etc.). [SL.3.1b]		
Contributes to discussions by commenting on the ideas of others, asking questions and explaining ideas. [SL.3.1c–d]		
Demonstrates understanding of the main idea from a given source such as read-aloud or other media and formats. [SL.3.2]		
Asks and answers questions in detail using information from a speaker. [SL.3.3]		
Reports on a topic, story, or experience with focus and accurate detail. [SL.3.4]		
Speaks clearly and at an understandable pace. [SL.3.4]		
Creates engaging audio recordings that demonstrate reading fluency. [SL.3.5]		
Uses visual displays to enhance presentations. [SL.3.5]		
Elaborates in complete sentences appropriate to the task and situation. [SL.3.6]		

APPENDIX 4.1   Core Message to Students

Everything happens for a reason! This means that there are causes for all actions and effects of all actions. You forget to brush your teeth, you might end up with a cavity. If you don't pick up your room, you can't find your book in the morning. Who else can think of a good example of cause and effect from their own lives? As readers we should always be thinking, "Why did this happen?" or "What caused this?" This is especially important when reading about things that happened in history.

Irena Sendler Story

Irena Sendler was 29 years old when her city, Warsaw, in Poland, was occupied by the Nazis. Because of this, everything changed. Life was suddenly dangerous for the city's Jewish families because they were all forced into an area of the city called the Warsaw Ghetto. Irena was Catholic, but she could still get in trouble easily. If she wanted to survive then the smart thing would be to keep her head down and try not to be noticed.

Irena did not do this. Instead, she smuggled Jewish children out of the Warsaw Ghetto to safety.

This required a great deal of courage. If Irena were caught, she would be in terrible danger. Yet, Irena was brave. By the end of the war, she had saved the lives of about 2,500 children.

She worked with about thirty other volunteers, mostly women. Sometimes the children were driven out in ambulances; one driver brought a dog with him whose barking distracted the soldiers. Sometimes they were disguised as packages, or put in potato sacks. They often traveled an escape route through underground corridors in an old courthouse at the edge of the ghetto.

Once they'd escaped the ghetto, the children were placed with families or in convents throughout the Polish countryside.

As a result, they were safely tucked away in villages, where they would wait for the war to end. But there was another problem: many of these children were very young, some were even babies. Not only that, but they'd been given new names, and therefore might forget their old ones. How would Irena keep track of who had gone where? How would she be able to reunite the children and their parents at the end of the war?

In order to remember, Irena and her friends wrote the old and new names of every child on lists. They put the lists in jars and buried them under a tree in Irena's garden. At the end of the war, they dug up the lists. So, it was possible to reconnect children with their families at the end of the war.

Years and years later, Irena told a newspaper reporter from The Independent, "Heroes do extraordinary things. What I did was not an extraordinary thing. It was normal." She was impatient with awards and honors; she told people the real heroes were the children's parents. Maybe Irena was so brave because her father was too. He was a doctor who treated all of his patients equally, even when there was a chance they would make him sick too. When Irena was young, he told her, "If you see someone drowning you must try to rescue them, even if you cannot swim."

Cause–Effect	Cause is why something happened. Effect is what happened.	©Benjamin Mercer/Fotolia
Problem–Solution	Tells about a problem. Then, gives a solution or more than one solution.	©cantor pannatto/Fotolia
Compare–Contrast	Shows how two or more things are alike and different.	©travis manley/Fotolia

Name: _____   Date: _____

Title: _____

Events across Time

Event:
Date:

Event:
Date:

Event:
Date:

Event:
Date:

Event:
Date:

Event:
Date:

Name: _____   Date: _____

Book Title: _____

Plan Your Topic Sentence: Include the book title and the main event that happened in your text.

Details about Causes: What caused this event to happen?

Details about Effects: What things happened as a result of the main event?

Conclusion: What finally happened in the end?

Name: _____   Date: _____

Book Title: _____

What was the main event? What image could you use to represent this event? Describe the image in writing.

What caused this event to happen? What image could you use to represent it? Describe the image in writing.

What thing(s) happened as a result of the main event? What image(s) could you use to represent this? Describe the image in writing.

What finally happened in the end? What image could you use to represent this? Describe the image in writing.

Now consider all of the events and images you have suggested. How will you represent these in your poster or book trailer? Think about sequence, placement, and any text or audio you might include.

????? Historical Headlines Leave Me Wondering ?????

Name: _____   Date: _____

Headline	What It Makes Me Wonder

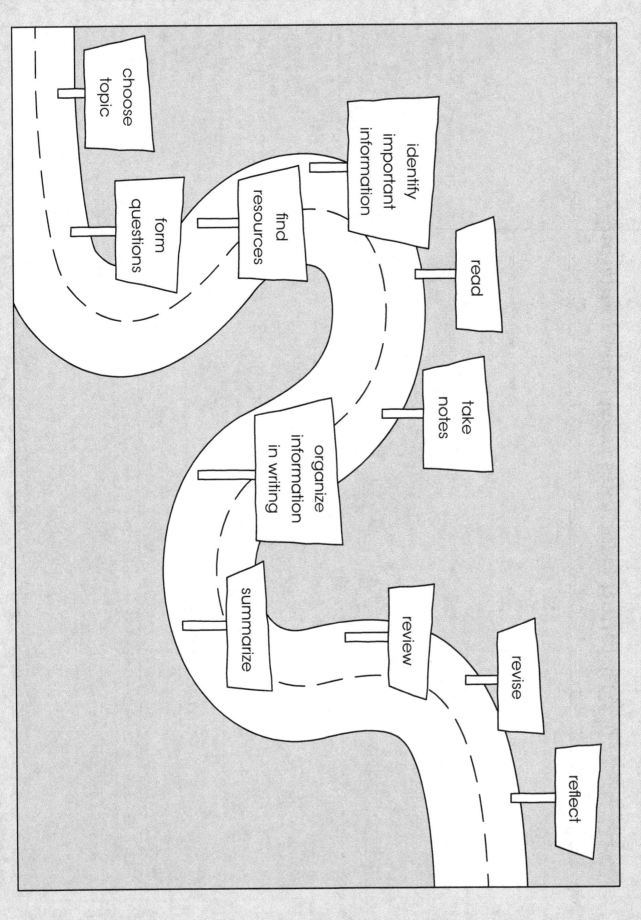

choose topic

form questions

find resources

identify important information

read

take notes

organize information in writing

summarize

review

revise

reflect

September 26, 1941

Dear Journal,

I wish everyone would stop telling me how brave I am. I don't feel brave. I feel very sad and very scared. Ever since my parents made me leave our apartment in Warsaw I have felt confused. I wake up in a strange room and don't know where I am until I remember my escape from the Jewish ghetto where I used to live. A week ago, my parents told me that it was not safe for children to live with them anymore because diseases were starting to spread and people were dying from sickness or hunger. The German soldiers that guarded the street were not afraid to shoot at residents who looked, talked, or dressed the wrong way.

A woman named Irena snuck me out of Warsaw. She is allowed to travel in and out of the ghetto because she is not Jewish. I don't understand why we had to move here in the first place. I grew up in a nice house and my mom and dad worked as teachers. Then a war started, our city was invaded, and we had to move to a tiny, cold apartment like all the other Jewish families in Poland. For some reason there are people that seem to hate me because I am Jewish. Not even my mom has been able to explain this to me, so I looked very closely at Irena when she came to pick me up. We both have two legs, two arms, two eyes, and a nose. We didn't seem very different at all. I couldn't find anything unusual about her. Once she arrived I had to get ready to leave so fast. Everyone was nervous and no one was talking much except to give me instructions, or to tell me they loved me, not to worry and of course, what a brave little girl I am. While Irena pulled me by the hand down the hallway of my apartment I looked over my shoulder, trying to memorize the faces of my mom and dad. I was not allowed to take a picture of them and no one could tell me when I would see them again.

Irena put me in the back of an ambulance in an old potato sack and we drove toward the exit of the ghetto. Writing it sounds like something I would read in a storybook, it's hard to believe it actually happened. The ride was bumpy and dark and seemed very long. The potato sack smelled like mold and the ambulance smelled like sweat and medicine. I was terrified that a soldier would stop the ambulance to inspect the inside and find me. I bit on my hand to keep from crying or screaming but I couldn't help shaking. Eventually I arrived at my new house. It is warm inside and I have my own room with a closet of clothes and a shelf of books. I can go outside and smell fresh air; I eat more than once a day and I even had a cookie for the first time in a year. The man and woman I live with are a nice old couple. I know I am lucky to be alive and safe, but I miss hugging my mother and the way she always smelled like soap. I miss my dad's silly stories about a dog named Pip Pop who always gets into trouble. I have no way to talk to them and I don't know if they are OK. I don't bother asking when the war will end and if I will see my parents again, because the answer is always, "I don't know."

APPENDIX 4.10 Sample Diary Entry 2

Dear Journal,

May 2, 1948

Ever since my teammate Lou Gibson woke up with a rat biting his ear I haven't been able to sleep at night. I'm twenty times the size of those disgusting rodents, but I can't forget the sight of Lou's ear with a chunk of skin bitten away. It happened in Chicago a few nights ago. Tonight I am in Detroit, but every boarding house for colored people is pretty much the same: uncomfortable and dirty. My body jumps every time I hear a noise and I have to inspect the area around my cot for creatures. Last night I tried pretending I was sleeping in one of those hotels for white folks. I imagined stretching out in a big bed with a thick mattress that would cushion my sore muscles and the soft blankets that I'd pull all the way up to my neck.

Instead of getting sleepy I got angry. Really angry. I run faster than half the players in the white leagues and I can hit the ball farther. If the coaches and managers of the white league picked players based on batting average, running speed, or number of strikeouts instead of skin color, how different would the teams look? Instead, it is skin color that determines if you are able to play in the professional league. I'm not sure how skin helps when you're at home plate trying to hit a home run. Wouldn't the games be more exciting for fans to watch with better athletes? Instead there must be separate leagues, separate water fountains, and separate restaurants. White players are paid a lot of money and get treated like heroes. As a colored player I just hope to be paid at all and try not to get spit on.

Someday everyone will realize that separating players based on skin color is as dumb as refusing to store strawberry ice cream in the same freezer as chocolate. Until then, all I can do is play baseball as well as I can, keep my head up, and believe in myself. In hopes of taking my mind off of ear attacks tonight, I will think about how much I love to play baseball. I love the smoothness of the wooden bat in my hands; the sound of the wind in my ears as I sprint toward home plate; the smell of popcorn floating to the field from the bleachers; the way all my muscles work together to swing the bat at exactly the right second; and the deafening cheers as I slide through the dusty brown dirt to home plate. If this doesn't work, tomorrow I'll sleep with a baseball bat next to my cot. Rats beware.

Name: _____ Date: _____

Book Title: _____

Event that happened in the story.

Why did this event occur?

Your thoughts on this event.

Your feelings on this event.

Name: _____   Date: _____

Book Title: _____

Facts about the Place	Facts about the People	Facts about the Time Period

Name: _____

Date: _____

Revising	Yes or No	Notes
Does my entry describe an important event?		
Does my entry include why this event happened?		
Does my entry make my point of view clear to the reader?		
Does my entry include facts about people, places, and events from the time period?		
COPS Editing Checklist		
Capitals—I remembered to use capitals correctly.		
Order and usage of words—I have reread my sentences, and they all sound right and make sense.		
Punctuation—I have used correct punctuation.		
Spelling—I have corrected my spelling errors.		

Standards Alignment: RI.4.1, RI.4.3, RI.4.5, RI.4.8

Reading Lesson 4

Milestone Performance Assessment: *Finding Cause and Effect*

Use this checklist to assess student work on What Happened and Why? chart

Name: _____   Date: _____

	Achieved	Notes
Identify effects cited in the text.		
Identify causes corresponding to the effects.		

Standards Alignment: RI.4.1, RI.4.3, RI.4.5, RI.4.7

Reading Lesson 5

Milestone Performance Assessment: *Cause and Effect across Time*

Use this checklist to assess student work on the Timeline Organizer.

Name: _____   Date: _____

	Achieved	Notes
Identify when events occur in a story on the timeline.		
Identify cause and effect relationships on the timeline.		

Standards Alignment: W.4.2a–d, W.4.4, W.4.6, W.4.10, SL.4.2

Reading Lesson 7

Milestone Performance Assessment: Summaries

Use this checklist to assess student summaries of effect and cause relationships.

Name: _____ Date: _____

	Achieved	Notes
Plan a topic sentence with main event.		
Plan supporting details about causes.		
Plan supporting details about effects.		
Plan a conclusion.		

Standards Alignment: W.4.4, W.4.6, W.4.10

Reading Lesson 8

Milestone Performance Assessment: Creating a Poster/Trailer

Use this checklist to assess student's ability to effectively use images to convey an historical idea.

Name: _____ Date: _____

	Achieved	Notes
Find suitable images to represent each historical event.		
Craft a poster/trailer that clearly illustrates cause and effect relationships.		

Standards Alignment: RI.4.1, W.4.4, W.4.10

Reading Lesson 10

Milestone Performance Assessment: Reflection

Use this checklist to assess student reflection on the text.

Name: _____   Date: _____

	Achieved	Notes
Craft responses to Core Questions posed.		
Use details from the text to support their ideas and thinking.		

Standards Alignment: RI.4.1, RI.4.2, RI.4.6, RI.4.9, W.4.4, W.4.7

Writing Lesson 3

Milestone Performance Assessment: Note Taking

Use this checklist to assess student note-taking skills.

Name: _____   Date: _____

	Achieved	Notes
Identify main points.		
Identify additional/supporting points.		
Take notes independently.		
Work with a partner to take notes.		

Standards Alignment: W.4.4, W.4.7

Writing Lesson 4

Milestone Performance Assessment: *Coding and Sorting*

Use this checklist to assess student ability to code and sort subtopics.

Name: _____   Date: _____

	Achieved	Notes
Group notes into logical categories.		
Name subtopic groups appropriately.		

Standards Alignment: W.4.4, W.4.7, W.4.10

Writing Lesson 5

Milestone Performance Assessment: *Planning Organizer*

Use this checklist to assess student ability to plan and organize thoughts.

Name: _____   Date: _____

	Achieved	Notes
Include an important historical event.		
Identify why the event happened.		
Develop point of view (thoughts and feelings) regarding an event.		

Standards Alignment: W.4.2a, b, d, W.4.4, W.4.6, W.4.10

Writing Lesson 6

Milestone Performance Assessment: Writing a Diary Entry

Use this checklist to assess student ability to assimilate facts to write a diary entry.

Name: _____   Date: _____

	Achieved	Notes
Identify facts about the place.		
Identify facts about the people.		
Identify facts about the time period.		
Begin writing diary entries.		

Standards Alignment: W.4.5, W.4.6, SL.4.6, L.4.1, L.4.2, L.4.3

Writing Lesson 9

Milestone Performance Assessment: Research Wrap Up

Use this checklist to assess student ability to make final revisions and edits.

Name: _____   Date: _____

	Achieved	Notes
Describe an important event.		
Include why this event happened.		
Make the point of view clear to the reader.		
Include facts about people, places, and events from the time period.		
COPS Editing Checklist		
Correct **c**apitalization.		
Correct **o**rder and usage of words.		
Correct **p**unctuation.		
Correct **s**pelling.		

This following checklist provides observable Core Standards–aligned indicators to assess student performance as speakers and listeners. Use it in its entirety to gather performance data over time or choose appropriate indicators to create a customized checklist to match a specific learning experience.

Name: _____   Topic of Study: _____   Time Frame: _____

Performance Indicator	Achieved	Notes
Actively engages in collaborative discussions in a variety of settings (student partnerships, student groups, teacher-led). [SL.4.1]		
Prepares for discussions in advance and uses this preparation to enhance discussion. [SL.4.1a]		
Follows agreed-upon rules and roles for discussions (active listening, taking turns to speak, etc.). [SL.4.1b]		
Contributes to discussions by commenting on the ideas of others, asking and answering questions and explaining ideas. [SL.4.1c–d]		
Paraphrases from a given source such as read-aloud or other media and formats. [SL.4.2]		
Identifies reasons and evidence a speaker provides to support a point. [SL.4.3]		
Reports on a topic, story, or experience with organization, focus, and accurate detail. [SL.4.4]		
Speaks clearly and at an understandable pace. [SL.4.4]		
Provides audio recordings and/or visual displays that effectively enhance ideas or themes of presentations. [SL.4.5]		
Uses either formal or informal English appropriate to task and situation. [SL.4.6]		

We have so much information at our fingertips. These days, when I want to learn something new or answer a question, I almost immediately turn to the Internet to get started. I search for websites, books to check out, articles to read. Researchers are such good readers and writers because they can take all this information, figure out what is the most important to them, and come up with a new way to look at it all. Over the next few days and weeks, we're going to dig into the topics that interest you the most—are you ready to research?

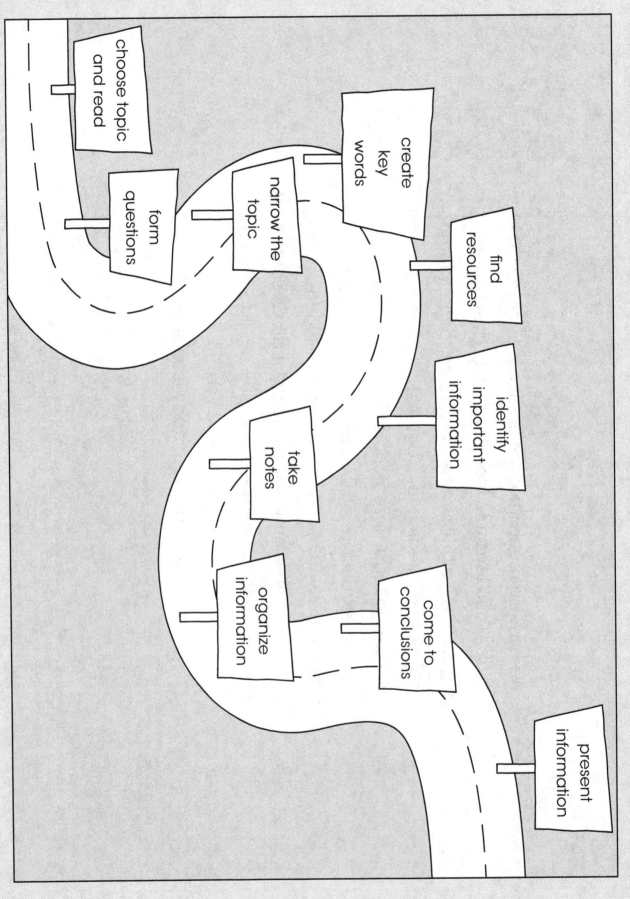

choose topic
and read

form
questions

narrow the
topic

create
key
words

find
resources

identify
important
information

take
notes

organize
information

come to
conclusions

present
information

Name: _____   Date: _____

Main Idea	Supporting Details	My Thinking

Name: _____   Date: _____

Topic: _____

Ideas	People	Events

APPENDIX 5.5 "5Ws, 1H" Graphic Organizer

Name: _____ Date: _____

Research Question: How were Legos invented?

Answer: Legos were invented by Ole Kirk Christiansen, a furniture maker who expanded his business to include wooden children's toys when his business was suffering during the Great Depression.

WHO: Who invented Legos?

- Ole Kirk Christiansen invented Legos
- Originally a furniture maker

Image:

WHAT: What are Legos?

- Legos are interlocking blocks
- Originally made of wood
- Now made of plastic and come in themed sets
- In Latin, Lego means "I put together"
- In Danish, Lego means "play well"

Image:

WHEN: When were Legos invented?

- 1940s

Image:

WHERE: Where were Legos invented?

- Legos were invented in Denmark
- OKC's furniture shop

Image:

WHY: Why were Legos invented?

- The Great Depression
- As people struggled, there were fewer customers and Christiansen had to find alternative ways to make money. He began to make children's toys. Christiansen started by making wooden pull toys and marionettes.

Image:

HOW: How were Legos invented?

- After World War II, plastics were available in Denmark
- Added hollow tubes to the backs of originally solid bricks and began making them out of plastic

Image:

APPENDIX 5.6 Research Wrap-Up Checklist

Revising	Yes or No	Notes
Did I include an informative and engaging introduction?		
Did I answer my research question(s) with enough details?		
Did I include information from more than one source?		
Did I include key people, places, and things related to my research questions and explain how they are related to each other?		
Did I include visuals that enhance my presentation?		
Are all my ideas clustered together logically?		
COPS Editing Checklist		
Capitals—I remembered to use capitals correctly.		
Order and usage of words—I have reread my sentences, and they all sound right and make sense.		
Punctuation—I have used correct punctuation.		
Spelling—I have corrected my spelling errors.		

Name: _____

Date: _____

Adding More

Also, _____

What is more, _____

In addition, _____

Furthermore, _____

Additionally, _____

Most of all, _____

Not only will _____, but _____

will also _____

Comparing (same)

Similarly, _____

Likewise, _____

In much the same way, _____

_____, _____

Contrasting (different)

However, _____

On the other hand, _____

Although _____, _____

Unfortunately, _____

In reality, _____

Ordering

First of all, _____

Second, _____

Third, _____ (etc.)

Then, _____

Next, _____

After that, _____

Finally, _____

Later, _____

Citing Sources

It says in the (name text)

that _____

As one can read

in _____

An example can be found

in _____

In (name text), it clearly

shows _____

Showing

For example, _____

For instance, _____

In this case, _____

It is obvious that _____

Clearly, _____

Cause and Effect

As a result, _____

As a consequence, _____

Because of _____

Therefore, _____

So, _____

Concluding

To sum up, _____

In conclusion, _____

In summary, _____

All things considered, _____

I have argued that _____

It is clear that _____

Standards Alignment: RI.5.1, RI.5.2

Reading Lesson 3

Milestone Performance Assessment: *Main Ideas and Support Details*

Use this checklist to assess student use of the Main Ideas and Supporting Details graphic organizer.

Name: _____   Date: _____

	Achieved	Notes
Identify and list main ideas from text.		
Identify and list supporting details from text.		
Record thinking about the ideas in the text.		

Standards Alignment: RI.5.1, RI.5.3

Reading Lesson 5

Milestone Performance Assessment: *Identifying Key Ideas, People, and Events*

Use this checklist to assess student use of the Key Ideas, People, and Events graphic organizer.

Name: _____   Date: _____

	Achieved	Notes
Identify key people from text.		
Identify key ideas from text.		
Identify key events from text.		
Explain the relationship between one or more people, ideas, and events.		

Reading *Lesson 8*

Standards Alignment: RI.5.1, RI.5.2, RI.5.6, SL.5.1a, SL.5.1c

Milestone Performance Assessment: *Compare and Contrast*

Use this checklist to assess student ability to compare and contrast information found in multiple accounts on the same topic.

Name: _____ Date: _____

	Achieved	Notes
Record similarities between sources.		
Record differences between sources.		
Provide reasonably logical reasons why sources differ from each other.		
Form connections with author's purpose and point of view.		

Reading *Lesson 10*

Standards Alignment: W.5.4, W.5.10

Milestone Performance Assessment: *How to Use Multiple Sources in Research*

Use this checklist to assess student written reflection on the Core Questions.

Name: _____ Date: _____

Speaking Skill	Achieved	Notes
Define research.		
Explain methods for answering reading questions.		
Explain how to synthesize and develop ideas using multiple sources.		
Explain how other media enhances the presentation of information with specific examples.		
Share examples of how researchers share their research in dynamic ways.		

Writing Lesson 3

Milestone Performance Assessment: Researcher Skills

Standards Alignment RI.5.1, RI.5.2, W.5.7, W.5.8

Use this checklist to assess student ability to summarize, paraphrase, and use a direct quotation.

Name: _____   Date: _____

	Achieved	Notes
Take notes that effectively capture the content of a larger piece.		
Attempt all three note-taking strategies.		
Explain decision to summarize, paraphrase, or quote with logical reasoning.		

Writing Lesson 5

Milestone Performance Assessment: Written Responses

Standards Alignment W.5.5, W.5.9b, SL.5.1a–d

Use this checklist to assess student ability to craft a strong written response.

Name: _____   Date: _____

	Achieved	Notes
Identify and describe the relationship between two or more key individuals, events, or ideas.		
Explain why this relationship is important.		
Provide details/evidence from the text to support thinking.		
Provide improvements to strengthen a partner's work.		

Standards Alignment W.5.5, W.5.7

Writing Lesson 8

Milestone Performance Assessment: Revising

Use this checklist to assess student ability to revise for voice, look for places to clarify work, and edit.

Name: _____   Date: _____

Revising	Achieved	Notes
Include an informative and engaging introduction.		
Answer research question(s) with enough details.		
Include information from more than one source.		
Include key people, places, and things related to research questions and explain how they are related to each other.		
Include visuals that enhance presentation.		
Cluster ideas together logically.		
COPS Editing Checklist		
Correct **c**apitalization.		
Correct **o**rder and usage of words.		
Correct **p**unctuation.		
Correct **s**pelling.		

Standards Alignment W.5.6, W.5.7, SL.5.6

Writing Lesson 10

Milestone Performance Assessment: Research Process Reflection

Use this checklist to assess student research process reflections.

Name: _____   Date: _____

	Achieved	Notes
List two lessons to carry into future research.		
Identify what felt hard and why.		
Identify favorite part and why.		

APPENDIX 5.9 Speaking and Listening Performance Checklist, Grade 5

This following checklist provides observable Core Standards–aligned indicators to assess student performance as speakers and listeners. Use it in its entirety to gather performance data over time or choose appropriate indicators to create a customized checklist to match a specific learning experience.

Name: _____   Topic of Study: _____   Time Frame: _____

Performance Indicator	Achieved	Notes
Actively engages in collaborative discussions in a variety of settings (student partnerships, student groups, teacher-led). [SL.5.1]		
Prepares for discussions in advance and uses this preparation to enhance discussion. [SL.5.1a]		
Follows agreed-upon rules and roles for discussions (active listening, taking turns to speak, etc.). [SL.5.1b]		
Contributes to discussions by commenting on the ideas of others, asking and answering questions. [SL.5.1c]		
Reviews key ideas and conclusions generated by discussion. [SL.5.1d]		
Summarizes ideas from a given source such as read-aloud or other media and formats. [SL.5.2]		
Identifies main points and links to supporting evidence provided by a speaker. [SL.5.3]		
Reports on a topic or text or presents opinion with organization, focus, and accurate detail. [SL.5.4]		
Speaks clearly and at an understandable pace. [SL.5.4]		
Provides multimedia components and visual displays that effectively enhance ideas or themes of presentations. [SL.5.5]		
Uses either formal or informal English appropriate to task and situation. [SL.5.6]		

References

Allington, D. (2012, in press). Private experience, textual analysis, and institutional authority: The discursive practice of critical interpretation and its enactment in literary training. *Language and Literature, 21*(2).

Allington, R. L. (2009). If they don't read much . . . 30 years later. In E. H. Hiebert (Ed.), *Reading more, reading better* (pp. 30–54). New York, NY: Guilford Publishers.

Carrier, K. A., & Tatum, A. W. (2006). Creating sentence walls to help English-language learners develop content literacy. *The Reading Teacher, 60*(3), 285–288.

Collins, A., Brown, J. S., & Newman, S. E. (1989). Cognitive apprenticeship: Teaching the crafts of reading, writing, and mathematics. In L. B. Resnick (Ed.) *Knowing, learning, and instruction: Essays in honor of Robert Glaser* (pp. 453–494). Hillsdale, NJ: Lawrence Erlbaum Associates.

Cummins, J. (2010). *Five principles for teaching content to English language learners.* New York, NY: Pearson.

Duke, N. & Pearson, P. D. (2002). Effective practices for developing reading comprehension. In A. E. Fastrup & S. J. Samuels (Eds.), What research has to say about reading instruction (3rd ed.). 205–242. Newark, DE: International Reading Association.

Dymock, S. & Nicholson, T. (2007). *Teaching text structures: A key to nonfiction reading success.* New York, NY: Scholastic Teaching Resources.

Ehri, L. C., Dreyer, L. G., Flugman, B., & Gross, A. (2007). Reading rescue: An effective tutoring intervention model for language-minority students who are struggling readers in first grade. *American Educational Research Journal, 44,* 414–448.

Gardner, H. (2007). *Five minds for the future.* Boston, MA: Harvard Business Press.

Goldenberg, C. (2008). Teaching English Language Learners: What the research does—and does not—say. *American Educator, 32*(2), 8–23, 42–44.

Hoyt, L., Mooney, M., & Parkes, B. (2003). Part 1: Bringing informational texts into focus. In L. Hoyt, M. Mooney, & B. Parkes (Eds.), Exploring informational texts. From theory to practice (p. 1). Portsmouth, NH: Heinemann.

Johnson, J. C. (2010). *Seeds of Change: Wangari's Gift to the World.* New York, NY: Lee & Low Books.

Kuhn, M. R., Schwanenflugel, P. J., Morris, R. D., Morrow, L. M., Woo, D. G., Meisinger, E. B., et al. (2006). Teaching children to become fluent and automatic readers. *Journal of Literacy Research, 38*(4), 357–387.

Lewis, M. (1993). *The lexical approach: The state of ELT and the way forward.* Hove, England: Language Teaching Publications.

Mozchizuki, K. (1993). *Baseball Saved Us.* New York, NY: Lee & Low Books.

National Institute for Literacy. (2000). Report of the national reading panel: Teaching children to read: An evidence-based assessment of the scientific research literature on reading and its implications for reading instruction. Washington, D.C.: National Institute for Literacy.

Pacific Resources for Education and Learning. (2008). Pacific CHILD teachers' manual. Honolulu, HI.

Nattinger, J. R. (1980). A lexical phrase grammar for ESL. *TESOL Quarterly, 14*(3), 337–344.

Pacific Resources for Education and Learning. (2008). Pacific CHILD teachers' manual. Honolulu, HI.

Padua, J. (2011). Text Structure: Cause and Effect. Honolulu, HI: Pacific Resources for Education and Learning.

PARCC. (2011). *PARCC model content frameworks: English language arts/literacy grades 3–11.*

Pearson, P. D., & Gallagher, M. (1983). The instruction of reading comprehension. *Contemporary Educational Psychology, 8,* 317–334.

Tovani, C. (2000). *I read it, but I don't get it: Comprehension strategies for adolescent readers.* Portland, ME: Stenhouse.

Index